THE LIGHT ON SYNANON

THE LIGHT ON SYNANON

How a Country Weekly Exposed a Corporate Cult–And Won the Pulitzer Prize

DAVE MITCHELL,
CATHY MITCHELL, AND
RICHARD OFSHE

Seaview Books
NEW YORK

Manufactured in the United States of America.

FIRST EDITION

Designed by Tere LoPrete

Library of Congress Cataloging in Publication Data

Mitchell, Dave.
The Light on Synanon.

Includes index.
1. Point Reyes light. 2. Synanon Foundation.
I. Mitchell, Cathy, joint author. II. Ofshe, Richard, joint author. III. Title.
PN4899.P575P65 071'.947 80-5199
ISBN 0-87223-613-7

To all our parents

CONTENTS

ACKNOWLEDGMENTS

We wish to thank people at the following institutions for having the courage to help us get this book into print:

The Hewlett Foundation, Palo Alto, California, for a $15,000 grant to support the writing and research; the University of California at Berkeley for housing the grant; the San Francisco law firm of Heller, Ehrman, White and McAuliffe for donating a *pro bono* defense in the legal actions that were brought against us while we were writing the book; the Virginia Barber Literary Agency in New York City for seeing the merit in the book long before anyone else did; and Seaview Books in New York City for wanting to publish us despite a climate of legal threats.

Many people were closely involved in helping us acquire the information to write this book. We do not acknowledge them here by name since they are named in the pages which follow.

PREFACE

This book tells how several people in a small community saw an event unfold and how they got caught up in it. For the most part, it is told from our point of view in Point Reyes Station, a rural town on the Northern California coast. The story is not over, but time has passed since the events we describe. Research we have done to write this book reveals how limited our point of view was. The residents of the small Central California town of Badger, for example, could tell their own story about dealings with Synanon. Several broadcast stations, newspapers, and magazines were also making revelations. And we have now come to realize how little various newsrooms knew about the discoveries of newsrooms elsewhere. Synanon, by virtue of self-interest and a subscription to a clipping service, must have had a much more complete picture. While *The Light* and other newsrooms often felt like voices crying alone in the wilderness, Synanon leaders, in contrast, must have perceived a cacophony of revelations being sounded about them.

We started to write *The Light on Synanon* in the third person. However, this approach began to seem awkward and contrived as we worked, and we decided to write it through the eyes of Dave Mitchell. This was a decision based on convenience: Dave was present at much of what we wanted to describe. We could have written from the viewpoint of Cathy Mitchell or Richard Ofshe and found ourselves with an equally important but somewhat different story to tell.

THE LIGHT ON SYNANON

CHAPTER

1

RUMORS AT A PARTY

December 30, 1977, was a seasonably cold night on the coast of Northern California. As I looked down from an open loft, guests were warming themselves before our Franklin stove, laughing and chatting. It was a cozy scene of happy friends and home.

The occasion was Cathy's and my tenth wedding anniversary. We had lived in Point Reyes Station (population 425) nearly two and a half years and were beginning to have a circle of friends. As was typical in small towns—we had lived in several previously—our friends were a varied group. In our living room, below me, Cathy was passing out champagne glasses to Realtor Cecil Asman and his fiancée, Ann Schecter. Sheriff's Lieutenant Art Disterheft and his partner, Susie Sasso, were sitting on the floor in front of the fire discussing carpentry with two stained-glass artists, John and Darlene Leighton.

Cathy and I had moved to Point Reyes Station in August, 1975, when we bought the town's foundering weekly newspaper. Our own careers had been foundering at the time. And, like many others who had moved to this scatter of coastal towns in recent years, we had arrived hoping to begin a new life in beautiful surroundings.

West Marin, as this stretch of coast is known, makes up the western half of Marin County. It is a region of dairy ranches with a dozen towns ranging from fifty to two thousand people tucked into valleys and coves. Ranching and commercial fishing had long dominated the economy of the area, but its proximity to San Francisco—only an hour's drive to the south—had in the 1960s and '70s made it increasingly attractive to artists and writers. In their path, an immigration of the counterculture had followed. By the mid-1970s, Point Reyes Station was fairly evenly divided between longhairs and cowboy hats.

Marin County had a reputation for wealth and chic lifestyles, but that image better fitted the eastern half of the county than West Marin. Because of its geographical isolation from East Marin (thanks to the hilly Coast Range), several county departments had regional offices in West Marin. All this had caused residents to think of West Marin as a separate region and at times to even talk of splitting off from the rest of Marin County. However, the population of West Marin was too small for secession to be financially practical, even if the concept could win political approval.

From a newspaper's point of view, West Marin offered only one problem, but it was a significant one: very few potential advertisers. Point Reyes Station was the business hub of West Marin, and its main street was only three blocks long. The biggest business in town was Toby's Feed Barn. Since 60 to 80 percent of most newspapers' income comes from advertising, *The Point Reyes Light* had never been more than marginally profitable since its founding in 1948. When we bought *The Light*, it was on the verge of bankruptcy. We were its sixth set of publishers in twenty-seven years.

Naive and idealistic, Cathy and I had bought the paper convinced we would make it *The New York Times* of West Marin. We had ten years of journalism experience between us and had developed a vision of what a weekly newspaper could accomplish. If we kept *The Light*'s focus narrow enough—covering only news involving the ten thousand people of West Marin—we could, we believed, be small and yet professional. We would provide readers not only with an objective record of local events, but also with editorials and features interpreting the significance of West Marin happenings. We would not be afraid of angering readers, only of boring them. Cathy and I never doubted we could do all this. The one thing we were unsure about was whether we could do it at a livable profit. That was a genuine worry since neither of us had any experience running a business.

We had held quite a variety of other jobs, however, since meeting in the graduate school of journalism at Stanford University eleven years earlier. Cathy had grown up in prosperous towns of Tennessee and Florida, graduating from Florida State in political science in 1966. I was an English major from Stanford, having been raised in a neighborhood of beige living rooms and tweedy residents uphill from the University of California campus in Berkeley. Both our families were solidly middle class. Cathy's father managed research nuclear reactors in Oak Ridge, Tennessee; her mother ran a drapery store in Florida. My father was vice-president and minor partner in a San Francisco printing company; my mother had sold advertising for *The Christian Science Monitor*.

Cathy and I first took note of each other in a seminar on mass communications in graduate school at Stanford, and it was not love at first sight. She was offended that the 200-pound, six-foot-five-inch fellow sitting across from her so often defended the professor's point of view against the rest of the class. He's probably a football player buttering up the prof to get an easy ride through school, she mused.

My initial impression of Cathy was no more charitable. At Stanford, I had co-produced a weekly civil rights broadcast for the student radio station, KZSU, and Cathy's southern accent made me suspicious of her racial views. But when I eventually learned that she had once tutored black ghetto children, I gave her a second look. She's cute, I observed, but what a frumpy dresser!

This casual, mutually critical acquaintanceship might have continued the rest of our graduate year were it not for a $45 check, an unexpected present from my parents, that found its way into my mailbox one day. Wandering away from the campus post office, I bumped into Cathy and blurted, "How'd you like to go to dinner in San Francisco?" Perhaps she has something less dowdy in her wardrobe, I speculated. Cathy quickly said yes. As she revealed years later, she thought: for a dinner in San Francisco, I think I can put up with him.

In the 1960s, forty-five dollars went a long way in San Francisco. We dined on roast duck with cherry sauce in a German restaurant overlooking the city's waterfront. Dinner was followed by drinks at a jazz club in North Beach. At the end of the evening, I shook her hand and said good night.

I later discovered that it was the handshake rather than the roast duck that had won her heart. "It was my first date at Stanford to end without my feeling I was fighting off an affectionate rapist," Cathy later explained. "I decided that I liked you." I, in turn, was pleased to discover this southern non-belle had at least one dress that became her. And so we started dating.

We both received our master's degrees in communications during the summer of 1967, and on December 30 that year, we were married in the home of Cathy's father. Eager to return to the West Coast, but out of work and desperate for money, we began looking for the closest jobs available. Somehow, we kept heading south, finally landing in Leesburg, Florida. There Cathy got her first newspaper job. She went to work for $71.50 per week as a full-time reporter for *The*

Leesburg Daily Commercial. I took a slightly better-paying job teaching at Leesburg High.

We lasted in Leesburg exactly one semester. Leesburg in Central Florida was still largely segregated when we arrived in 1968. It had been fourteen years since the U.S. Supreme Court had outlawed segregation, but Leesburg still had an all-black high school and a nearly all-white high school. Cathy ran up against the city's conservative racial views when her paper refused to let her reveal that racial friction was behind a black man's being fired from his teaching job. Clearly, we could not remain in Leesburg.

After weeks of applying by mail for jobs throughout the country, especially on the West Coast, we both were hired by a small private college we had never heard of before: Upper Iowa College in rural, northeastern Iowa. There followed for us two comfortable years back in the secure womb of academia. I taught journalism and English. Cathy wrote for the college's public relations department. Our days were spent among liberal, intelligent students, our evenings with liberal, intelligent colleagues. By the end of two years, the routine had become dull.

Again we wrote for jobs throughout the country, and again we focused on the West Coast. We both applied to newspapers and colleges, and this time I got an offer from a newspaper in Iowa, Council Bluff's daily, *The Nonpareil*. Cathy soon after found a job writing for an employee magazine for Northwestern Bell in Omaha, across the Missouri River from Council Bluffs.

My four-month stay at *The Nonpareil* was as frustrating as my two years at Upper Iowa had been tranquil. It was my first newspaper job, and I soon realized how far I was from mastering the craft of news writing. My articles often read like college essays, and *The Nonpareil*'s city editor professed amazement that I could have taught journalism for two years without being better at it. I felt both hurt and guilty.

But even after mastering the rudiments of newspaper writing, I still found *The Nonpareil* unpleasant. An exposé I had written on three restaurants polluting a creek with their septic tank runoff was downplayed and rewritten; two of the restaurants, the managing editor explained, were "a couple of our best advertisers."

"I have to get out of here," I told Cathy in disgust. "I'm going to start looking again for jobs in California. As long as I'm writing, we might as well try once more to head west." Cathy wasn't altogether happy about moving again so soon. She liked her job, and she was working for a demanding editor who taught her much about writing. But, realizing my discomfort, she finally acquiesced: if I could find a job on the West Coast, we'd move.

Now able to claim some experience as a reporter, I had better luck this time. A small daily in the Sierra foothills of California offered me a job. The salary was only $125 per week, but I was desperate to leave *The Nonpareil*. In October, 1970, we moved to Sonora, in the historic gold rush area known as the Mother Lode.

The Sonora Union Democrat was the best—and most demanding—newspaper I have ever worked for. During my two and a half years as part of its four-person newsroom, I learned the secrets of writing that I had somehow failed to uncover in school. In those days *The Union Democrat* was something of a legend in California journalism. It came out five days a week, yet it had no wire service. Staff reporters wrote every word in the newspaper every day. *The Union Democrat* covered only the doings of Tuolumne County (population then 22,000), and probably no community in American history was so well informed about itself as was Tuolumne in the early 1970s. With a twelve-page broadsheet newspaper to fill every day (eighteen pages on Wednesdays, when most of the grocery ads ran), few public happenings were too insignificant for full coverage in *The Union Democrat*.

Every baby born in Tuolumne County had its picture in the newspaper on its first birthday. If the county treasurer changed bookkeeping practices, there was a story in *The Union Democrat*. If a man quarreled with his neighbors over how high he should build a fence, the newspaper covered the debate.

This is not to say that *The Union Democrat* covered only small news. The publisher, Harvey McGee, had been an aide to former California governor Goodwin Knight. He could recognize a political struggle brewing even before the good old boys who warmed the benches around the courthouse had begun to whisper about it.

As a young reporter, I both admired and hated Harvey McGee. It was over a year after I left his newspaper before I realized how much I also liked him. I admired McGee because he could write so well and so fearlessly. He was at his best hammering out front-page opinion columns that slashed away at popular community views.

I hated McGee partly because of his frequent flashes of temper and partly because he had no patience with my ponderous writing style. "This story's okay," he would say. "It covers all the points. But it lacks impact. Tighten it up! Tighten it up!" McGee's own style was often a staccato of sentence fragments. Read like a burst of machine-gun fire. I never did completely accept his style. But I did tighten up.

The Tuolumne County Board of Supervisors met at 10:00 A.M. every Tuesday, and I was assigned to cover the first hour of discussion. At 11:00, another reporter was supposed to spell me so I could return to the newsroom and write up the early discussions for that day's paper. My deadline for filing the story was noon. Unfortunately, many board discussions did not end promptly at 11:00.

There were many Tuesdays when it was almost 11:30 before I could get up from the press table and start my two-block sprint back to *The Union Democrat*. As I dashed down a back alley, I would be composing in my head the lead to the main story. By the time my hands were on the old manual typewriter at my desk, I usually had the first half dozen "graphs" of my story figured out. Once my copy was in, I was supposed to help with proofreading. Afternoons were for feature writing and picture taking. In the evening, I often had a meeting to cover.

It was an exciting, frantic life. I covered environmental debates and airplane wrecks. I interviewed state politicians and murder suspects. And on my salary, which slowly climbed to $165 per week, Cathy and I were slowly going broke. Sonora in those days had a population of five thousand, and Cathy could find no full-time work. She tried a little part-time teaching and wrote some promotional articles for the local fair, but mostly she read, and quilted, and read, and learned macramé, and read. I was exhausted. She was restless.

As our small savings—banked during our years at Upper Iowa—began to give out, Cathy increasingly pressed me to move on again. I was of mixed mind. By now I had won a national feature writing award, and one of my exposés had resulted in the state's filing civil complaints against thirty-one people. At the same time, I hoped someday to be an editor—if only to get out of attending so many night meetings—and to be an editor, I would have to leave Sonora.

Cathy was elated when at last I agreed to resume job hunting. Her only condition was that our new home be in a community large enough for her to find work. Macramé, she had concluded, was a bore.

Again I blanketed the California newspaper industry with applications. After months of turndowns and regrets, I was finally invited to a job interview at *The Sebastopol Times*, a medium-sized weekly on the northern coast of California.

"I've received over a hundred applications for the editor's position," revealed *Times* publisher William Potter Johnson at the start of the interview, and my hopes walked back out the door. "I see you won a pretty nice award," he remarked, skimming through my résumé. "That's good. I want *The Times* to win awards." My hopes poked their head back in. "Whoever gets the job has to be able to get along with the longhairs as well as the business community. We have a lot of hippies in western Sonoma County." I made a show of stroking the moustache I then wore. "But the businessmen, of course, are the ones we're ultimately dependent upon," he added. I adjusted my necktie.

Thus began a remarkably happy employment. Johnson, in contrast to McGee, was the easiest publisher to work for I ever knew. Once he had decided I knew what I was doing, he left me alone to run the *Times*' newsroom pretty much as I saw fit.

About a month after I had gone to work for him, *The Times*' part-time feature writer resigned to take a full-time job on a nearby daily, and Cathy was hired to replace her. A few months later, another part-time reporter resigned, and Cathy's job became full-time. Johnson gave her the title Feature Editor.

For the next couple of years we were satisfied and usually happy. Johnson was in his office, and all was right with our world. Moreover, we were, as Johnson had hoped, winning awards. Cathy's feature section was judged second among California weeklies. The one reporter we supervised, Lindajoy Fenley, also won a second-place state award, for a series on the local Chicano subculture. A photographic series I shot on hang gliding took first place in regional competition. And *The Times* won state and regional awards for typography.

Typography—the design or appearance of a newspaper—was Johnson's forte. McGee in Sonora had taught me news writing. Johnson was determined to teach the Mitchells typography. As Johnson saw it, the front page of a newspaper was its packaging. The arrangement of stories, headlines, and photos should be "clean" and dramatic. He was disdainful of the gray, cluttered front pages of most weekly newspapers. It was an aspect of newspapering I had never thought much about. Now I can't pick up a newspaper without taking note of its headline sizes, overall balance, and use of photographs.

We worked for Johnson two years, and would have worked for him another ten, but he sold *The Times* after buying a more profitable weekly in Colorado. Within a month, one of the new owners laid off Cathy as "too expensive" an employee. I quarreled with the owner over his treatment of Cathy and was fired. That same week, my mother died of cancer.

I remember the week as a crescendo of misery. My mother, Edith Vokes Mitchell, was a native of Canada and had immigrated to the United States during the Depression. She had known what she wanted for her life. And mine. For fifteen years I struggled against her to find my own way, but in the year before she died, the struggle lost its importance. Then we were happy just to see each other when we could. She suffered a great deal of pain in her last months, so I was sad but not distraught at her death.

The loss of our jobs was harder to adjust to, although the blow was more emotional than financial. Cathy and I were entitled to substantial unemployment insurance; together we had been making over $350 per week before the gravy train derailed. But I was mortified at being fired, and frantically we began applying for jobs all over Northern California. There were still a hundred or more applicants for every opening, and this time neither of us was lucky.

As weeks went by without a job offer, we began discussing buying a small newspaper of our own. I called Johnson and asked how to go about purchasing a newspaper—and if it would even be possible for someone with our limited finances. Johnson said the equity in our home might be enough for a down payment on a weekly. With some trepidation, we placed classified ads in a couple of newspaper trade magazines, saying we were looking for a small West Coast paper to buy. Responses came in from Idaho to San Diego; most were from publishers trying to unload dying businesses. A few sounded intriguing, and we wrote for more information. The details invariably revealed financial disasters.

Ownership was beginning to look no more promising than employment when one day we got a letter from Michael Gahagan, enclosing a copy of the weekly newspaper he owned in Point Reyes Station. "Point Reyes Station!" exclaimed Cathy with distaste. "That's the most desolate town around here." We had driven through the town a few times when taking the scenic route into San Francisco. I remembered Point Reyes Station as a bleak, windswept conglomeration of buildings between two bends in State Highway 1. The hodgepodge of brick, corrugated steel, and wooden structures, all shedding paint, seemed to exist only to interrupt the natural beauty along the coast highway.

With a ruler we measured the inches of advertising in *The Point Reyes Light*, multiplied that by $2 (the column inch price listed in the paper), and multiplied that by 52 weeks. "At best, this paper's grossing fifty thousand dollars a year," I told Cathy. "That's pretty small, but at least we could probably afford it."

Point Reyes Station was less than an hour to the south, and we decided to drive down. It was a late spring day in 1975 when we drove into Point Reyes Station. Promise had replaced the desolation we remembered. Fewer vacant storefront windows stared out at the three-block main street. There were more people, and some of them had planted street trees throughout the business district.

On the south end of town, we found the offices of *The Point Reyes Light*, a frontier-style building complete with false front. Its oak-paneled front office was cluttered with potted foliage. Behind a heavy oak railing was an old-fashioned, two-fronted newspaper desk. A receptionist sat on one side; there was no one sitting at the facing front.

Gahagan, the owner, was out, so we asked the receptionist

to tell him that Dave and Cathy Mitchell from Sebastopol had dropped by and that we had gotten his letter.

Through an interior window next to her desk, we could see an antique flatbed press webbed with newsprint. Would she mind if we peeked into the newsroom? We had been in the newspaper business ourselves, we told her, and were "just curious."

She showed us past some oak filing cabinets and into a sunny room dominated by a huge rolltop desk. The opposite wall was covered by oak shelving. Next to the door on a brick hearth sat a potbellied stove. The only blemish on this nostalgic scene was the ceiling and part of one wall. Whoever had painted the room apparently ran out of paint and quit. The furniture had been pushed back in place, leaving patches of pink in an otherwise green room.

When we finally did meet Gahagan some days later, it turned out *The Light*'s financial problems were even worse than its color scheme. Gahagan and his wife, Annabelle, had owned the paper five years and lost money in every one of them. Money that might have been spent replacing ancient equipment had instead been used to buy more of it. Gahagan told us it was he who had erected the false front on the building and had paneled, floored, and furnished the front office in oak. He had created an antique newspaper out of one that, when he bought it, had been merely obsolete. *The Light* was a museum of newspapering in the 1920s.

We asked for copies of *The Light*'s financial records and found that our $50,000 estimate was close—but high. *The Light* had taken in $41,000 in 1974, so that was the price Gahagan had set on his paper. A few weeks later, we offered $37,500. Gahagan could keep the building, and we would rent from him. After the briefest of negotiations, the Gahagans accepted our offer. We set the change in ownership for August 1.

The Light, when we bought it, was still hot type—that is, articles were set in hot lead on a Linotype machine. The paper was printed on a 1910 Goss flatbed web press. The press was so old that it had been geared down to run at half speed lest it fly apart. Even so, our predecessor had spent much of each week repairing the press just so it could handle the next press run. Looking at his antiquated production methods, we could see how he had little time to attend to financially managing the business.

Neither of us knew how to operate the old equipment, and so before our first issue we converted the paper to offset reproduction. With modern technology, articles could be typeset on paper rather than in lead. Scissors could replace saws. An average typist could set the entire paper in two days where it had taken a Linotype operator a week. The production staff could be cut in half, and by that saving of wages alone, we hoped to turn a profit. The principle was sound, but we soon found out how little we knew about what would be required to carry it out.

Preparing to take ownership of *The Light*, we bought darkroom equipment, hired a typist, and—after Gahagan printed his last issue—moved tons of the old production equipment to make space for new equipment. The old Goss press we sold for $1, on two conditions: that the buyers immediately remove it, and that they restore the newspaper building to its usual condition. The second condition was the more difficult. The press was so large, filling an entire room, that the front of the building had to be cut open and hinged back, and the press rolled out on steel bars. But the project was accomplished in one weekend. The buyers—a group of local residents with a fondness for antique machinery—closed the building up and plastered over the cuts. But we still weren't ready for business.

In fact, we didn't go to bed at all the two nights before our first issue came out. We had arranged with a much larger weekly, *The Sonoma Index-Tribune* in Sonoma, forty-five minutes away, to print *The Light*. Our maiden issue was to go to press the first Wednesday of August.

Cathy wrote almost that entire issue. I shot a photo feature on local hang gliders to show off the new *Light*'s improved reproduction, and huddled with salesmen, learning how to operate our new production equipment. The most difficult offset skill to master, I quickly learned, was converting photographs to good halftones, the dotted pictures used in newspapers.

A friend named Smitty, a former production manager at *The Sonora Union Democrat*, dropped by to help us get the issue out. *The Light* in those days was only twelve tabloid pages, but it took us all Tuesday night to paste it up and then to make the page negatives, from which plates for the press were burned.

Gahagan, the former publisher, was curious about offset printing and on Wednesday morning joined us for breakfast and the trip to the printer. *The Index-Tribune*'s press was over thirty feet long, and it was with excitement that Cathy and I watched the first pages of our first issue wind their way through the press and then drop down into the folder, emerging seconds later as our newspaper.

Back at *The Light*, the excitement continued. We popped bottles of cheap champagne while our ad manager, Melissa Sweeney, played and sang Bessie Smith renditions at an upright piano, which we had jammed into the newspaper office along with the rest of our belongings.

The next issue required us to work through only one night. The following Tuesday night, we got two hours' sleep. By the end of three months, we could almost always put the paper to bed with no more than a sixteen-hour shift on Tuesday.

Before we bought *The Light*, it had been geared to college-educated, environmentally concerned readers in their twenties and thirties—people like us. But we quickly realized that if *The Light* was going to attract more readers, we would also have to appeal to the more conservative segments of the community, such as ranchers. And we would have to start covering more news in Stinson Beach and Bolinas, two of the larger towns in West Marin.

Circulation was a problem. Gahagan had listed his total circulation—newsstand sales and subscriptions combined—as 2,000. But that, we discovered, included about 300 readers whose subscriptions had expired at least six months earlier. Paid circulation was really about 1,700.

Before we dropped the 300, we gave them a few weeks to see the changes we were making in *The Light*. Determined to make the paper a general-interest weekly, we dropped readers' poetry, which had once filled almost a page of the paper. We dropped an astrology chart. We stopped listing readers' birthdays. In their place, we provided increased coverage of outlying towns and the ranching community. We put more emphasis on dramatic photography, and we redesigned the appearance of the paper.

The changes were not universally accepted. Some of West Marin's counterculture were offended by the loss of poetry and the astrology chart. We received a spate of angry letters to the editor, but the longtime families of West Marin were enthusiastic. Many of them were descendants of Italian and Swiss-Italian immigrants. Two months after we took over *The Light*, Cathy conducted a subscription drive, and we were delighted to see a succession of little old Italian ladies in black dresses troop into the newspaper office to buy a subscription.

Cathy and I thought of ourselves as environmentalists, and at our previous jobs on *The Sebastopol Times* we had been dubbed "hippie editors" by several Realtors. Our call for Sonoma County to put more limits on new home building had irked the real estate community. Sonoma County at the time had the highest growth rate of any California county. In West Marin, however, we found ourselves under attack from environmentalists, and viewed by Realtors as their champions.

The change occurred in part because environmentalism was more firmly entrenched in Marin than Sonoma County. Public environmental policies we had called for in Sonoma County had already been adopted in Marin County. Some of the regulations created snarls of red tape, and our editorials denouncing the regulatory problems were read by some people to mean we also disapproved of environmental goals.

Our experience, we later learned from other publishers, was not unusual; it is typical for readers to be suspicious of new owners when their paper changes hands. However, we were ill prepared for the barrage of angry letters that arrived the first few months we owned *The Light*. I walked into the newsroom one October day in 1975 to find Cathy with an angry reader. "How can you say that in the paper?" he challenged her repeatedly. Finally, in exasperation Cathy replied: "Because we own it!"

There was so little money left after buying *The Light* and its new equipment that we could not afford to rent a house in Point Reyes Station. Various buildings had housed *The Light* over the last couple of decades, and the publisher who had built the present office had included a tiny living area in the back, with a minuscule kitchen and bathroom. Cathy and I moved in.

The room was too small to hold a bed, so in the adjoining newsroom we put a couch that at night unfolded to become a bed. This arrangement insured our being up and showered by 8:00 A.M., when our employees reported in to share our bedroom cum newsroom. But living and working in *The Light*'s office soon became unbearable. Newsroom phones started ringing some days before 6:00 A.M., with callers wanting to place a classified ad before going to work. Cathy took the copy, but without her contact lenses in she has the vision of someone legally blind; the result was several garbled ads.

To supplement our income, Cathy had taken a part-time job teaching journalism at Santa Rosa Junior College near Sebastopol in Sonoma County. When her paychecks began arriving, we used them to rent a cottage in nearby Inverness.

A year later, we began building a cabin on a hillside pasture above Point Reyes Station.

When we moved into the cabin in March, 1977, we were still poor, but to me life seemed bountiful. Our income from *The Light* for 1976 had come to only $13,000; for two people working long hours and having over $40,000 tied up in the business, $13,000 was a very low return. But we were pleased. It was the first year in seven *The Light* had made money, and we knew the paper would survive.

Publishing *The Light*, moreover, had become pleasant work. We had put into practice our theories of good newspapering, and our steadily growing circulation indicated that readers liked what we were doing. We were also receiving occasional compliments on our improvements to *The Light*, even from members of the counterculture, and the paper had won a few journalism awards. We had hired a reporter, Keith Ervin, allowing me to shift most night meetings onto him. But even when I wasn't at *The Light*, my mind was still on the newspaper.

In the newspaper office, I was in my element. The atmosphere of weekly newspapers, such as *The Light*, is more personal than that of dailies. Dimensions make the difference. Dailies have more employees; they work in bigger rooms; the editor's desk is farther from the front door. Every newspaper gets continual visits from readers who want "to see the editor." At *The Light*, they usually got to, for I thrived on that sort of casual socializing.

Often when a reader dropped by late in the week—when deadline pressure was off—I got us beers from a refrigerator in the back shop to make our discussion more convivial. Some conversations required me to take notes, but for the most part my role was merely to puff on a pipe or suck on a beer while the visitor described for me some new intrigue in local politics.

By the summer of 1977, the office had become more comfortable for me than home. At home, Cathy and I were arguing. "You're obsessed with *The Light*," Cathy complained. I was angry that she didn't share my obsession. "All we ever do together is work on the paper," she added with bitterness. "You never have time for us." I countered that *The Light* belonged to and benefited both of us. "Because I'm at the college three days a week and only at *The Light* two days, it's become your newspaper," she responded.

Six months after we moved into our cabin, Cathy moved out. She rented a bungalow in Sebastopol not far from the junior college, and we began making plans to sell the cabin. I would continue operating *The Light*, and Cathy would go her own way.

Somehow we never got around to burning bridges. On a few weekends, Cathy drove down to *The Light* to fill out financial forms required by the government. For a while I dated other women, but in October she and I started going out together occasionally. Just before Thanksgiving, Cathy moved back to our cabin.

By then we had reached a compromise. Each of us would be free to pursue our own interests, but we would set aside time each week to enjoy non-business activities together. The key to the compromise was scheduling.

Our tenth anniversary party, coming as it did a month after our reconciliation, was in part a celebration of our reunion. With our differences for the moment resolved, we could look back over ten years together with the same good cheer with which war veterans can recount their adventures in battle. What was fun could be laughed about; what wasn't we could take pride in surviving.

The guests at our anniversary party all had known us long enough to witness our struggles to survive in business and in marriage. I observed with bemusement that their congratulations this evening seemed exceptionally hearty. Leaving the loft, where I had momentarily gone to change a record, I rejoined the party.

The guests who had been sitting in front of the Franklin stove had gotten too hot and moved off. In their place was a friend from out of town, Sue, and her date. Talking to several of us, the date remarked that while he also was from out of town, he was familiar with West Marin. His father, he explained, had been involved with Synanon, a drug rehabilitation center six miles up Tomales Bay in Marshall.

The mention of Synanon prompted several other guests to join the conversation. Synanon had bought the first of its three West Marin facilities in 1964, and Synanon's arrival had been greeted by local residents with a mixture of suspicion and respect. Some neighbors claimed Synanon had arrogantly ignored local zoning laws, but others were impressed by news stories on Synanon's success in curing narcotics addicts.

Among those most suspicious of Synanon were several members of West Marin's environmental movement. The movement had grown in strength during the thirteen years Synanon had been in the area, and Synanon's steady construction—some of it done without the necessary permits—angered environmentalists who were arguing for even stricter controls on new construction.

One of our guests asked Sue's friend what Synanon was up to now. "There's a lot of changes going on," he answered, giving us an uncomfortable look. "It looks to a lot of people like Dederich's going crazy." Charles Dederich, the leader of Synanon, was a recovered alcoholic who had founded the organization in 1958. Dederich's start in a Santa Monica (Los Angeles County) storefront and his subsequent development of a wealthy organization with nearly two thousand members was a story well known in West Marin.

Sue's friend gave only a vague account of what was happening in Synanon: several responsible members had quit; his father was ready to drop his support of Synanon. Guests pressed for more details—what was Dederich doing? Sue's friend indicated he had said too much already, but noted,

"*Time* magazine this week has a story all about Synanon's troubles." He got up to get a drink, and the conversation turned to other topics.

The next morning, Cathy woke with Synanon on her mind. Over breakfast we discussed what Sue's date had said, and I suddenly remembered that *The Los Angeles Times* supposedly had done a long article on Synanon sometime in the fall. "Lee over at the garage told me some woman reporter from *The Times* was up here last summer asking questions about Synanon," I told Cathy.

Cathy responded that it was time *The Light* did an in-depth piece on Synanon. I had written a dozen or so stories on Synanon in the two and a half years we had owned *The Light*, the longest published a month after we bought the paper. The article was generally favorable but noted, "Above all it is big—much bigger than most people imagine. . . . Some 900 people are now residing at Synanon's three properties in and around Marshall. . . . Synanon boasts a fleet of about 400 vehicles, not including scores of motorcycles. It also has three large boats moored in Tomales Bay, with more on the way, and six airplanes tied down at Gnoss Field in Novato. . . . At the core of the commune is a computer center appropriate for a large corporation. The kitchen which feeds local Synanon residents can serve more than 2,700 meals per day."

Cathy's suggestion that we do another lengthy piece on Synanon struck me as a waste of time. I doubted many of our readers gave a damn about Synanon or Charles Dederich—even if he were going crazy. Cathy had just finished reading *The Investigative Reporter* by James Dygert; I thought she was now looking a little too hard for something to investigate in West Marin. I was aware how closed off Synanon was from the rest of the area, and told her, "I can't just walk in and start asking questions—not when there is a Synanon security force to watch for trespassers and keep tabs on visitors. Even if something big is happening in Synanon," I argued, "we'll find out only if they want us to."

Cathy reminded me of the *Time* article on Synanon, and I agreed to try to get a copy. But I still wasn't that interested, and never got around to buying the magazine. At Cathy's insistence, I also agreed to call the father of Sue's date to find out what he knew, but somehow I never got around to that either.

Of more concern to me was a vacation to Mexico we had scheduled for the end of January. I had agreed to go as part of our reconciliation. This would be the first time we had left the newspaper in someone else's hands. We had promoted Keith Ervin from reporter to news editor, but tales told by the previous owners were making us nervous. In his five years at *The Light*, Gahagan had taken two vacations. Both were disasters for the paper. While Gahagan was gone the first time, his editor in a column had gratuitously insulted en masse the restaurants of West Marin. Most had canceled their advertising as a result. His second trip, Gahagan had said, cost him most of his real estate advertising.

Roughly 80 percent of *The Light*'s income was from advertising, with the other 20 percent coming from subscriptions and newsstand sales. On occasion, we had published stories in *The Light* that we knew in advance would offend some advertiser. The year before, we had lost a regular ad when we covered a story an advertiser had demanded we ignore. But *The Light* was a business, one we depended on for most of our income. While we might sacrifice advertising on a matter of principle, we were determined not to lose any through mere blundering.

"Be conservative," we told Keith as we prepared for our nine-day trip. "If something is likely to get the paper into trouble, hold it until we get back."

Our plane was to take off Wednesday morning. Tuesday evening, Keith and I were pasting up *The Light* when Cathy returned home from teaching at the junior college. She clicked on the evening news of KGO-TV, the ABC station in San Francisco, in time to catch a report that Synanon had just bought over $60,000 worth of guns and ammunition from a gun dealer in San Francisco. Immediately, Cathy called *The Light*. I told her it was too late to get the story in that week's paper. The typesetter had already gone home; Keith and I were almost done with paste-up. We agreed it would be a good story for Keith to work on while we were gone—interesting but unlikely to cause any troubles for the paper.

CHAPTER 2

WHAT A GRAND JURY FOUND

Wednesday morning, January 25, 1978, Cathy and I flew off to Mazatlán for a week in the sun. By the time our plane landed in Mexico, Keith had picked up a sheriff's department broadcast on *The Light*'s scanner, which monitors police and fire channels.

The West Marin sheriff's substation wanted any patrol car in the area to stop a pickup truck eastbound on the Point Reyes–Petaluma road. The occupants were suspected of "brandishing" a handgun at five Synanon members in a van. When Keith heard deputies report in that they had the pickup, he jumped into his battered Datsun, and arrived on the scene in time to take a photograph of three men spread-eagled on the pavement as deputies searched them for weapons.

The officers found only a pellet gun, but took the three to the substation for questioning. There the three claimed that they—not the Synanon members—were the victims. The Synanon van had repeatedly blocked the road in an attempt to stop their pickup, they said.

The Synanon members, in turn, said the confrontation occurred because the three had tried to "hassle" Synanon members near Synanon facilities. "People cannot hassle Synanon residents and get away with it," deputies quoted one Synanon member as saying. Noting that he had only "one word against another," a deputy let the three go without charging them.

Keith realized the incident was similar to other heated disputes Synanon members had had with motorists in West Marin. Most of the incidents had gone unreported in *The Light*. Now, with a huge weapons purchase making Synanon look more militant, this latest dispute seemed to Keith to take on significance. He combined an account of the incident with his story on the gun buy.

Synanon spokesmen refused to talk with Keith about the weapons purchase, and he was reduced to summarizing Synanon statements to other news media. Synanon founder Charles Dederich had told selected reporters the arms purchase was prompted by threats against his life in the wake of the *Time* article on Synanon. Reports in other papers said Synanon planned to train a 30-member "private police force" and 120 reservists. They would be armed with pistols, shotguns, and rifles of various gauges—including a number of semiautomatics. Altogether, 172 weapons had been bought, along with $34,000 worth of ammunition.

Keith's article quoted Marin County Undersheriff Larry Kelly as saying that there was nothing illegal about the arms purchase and noting that the sheriff had "pretty good communications" with Synanon. Keith went on to write, "Local reaction to Synanon's arms buildup was almost universally negative." He quoted several West Marin residents upset by the arsenal and private police force.

One of the people Keith interviewed suggested he talk to Alvin Gambonini, whose cattle ranch bordered on Synanon property. There had been repeated friction between Gambonini and Synanon over an access road, for which Synanon had an easement across Gambonini's land. In June, 1975, some Synanon members had jumped Gambonini on his own property. Gambonini lost a tooth and suffered other injuries when Synanon members punched him and tried to pull him from his car. Three Synanon members later pled no contest to misdemeanors in connection with the attack.

Gambonini told Keith about his problems with Synanon and also about dozens of runaway children from Synanon whom he had helped reunite with relatives elsewhere. Mindful of our admonition to "be conservative," Keith quoted Gambonini only briefly and did not mention the runaway children.

When Keith laid out page 1 of the February 2 *Light*, he put the Synanon story at the bottom of the page. His lead story concerned county officials' dim view of Proposition 13, a property-tax-cut measure that California voters were obviously about to pass.

In the paper following our return, there was another story about Synanon, but this one ran only four inches long. It reported that Synanon founder Dederich planned to step down as chairman of the foundation's board of directors in March, when he would turn sixty-five. The last sentence of the article noted, "State Department of Justice officials last week confirmed they are investigating Synanon's finances but released no details about the probe."

I anticipated no further stories on Synanon for a while, and was relieved that Keith had written a lengthy piece on the weapons purchase. I hoped it would satisfy Cathy's demands for an in-depth article on Synanon.

Our reconstituted marriage was having problems. It turned out that Cathy had not caught an employee's thousand-dollar mistake in the newspaper's bank account, and a corrected balance revealed we were broke. Angrily I accused Cathy of using "optimistic bookkeeping" to convince me that we could afford the Mexico trip. Cathy insisted the mistake was not her fault, and was hurt by the accusation. For a week, we sulked around the cabin.

As had happened after past arguments, our anger faded not through any reconciliation but by our becoming busy on a project. As February, 1978, drew to an end, we were reminded by a local historian, Jack Mason, that *The Light* was about to turn thirty years old. We decided to celebrate with a special issue reviewing the newspaper's past. The special issue would recap West Marin history over the last thirty years and would include historic photographs of the area going back to the turn of the century.

Because of its marginal (at best) success as a business, the newspaper had gone through five sets of owners in its thirty years. We were the sixth publishers. "Newspapering in West Marin has always been chancy business," I wrote in the commemorative issue, which came out March 2. "Five papers have been born here. Three lasted a year or less: The West Marin Star (1928), The Point Reyes Beacon (1947), and The Tomales Bay Times (1976–77). One moved away: The Pacific Sun. And one survived here; you're reading it. For its first 18 years, The Point Reyes Light was known as The Baywood Press; some oldtimers still haven't gotten the name change straight."

The commemorative issue was the biggest in *The Light*'s history: 24 tabloid pages. Readers loved it. The issue went on sale Wednesday afternoon, and by Thursday afternoon some newsstands had sold out.

Looking back on that week, I am struck by the way events followed the pattern of the adventure cartoons I am fond of in the daily papers. After weeks of some improbable adventure, there finally comes the strip that contains the denouement. For me the happy moment comes in the frame with the first hint of some new escapade that in future weeks will have my hero again embroiled in troubles.

So it was with *The Light*'s commemorative issue. The issue seemed to climax not only the first thirty years of *The Light*, but also Cathy's and my efforts to make it a profitable and professional newspaper. The Wednesday and Thursday panels of that week were happy ones. Friday's panel contained an "Interim Report on Synanon" from Marin County's 1977–78 Civil

Grand Jury. The adventure launched in that panel has not yet ended.

Grand juries are appointed yearly in each California county by judges of the superior court. Traditionally the juries have had two roles. District attorneys take controversial criminal cases to grand juries, so that jurors—and not the district attorneys—are responsible for indicting the defendants. Grand juries are also responsible for watchdogging county government to make certain all county departments are honest and efficient. The jury's only power in this regard is to issue reports on its findings.

The first Marin County grand jury to visit Synanon was the 1976 panel. Synanon by then had developed impressive tours of their facilities, and frequently invited officials and selected newsmen for visits.

I had taken such a tour in October, 1975, shortly after we bought *The Light*. The article I had written on my visit pointed out how big the operation was. But mostly I was impressed by what I saw: happy, articulate people seemingly living productive lives. Many of those I talked to told of drug and criminal problems before joining Synanon.

The 1976 grand jury had a similar reaction to their tour, and afterward criticized the county probation department for not sending juvenile delinquents to Synanon for rehabilitation. The probation department had refused to do so because of the large number of juvenile runaways from Synanon. The 1976 grand jurors, however, accepted Synanon's explanation that children ran away "mostly because of the rigor of the program. . . . There is no permissive attitude in Synanon. Running away and deserting has always been part of our society."

The following year, 1977, Marin County experimented with its grand jury system. Two grand juries were named—one to deal with criminal matters, one for civil matters. On Friday, March 3, 1978, the civil grand jury shocked the county by issuing a scathing report on Synanon.

The 1977–78 grand jurors had begun investigating Synanon

in August, 1977, after the daily newspaper in Marin County, *The Independent-Journal*, reported runaway children had claimed they were abused in Synanon. The report ran as a series, carefully balancing the youngsters' stories with Synanon's explanation that it had only used necessary discipline. The *I-J* attempted to make few independent findings, and I had read the series more as a dispute than as an exposé of a major problem.

Two harder-hitting stories had followed in *Time* magazine and *The Los Angeles Times*, but neither Cathy nor I had seen them. After the grand jury report was issued, I got copies of both from the clerk of the grand jury. The *Times* article, published in October, 1977, described allegations in a Los Angeles civil case of child abuse at Synanon. The *Time* story, published in December, 1977, described Synanon as "a once respected drug program" that had turned into "a kooky cult."

Drawing on these articles and their own research, the 1977–78 grand jurors issued a ten-page report criticizing state and county officials for failing to properly regulate Synanon and thereby allowing a variety of problems to develop. The jurors noted:

> . . . Recent events such as the runaway problem, the lawsuits against Synanon to obtain the release of children and others, intemperate statements by Mr. Dederich, the arming of Synanon people, the altercations with neighbors at Marshall, the reports of child abuse, have placed Synanon in the public limelight. The people of West Marin are worried and uneasy. They don't like having as neighbors an organization that has changed from a benevolent group of rehabilitated addicts, who presented a low profile in the community, to an autocracy, which refuses to observe the rules of the very society it proposes to help.
>
> There is no question that Synanon as originally conceived and operated provided a lifestyle alternative for

> those suffering from narcotics addiction. As such, the organization was acceptable to the people of West Marin. However, over a period of years obvious changes have taken place, and materialism seems to have altered the underlying philosophy.

I rather doubted that West Marin residents were all that "worried and uneasy" about Synanon, although I was certain many residents considered Synanon arrogant and unconcerned about zoning laws. I also was vaguely aware that Synanon claimed to have been libeled by the *Time* story and had filed a $76 million lawsuit over it.

Nonetheless, the report seemed to warrant a major news story, and I decided to make it the lead story on page 1 of the next issue. The grand jury report had arrived in Saturday's mail, and I realized that more than half a week would go by before *The Light* could get the story in print. By then it would be old news for some people—one of the frustrations of weekly newspapering.

Friday's *Independent-Journal* had covered the report—but only with an eight-inch story on page 5, and half of that was a rebuttal to grand jurors from Sheriff Louis Mountanos.

In Marin County, the sheriff and his deputies are the police force for all areas not inside city limits. Since none of the towns of West Marin have city governments, the entire region is patrolled by the sheriff's department. Several years earlier, Marin County Sheriff Mountanos had named two Synanon men reserve deputies. As such, the two rode in patrol cars with regular deputies and while on duty had all the police powers of regular deputies. Unlike regular deputies, however, the reserves lost their police powers when they went off duty.

The grand jury report called Sheriff Mountanos's deputizing of the two Synanon men "inappropriate." One of the jurors' nine recommendations at the end of their report was for Mountanos to "review the deputy status of Synanon residents."

Another recommendation urged the sheriff to "investigate reports of child abuse at Synanon." A third recommendation aimed at the sheriff's department, along with other agencies, said the Synanon security force and arsenal should be investigated.

The Friday *Independent-Journal* story quoted Mountanos as saying the child-abuse reports were "unfounded" and that the sheriff's office had "no problems with Synanon."

I was surprised at how little attention our nominal competitor, *The Independent-Journal*, had given the report. Figuring that the daily must have received the report not long before its noon deadline, and therefore could do little on it in that day's issue, I waited to see what *The I-J* would do next. The Monday *I-J* carried a slightly longer story on the report, sixteen column inches. Synanon had by now responded to the grand jury: spokesman Mike Kaiser called the jurors' request for investigations "an expensive fishing expedition in the worthy tradition of McCarthyism." Tuesday's *I-J* contained a third Synanon story, this one quoting the county district attorney, Bruce Bales. The grand jury had named the DA as one of those who should investigate. Bales said he wouldn't. Any investigating, Bales said, should be done by other agencies.

The Independent-Journal's coverage continued to puzzle me. The paper had now run three stories. None had much depth. In fact, *The I-J* had given more details of Synanon's, the sheriff's, and the DA's rebuttal to the report than to the report itself. "We're going to do it right," I told Keith Ervin, our news editor, as I sat down to type what turned out to be a thirty-three-inch story covering all facets of the report.

> The biggest section of the grand jury report [I wrote] deals with children at Synanon—especially with the corporal punishment they receive. "While the grand jury does not have at this time the direct evidence to bring legal accusations against the offenders, we are very concerned at the number of reports we have received that

point to degrees of punishment far exceeding the standards set by the Supreme Court or by the State of California," says the report. Aside from a runaway child's black eye, which was reported by a West Marin rancher, the grand jury offered "no physical evidence of injury" from corporal punishment. However, noted grand jurors, "A small sobbing girl forced to stand outside in the rain, receiving periodic verbal abuse from adults, was observed by a social worker."

Sheriff Louis Mountanos Monday told *The Light* his office has investigated reports of child abuse at Synanon but found no evidence of any.

Synanon's "games"—no-holds-barred group encounter sessions—have long been the organization's primary way of shaping members' behavior. But the grand jury writes, "It is questionable whether the game is a suitable instrument for the training of very small children. We understand that children are frequently subjected to its rigors from the age of four or five. In addition, Synanon teaches children its philosophy that only life at Synanon is good, and that the outside world is bad and filled solely with malevolent people who wish them harm. This attitude could be extremely damaging to children."

The grand jury also notes, "There have been occasional threats to enter the children in the public school system. This, of course, would be a major problem for the Shoreline Unified School District. It would mean almost doubling the attendance at Tomales Grammar School . . .We understand that only the children of Synanon residents or court-placed children would be eligible to attend local schools."

Not included would be delinquent children placed at Synanon by their parents.

"The district would be obligated to take the children although feeling against such a prospect runs high in the West Marin community." Synanon pays no property

> taxes [to support the school district] and has not offered to finance such a move, grand jurors note.

My article also quoted grand jurors that "top (Synanon) executives received substantial salaries, large retirement bonuses, and other executive benefits. Synanon operates a profitable souvenir business among others, and the character of the organization has undergone a change. (Founder) Charles Dederich has allegedly stated, 'I like to be paid for what I do like any other American. I don't work for nothing. I'm an American businessman.' This attitude is interesting in light of Synanon's claim that it is tax-exempt. The IRS and State Board of Equalization should reappraise the tax-exempt status of this organization."

A third part of my article dealt with the grand jury's charge that Synanon was not obeying county zoning laws. And I noted that "*The Light* contacted local Synanon headquarters for a comment but was told no one there would speak for the organization."

Remembering that Synanon had filed several libel suits, I had Keith read through the article to get his comments. Keith approved and suggested a sidebar to accompany the larger article. Keith told me that when he interviewed rancher Alvin Gambonini for *The Light*'s article on the Synanon gun buy, Gambonini had mentioned helping dozens of Synanon runaways find their way back to their families. Many of the children Gambonini helped had problems that ranged from hyperkinesia to delinquency. Some of the children had been placed in Synanon by parents; a number of the parents apparently believed Synanon's children's program was similar to that of many private or special schools. Months later, we were to learn that two civilian counselors in the Las Vegas police department had urged numerous parents to send their children to Synanon. One of the two counselors in particular turned out to have close ties to Synanon.

Other children were sent to Synanon by criminal justice agencies throughout the United States. Agencies in Michigan were particularly fond of sending delinquents to Synanon. Later, the Fresno County (California) Probation Department was one of the agencies most active in supplying Synanon with children.

Some of the children came to Synanon without any previous problems. The late band leader Stan Kenton had had his son, Lance, accompany a sister to Synanon when she began to have problems at home. In other cases children were sent to Synanon as a result of their parents' separating.

The children were often led to believe they were going to an avant-garde program in which they would enjoy life in the country, with opportunities to ride horses and motorcycles. Many were shocked by what they found. Synanon placed juvenile newcomers in a "punk squad" more military than avant-garde. The children learned it would be months, if not years, before they could enjoy such pleasures as horseback riding. Instead they were assigned menial work and, in effect, became part-time members of the maintenance crew for Synanon.

Not surprisingly, many of the children quickly tried to run away. Ranchers and commercial fishermen living in the Marshall area received Synanon runaways almost daily. The grand jury quoted a Synanon member as saying "30 children had attempted 'splitting' during the month of June, 1977."

The Gambonini ranch is one of the closest to Synanon, and despite efforts by Synanon to frighten children into staying, many runaways sought help from the Gamboninis.

I told Keith that Gambonini seemed to be running an "underground railroad" and agreed with him this would be a good time to cover the story.

Keith's sidebar quoted the rancher as saying:

> "The kids that come here—every one—said the adults [at Synanon] told them we'll shoot them. But one girl

> came in here at two in the morning, and she told me, 'What have I got to lose?' "
>
> Most of the runaways are between ages 11 and 20. Usually the Gamboninis let the kids call their parents. The sheriff's deputies are notified, and they often take the youngsters to Juvenile Hall.
>
> Gambonini's wife, Doris, keeps a collection of letters from grateful parents whose children have returned home from Synanon . . . An earlier runaway complained to Mrs. Gambonini, she says, that he had been boxed on the ears for bad behavior. "I can hardly hear," she quotes him as saying.
>
> Now that Synanon has bought weapons to defend members, Gambonini says he's scared to plow his fields near his border with the rehabilitation center.

Reading through Keith's sidebar, I began to suspect there might be more anxiety in West Marin about Synanon than I had realized. Perhaps I was not enough in touch with community feelings in Marshall, I mused. I called several people I respected to get their observations.

One of those I talked to was Howard Brose, principal of West Marin School in Point Reyes Station. Brose had his criticisms of Synanon but warned, "Don't forget the people who need Synanon. Some of them have nowhere else to go."

I also called a ranking county staffer and asked why county government hadn't taken action despite fairly obvious zoning and building-code violations at Synanon. At first, the staffer was reluctant to answer. "Tell me off the record," I urged. The staffer finally agreed but warned, "If you quote me on this, I'll deny it." I assured him of anonymity, and he then revealed, "It's the county counsel's office. They're afraid of a lawsuit."

The staffer explained that Synanon supposedly had about forty people in its legal department. The county counsel's office, he said, was aware that Synanon would file lawsuits "at the drop of a hat." County Counsel Doug Maloney didn't want to have his office tied up for years in a court fight with Synanon, claimed the staffer. And again he warned me: "If you quote me on this, you'll never get any information from me again."

From all this, it became obvious to me that *The Light* needed to say something editorially about Synanon; the problem was more complex than I had at first realized. The editorial should pressure both Synanon and county government to behave better. But the message should be moderate in tone, since I did not want to inflame readers—or to draw a Synanon lawsuit. I wrote:

> We have mixed reactions to the Marin County Grand Jury report released Friday which lambasts Synanon on a wide range of topics.
>
> As was true of past grand jury reports, this one promises more than it delivers. It offers much general criticism but cites few specifics.
>
> But even in its inconclusive form, it is bound to be welcomed by many West Marin residents. There is a widespread feeling here that Synanon for a long time has "gotten away" with questionable activities.
>
> As the grand jury report notes, county supervisors in 1965 issued Synanon a use permit to "allow its present use," which was essentially a drug-rehabilitation and residential center on the 65-acre Bay Ranch at Marconi Cove. Since then, Synanon has bought two more local ranches; it is about 50 times the original size; and activities there have broadened.
>
> County supervisors periodically have claimed Synanon has mushroomed far beyond what their permits authorize, that growth there has been largely unregulated. To assuage the county, Synanon three years ago promised to offer the county a master plan for Synanon development. It was never written.
>
> Meanwhile, depending on what tax or permit Synanon

was at the time claiming exemption from, the organization has alternately billed itself as a rehabilitation center, an educational center, an agricultural operation, and a religion.

Synanon has a well-publicized team of lawyers who may be able to show in court that the organization technically can be considered all these things. But the impression left with West Marin residents is that a scam is being pulled off at their expense.

Synanon's gaggle of attorneys may also explain why the organization has not been called to account for some developments there. Even the county would find it expensive to wage a legal fight against Synanon. As a result, county agencies that regulate others merely negotiate with Synanon.

Perhaps mindful of this, the grand jury calls for various state agencies (who are less intimidated by cost) to investigate Synanon.

Synanon's relations with the West Marin public have always been mixed. There have been repeated hassles between Synanon and neighbors, between Synanon and motorists on local roads. Their recent weapons purchase alarmed many people here. At the same time, the organization has provided West Marin with ambulance and fire fighting services and has provided crews during rescues and emergencies.

There are a number of West Marin residents convinced that the best thing for both West Mariners and Synanon residents would be for the organization to be destroyed by its present troubles. We're not so sure.

As far as Tomales Bay area residents are concerned, there would be problems. Such an event would dump scores of children into the Shoreline Unified School District—many more than the district has room for. There is no reason to assume that Synanon families would all "go home" if the organization collapsed. For many Synanon folks, this is their only home.

Which gets us to a second concern. Regardless of the problems the Synanon organization finds itself in, the community provides many of its residents a much better life than they ever found—or may find—elsewhere. A collapse of Synanon would mean hundreds of personal tragedies.

We doubt Synanon will go under. We hope—and expect—the organization will make major changes. A good place to start would be in its dealings with West Marin and the rest of Marin County.

To my surprise, the editorial drew more comments than the two news articles. Readers stopped me on the street to say they agreed. Several added, "I'm telling you this in person, rather than writing a letter to the editor, because I don't want to get in trouble wih Synanon." Again I realized I had underestimated community concern. But in any case, the story had been covered, and I felt *The Light* had said editorially what needed to be done. The supervisors that week had voted 4-to-1 to hold a hearing on Synanon and the grand jury report in a month. I planned to forget about Synanon until the hearing.

However, I was a bit puzzled by the 4-to-1 vote. The negative vote was cast by Supervisor Arnold Baptiste, who called the grand jury's accusations "unfounded" and worried aloud that the public would interpret the hearing as "an attack on Synanon." The supervisor from West Marin, Gary Giacomini, had voted to hold the hearing but had joined Baptiste in criticizing the grand jurors. Their report, he said, amounted to "rank hearsay, triple removed."

Giacomini had a reputation for being sensitive to community feeling and representing it strongly. Surely he knew how West Marin residents felt about Synanon. I had once covered a meeting in Inverness where West Marin residents told the supervisor they resented Synanon's flouting county zoning laws. So why was he now taking Synanon's side, I wondered.

But I had more pressing concerns and so for the time being put the Giacomini puzzle aside. My immediate problem was the new post office planned for Point Reyes Station. The town had outgrown the old post office with its antique brass-and-oak lobby. I had gotten copies of the architect's plans for the new post office and in dismay discovered it would have a plastic counter area. The lobby of the new post office, I grumbled to myself, would be more suitable to a suburban McDonald's than Point Reyes Station, with its turn-of-the-century western architecture.

I called several postal officials about the plans, and with their agreement undertook a public opinion poll to see if townspeople really wanted the suburban look. The newsroom's deadline for the March 16, 1978, issue had nearly arrived by the time I had finished the post office story and drafted a poll to run in *The Light.*

Suddenly I remembered I still hadn't written that week's editorial. It was fairly common for me to write my editorial last—mainly because I was not fond of writing it. Only when I had an insight not generally shared could I get excited about writing editorials. I never saw much value in an editorial that merely took one side or another in a controversy. Sometimes I spent half a day trying to come up with a topic. On those occasions when I still came up with nothing, Cathy wrote the editorials. More than I, she felt each issue of *The Light* should carry an editorial.

On Tuesday, March 14, Cathy was teaching at Santa Rosa Junior College, and I could not dump the editorial burden on her. Casting about for a topic, I hit upon Synanon. It's absurd, I thought, for the district attorney, sheriff, and two county supervisors to reject the grand jury recommendations out of hand. Several issues raised by the grand jurors, such as child abuse and the "materialism" of Synanon's leaders, I knew little about. But I was aware of zoning violations at Synanon, and the grand jury report's comments about county failure to enforce zoning laws at Synanon seemed accurate to me. I reread the attacks various county officials had leveled against the report and wrote:

> Ever since the grand jury report harshly criticizing Synanon became public March 3, there has been a flurry of attacks on the report by county officials—supervisors and department heads . . .
>
> In contrast, the reaction of West Marin residents has generally been "it's about time" misdeeds at Synanon came to public attention.
>
> Interestingly, middle-level staffers in several departments have told us privately they share this reaction. The problem, it appears, is that the grand jury report by implication—and occasionally directly—accuses county departments of not doing their job to regulate Synanon. So it is not surprising county officials are defensive . . .
>
> Unfortunately, county officials feeling defensive about the report may merely attempt to rebut it—and thus end up Synanon's most powerful allies. Such an alliance will not sit well with many West Mariners.

It was a short editorial, but I was satisfied. *Now,* I thought, Synanon can be forgotten about for a while. The editorial had taken care of the one remaining problem. No one at *The Light* wrote anything else about Synanon for the March 16 issue.

There would have been no mention of Synanon in the March 23 issue either had it not been for an unusual bit of news. An article in *The Independent-Journal* reported grand jurors had complained of harassment in their homes from Synanon members.

Synanon members had begun showing up at jurors' homes demanding to discuss the report. In some cases, the jurors were not home when Synanon members arrived. The members with their shaved heads and overalls then waited for the jurors to return. In at least one case, children of a juror were frightened to be at home alone with such unusual, somewhat threatening-looking people hanging around the house. The jurors asked County Counsel Maloney to get a court order restraining Synanon members from harassing them.

Maloney refused and commented, "What was Synanon doing? Ringing doorbells? That's not harassing anybody." Maloney's assistant, Deputy County Counsel Tom Hendricks, however, managed to get a commitment from Synanon to keep members away from jurors' homes.

Meanwhile, Synanon attorney Dan Garrett issued a statement that the grand jury report was "full of lies, innuendos and cheap shots and filthy venom. . . . We're not going to take this lying down." Synanon, he said, was investigating whether the grand jury had exceeded its legal authority in issuing the report. He implied Synanon might sue the jurors.

Garrett's comments, while extreme, were less perplexing to me than County Counsel Maloney's. Here was another county official publicly siding against the grand jurors. And what did Synanon hope to gain by harassing grand jurors—especially in a county such as Marin?

For Marin County in the minds of many residents has arrived at mankind's goal throughout its five thousand years of civilization. It is the end of the rainbow. Marin County is linked to San Francisco by the Golden Gate Bridge. Motorists from San Francisco enter Marin County through a tunnel at the north end of the bridge, and to make them realize they are entering a chosen land, the arched tunnel entrance has been painted as a rainbow. There are solid economic reasons for Marin residents to feel as they do about themselves. The 1970 census found Marin County to have the highest average income in California. In fact, in terms of family income, Marin is the fifth wealthiest county in the United States, the census found.

So Marin County has tried to govern itself in an especially civilized manner, with county government working out of a civic center designed by Frank Lloyd Wright. It's almost as colorful as the tunnel entrance. West Marin, which is still mostly agricultural, is less carried away by this vision of a new society, however. Farmers more than most people are aware of roots. But even if West Marin is prosperous, its ranchers feel strongly about what is proper and what ain't.

In a civilized society such as Marin, I reasoned, Synanon couldn't truly imagine it would be able to intimidate grand jurors from their duties—could it? There was something happening I didn't understand, and it seemed to involve Synanon and many county officials. On Tuesday, March 21, I called one county official who might suggest an explanation, Supervisor Barbara Boxer. She and Supervisor Denis Rice were the two board members most outspokenly critical of Synanon.

Supervisor Boxer agreed relations between Synanon and several county officials were strange, but didn't know why. "Is somebody getting paid off?" I asked her. Supervisor Boxer didn't know. Then, referring to Rice and herself, she added, "Sometimes it feels like we're hanging out here alone—with the grand jury."

I had planned to include Supervisor Boxer's comments in a story on harassment of the grand jury, but again it was almost deadline and I hadn't yet written an editorial. To save time, I decided to combine the two.

The editorial reviewed various officials' attacks on the grand jury, Supervisor Boxer's comments, Synanon's harassment of the jurors, and Synanon's investigating the possibility of suing the grand jury. It concluded: "What started as a grand jury attack on alleged misconduct at Synanon and a call for county and state investigations is becoming a county attack on grand jurors with investigations by Synanon. It's indeed curious."

That evening, Cathy, Keith, and I were pasting up the paper when Art Disterheft, the officer in charge of the West Marin sheriff's substation, dropped by to chat, as he sometimes did on Tuesday evenings. Paste-up at *The Light* was often the most pleasant part of the week, for the work was easy and mechanical. A machine coated the backs of news columns, photographs, and headlines with wax. Paste-up involved merely arranging these pieces attractively on a layout sheet and then making the wax stick by running a roller over the pieces. While this was going on, the staff usually chatted and listened to the radio. Meeting the weekly deadline often put considerable pressure on the staff, but once paste-up began, the pressure was pretty much over. I often bought a six-pack of beer for the workers, and friends who had just gotten off work often dropped by.

Art poured himself a cup of coffee and commented there was something Keith or I might want to look into for next week's paper. He didn't have any details yet, having got word of the incident just as he went off duty, but there had been some kind of an assault at Synanon the day before.

From Art's brief account I did not realize this was the first hint of a story that would commit *The Light* to an investigation of Synanon, an investigation that would run not only through 1978 and 1979 but into the 1980s. Instead I muttered to Art that I'd probably be reading about the assault in tomorrow's *Independent-Journal.*

When Cathy and I first bought *The Light*, the excitement of late-breaking news had often prompted me to squeeze stories in after deadline. Too often the result was a late night, with staff exhausted and resentful. At Cathy's insistence, I had begun adhering to the deadline, and I forced myself not to think about the story going uncovered—until after the paper was out.

The next morning, as I did every Wednesday morning, I drove to Sonoma with the negatives for the paper. At *The Sonoma Index-Tribune*, the negatives were used to make printing plates for the press.

The process took about an hour and a half, during which I went out for breakfast. Somewhere between 9:30 and 10:00 A.M., the plates would go on the press. I always tried to be back in time for the press run in case there were problems. The run was so small (only 2,900 copies) that it usually took less than twenty minutes. Papers going to subscribers were then addressed, and all the papers were tied in bundles. These I loaded into my small Ford Fiesta, and then I drove back to Point Reyes Station, arriving about noon. I spent most of Wednesday afternoon delivering bundles of papers to various West Marin merchants, who kept stacks of *Lights* for sale on their counters.

Not until Thursday that week did I have time to look up Art at the substation and ask about the assault at Synanon.

CHAPTER 3

TIPPED TO A BEATING

When I arrived at the sheriff's substation on Thursday to find out about the Synanon incident, Art Disterheft seemed worried. The deputy had been almost nonchalant Tuesday evening when he first brought up the "assault." "What's up?" I asked now.

"Just between us guys," said Art, "I got a call from the main office. I was told not to bring our report to the press's attention." I was annoyed but said nothing, and Art continued, "It's too late for that, but so I can cover my ass, here's what I want you to do. Check the log as you usually do. When you find the Synanon entry, note the case number and ask about the report."

There were only three officers over Art in the sheriff's department: a captain, the undersheriff, and Sheriff Louis Mountanos. Art was really spooked; his orders must have come from one of them, I reasoned. Art explained that while he had orders not to volunteer the report, no one had told him to withhold the report if the press requested it. Realizing the lieutenant was in a difficult situation, I agreed to act out the charade.

I found the case number on the log, which listed all calls handled by deputies at the substation. "Can you pull the report on C78-3996?" I asked him, as the officer on duty. "The log says it's a 207-PC. What's that?"

"A 207 is kidnapping," replied Art coolly.

The report was fairly long, nine pages. It described an incident on March 20, 1978, at 10:45 A.M. The incident had been reported at 1:30 P.M. the same day by the victim, Thomas Joseph Cardineau, twenty-four, of Coram, New York, a factory worker. There was a witness, Donna Evelyn Cardineau, twenty-four, of the same address. Her occupation was listed as "teacher."

"Location of Occurrence" was given as "Synanon Walker Creek Ranch, Marshall-Petaluma Rd." Four Synanon residents were listed as suspects: Phil Black, Harvey Litwin, Floyd Egan, and Chris Benton. In addition to the kidnapping charge, the report also mentioned a "245-PC—assault with a deadly weapon."

The deputy who wrote the report had included a brief summary of the incident: "Suspects beat victim with fists and feet as they felt the victim was sent to spy on Synanon by *Time* magazine in New York. . . . Suspects state victim was an agent for *Time* magazine in regards to recent threats on Chuck Dederich. . . . Major injuries to victim's face, head, and body (cuts, bruises, etc.)."

There followed a lengthy narrative by the deputy who took the report, describing what the victim said had happened: Cardineau reported he was a member of Synanon from 1971 to 1975 and had just been married in New York. He was in California on his honeymoon and had decided to show his new wife where he once had lived.

As Cardineau drove up the access road to Synanon's Walker Creek Ranch, his car had been hailed by a Synanon member in a van, and the ex-member had stopped.

The van's driver, Phil Black, asked Cardineau why he was

on Synanon property. "We're just looking around," Cardineau reported answering. Black, he said, responded, "Well, I'm sorry, you'll have to leave. This is private property." Then he added, "Wait a minute. You used to live here." According to the deputy's report, "Suspect Black then started cussing at victim and called him a 'splitee.' "

On my tour of Synanon, almost three years before, I had learned that the organization encouraged hostility toward former members. "Splitees" were considered deserters, so it was not surprising that Cardineau had found himself in a dispute when he revisited the place.

The report added that when Black "started cussing at victim, he returned conversation with similar type of vocabulary." Cardineau said he then tried to drive away from Synanon, but Black in the van chased Cardineau's car and, with the help of another Synanon vehicle, forced Cardineau to stop again.

"Numerous subjects from the second vehicle," said the sheriff's report, forcibly removed Cardineau from his car and made him lie on the ground. He was then handcuffed and searched; his wallet was taken and the contents inspected. Cardineau later told the deputy he lay on the ground for half an hour while a Doberman dog, supposedly attack-trained, guarded him.

As a former member, Cardineau said, he recognized a number of the Synanon members present. One of those he recognized was Synanon member Buddy Jones, "who," noted the report, "the victim knew was a reserve deputy sheriff for Marin County."

One of the deputies from Synanon was there! To me, this was the most startling part of the report so far.

"Buddy Jones, the deputy, saw all this," I said to Art. "Hea-vy!"

The report continued, "Victim states that subject Jones did not attempt to assist the victim in any way. Victim and witness state that during this time, subject Jones questioned the witness about why victim and witness had come to the Synanon property."

Cardineau said he was eventually put in a covered pickup truck and taken to a room on the Synanon ranch. His wife was left with their car, and two Synanon members remained to guard her. Still handcuffed, Cardineau was left alone in the room for almost an hour, with the Doberman guarding him. Finally, the deputy's report said, four Synanon members came into the room talking among themselves: "He's a spy. Who sent him?"

Cardineau reported he was then interrogated for fifteen minutes and accused of lying when he denied being a spy for *Time*. "The suspects slapped the victim in the face numerous times," said the sheriff's report. Besides accusing him of trying to spy, the four Synanon members suggested he might also be involved "with recent threats made against the head of Synanon—Chuck Dederich," added the report.

Cardineau reported that after the interrogation he was taken to a barn, where his handcuffs were removed. One Synanon member, according to the deputy's report, "instructed others who were outside, 'Don't let anyone in.'" Several Synanon members, including the four suspects he could identify by name, then assaulted him, Cardineau related, kicking and knocking him to the ground and beating him repeatedly.

Cardineau estimated the beating lasted about five minutes, after which the assailants dragged him to his feet and "told me to let everyone in New York know that they weren't fooling around."

Cardineau told the deputy he was then taken back to his car, where his wife was being held. He reportedly asked for his wallet, and a Synanon man found it for him.

The report noted that Cardineau was then told to leave. He drove to the East Marin city of Novato, where he contacted the Novato police and was sent on to the sheriff's office. The report indicated one deputy had taken the report and another had photographed Cardineau's injuries. His cheeks and lips were puffed from the beating, Cardineau's wife had pointed out in her statement, included with his in the report.

"We've got a hot one," I exclaimed to Cathy when I got back to *The Light.* "Some ex-member of Synanon had the hell beat out of him at Walker Creek, and for some reason the sheriff's brass doesn't want us to know about it. It's just a guess, but Mountanos may be worried because one of his deputies from Synanon stood idly by and just watched the guy get grabbed."

"You're kidding!" said Cathy with a start that showed she knew I wasn't. "I'd think the story would be all over *The Independent-Journal* by now."

"They may not have it yet. No one's been arrested. I'm not about to call the main office or the DA till Tuesday morning. Once Mountanos knows we know, he's likely to issue a statement to the press, and *The I-J* for sure will beat us into print—"

I was interrupted by a voice in the front office saying to the receptionist, "Is Dave Mitchell in?" I walked into the front office, where a well-dressed man was talking to Gayanne Lathrop, our receptionist cum classified ad manager cum circulation manager. "Hi," said the man, "I'm —————— ——————. I'm on the grand jury. You got a minute?"

I invited him into the newsroom but wondered, "Is this guy for real?" Grand juries met behind closed doors, and I had assumed grand jurors were more secretive than this. "Do you have any grand jury identification?" I asked. The juror showed me his official card. "We're being a little careful these days," I apologized.

"I don't blame you," said the man. "I just wanted to let you know those of us on the grand jury really appreciate your coverage of the Synanon report and your editorials. You're the only paper that seems to know what's going on."

Despite the juror's friendly appreciation, I found it difficult to talk with him. We had never met before, and he seemed afraid of talking too freely lest he compromise his position on the grand jury. Instead of getting to know each other, we talked of current events. Eventually I led the discussion around to news coverage of Synanon.

We mentioned *The Independent-Journal*'s limited coverage of Synanon, and he brought up *The Pacific Sun*, a sophisticated alternative weekly that circulated throughout Marin County. That week's *Sun* was lying on a table in the newsroom; I hadn't opened it, but the juror pointed out an article written by *The Sun*'s assistant publisher, Hut Landon. The headline was: GRAND JURY STUBS ITS TOE ON SYNANON. Accompanying the story was a Synanon rebuttal to the grand jury report.

"In effect," claimed the rebuttal, "the grand jury is saying, 'We hate and despise Synanon because they are different and practice a religion different from ours, and we want to use county, state, and federal government agencies to deny them their constitutional guarantee of freedom of religion.' "

"What crap!" I remarked. "Synanon's no more a religion than *The Point Reyes Light*. The issue is child abuse and zoning violations. This religious junk is just a smokescreen."

I read Hut Landon's article. Much of it concerned relations between Sheriff Louis Mountanos and Synanon. The article noted grand jurors thought it "inappropriate" that the sheriff had deputized two Synanon members. "According to the sheriff," wrote Landon, "the two men in question are volunteer reserve deputies who have been trained for search and rescue missions, not unlike similar volunteers in towns throughout Marin; they have no power to perform normal police functions. Mountanos, pleased with the work of the two, said, 'They have been very helpful on searches in the West Marin hills, and they have been helped at times by as many as 200 Synanon resident volunteers.' "

"That bit about the reserves not having full police powers

is bullshit," I told the grand juror. "Mountanos is lying through his teeth. Lieutenant Disterheft says as long as they're on duty, the reserves have the same powers as regular deputies."

The more I thought about it, the angrier I got. "Those two deputies aren't being used for searches. I happen to know Mountanos has them working out of the main office in the detective division. They have access to all police intelligence in the county. They're working with the goddamn dicks!"

The grand juror raised an eyebrow. "Are you going to mention that in *The Light*?" he asked.

"I sure as hell will!" I fumed.

I went back to reading the *Sun* article. "Where did the grand jury get the idea that these reserves were official policemen?" Landon had asked rhetorically. "Even though he is credited as the source," Landon wrote, "Mountanos states emphatically that it did not come from him."

I began to have visions of an immense intrigue, involving Synanon, top county officials, and the two major newspapers in the county. "How does Synanon wield so much influence?" The grand juror didn't know, and added that as a grand juror it would be difficult for him to give an answer if he did. Was there *anything* he could say, I asked him. "Did you know that documents used by the grand jury are public records?" he asked. I shook my head. "Well," tipped the juror, "they are."

"I'll check to see what's there," I reassured him.

After the juror left, I tried to figure out why he had dropped by. Was it just to extend other jurors' appreciation for our defense of them? Obviously he wanted us to stay with the Synanon story but couldn't say so. Perhaps the article in *The Sun* had prompted his visit. Or was it to let me know about grand jury documents? Or all of the above? I never knew.

I was still annoyed by *The Pacific Sun* story when I finally got around to reading the previous evening's *Independent-Journal*. A front-page headline proclaimed: GIVEAWAY AT SYNANON—'ATTIC' YIELDS $250,000.

> Synanon Foundation put $250,000 worth of goods on the block today at two of its West Marin ranches and invited 60 California religious and charitable groups to help themselves.
>
> Larry Akey, who heads the Synanon Distribution Network, said the giveaway was timed to celebrate the 65th birthday of Synanon founder Chuck Dederich and the 20th anniversary of the founding of Synanon. . . . The distribution network arranges for disposal of food and other surplus goods donated by American industries. In its first year of operation last year, it distributed $2 million worth of goods, Akey said.

"There's no mention of anything going wrong at Synanon," I pointed out to Cathy. "It's obvious," she replied. "Synanon got *The I-J* to do a puff piece to counter the grand jury publicity."

Friday afternoon's *Independent-Journal* followed up with an even longer story on the giveaway, noting how appreciative recipients were.

By Saturday there still was no mention in any newspaper of the Cardineau beating. It began to appear that we might yet be able to break the story. "The tension," joked Cathy grimly, "is beginning to mount."

Saturday afternoon I was working at the newspaper office when Sergeant Ray von Savoye dropped by. "Have you seen this?" he asked, holding out a copy of the Cardineau report.

"I got a rundown on it from Art," I answered.

"Word from the main office was that we weren't supposed to bring it up," said the sergeant.

"Oh," I said offhandedly, "I asked about it."

Sergeant von Savoye looked relieved.

We chatted a bit about Synanon, and I began to realize the men at the sheriff's substation were more worried about

Synanon than was "the old man," as they referred to Sheriff Mountanos. First Art and now Sergeant von Savoye were risking their own positions to make sure I got the Cardineau story. I was impressed by their concern.

On Monday, I called Marin News Service, a small news agency that covered meetings at the civic center for weeklies in the county. When West Marin topics came up, Marin News Service wrote articles for *The Light*, just as Mill Valley topics were picked up for *The Mill Valley Record*, and so on. I asked an MNS reporter to start checking arrest warrants being issued. The warrants would indicate if any of the suspects in the Cardineau beating were being charged.

A little while later, the reporter called back. She had thought it over and decided she wouldn't do it: "If by any chance we were to make a mistake, Synanon could well sue us. That could bankrupt my husband and me." She said she had talked to a reporter for *The San Francisco Examiner* who knew something about Synanon, and suggested I call the *Examiner* reporter.

Once again I found the Synanon story exasperating. "Our own damn news service is too scared to make a routine check of county records!" I ranted in the newsroom. Keith just shook his head.

I called the *Examiner* reporter. *The San Francisco Examiner*, said the reporter, was not covering the grand jury report. Twenty months earlier *The Examiner* had settled a libel suit with Synanon out of court for $600,000, she reminded me. *The Light* was making a mistake in covering the grand jury report, said the *Examiner* reporter, since "those reports aren't privileged." Coming from a lawyer, that would have been a disconcerting bit of news, since newspapers can publish privileged information without risk of losing libel suits. Normally, privileged information includes such matters as courtroom testimony, public documents, and county supervisors' discussions. I felt certain the reporter was mistaken. And even if she wasn't, I remarked, newspapers have a duty to report on significant grand jury findings. (Cathy later looked up the law and found grand jury reports are indeed privileged.)

The *Examiner* reporter then suggested the grand jurors had been irresponsible, that they had listened to too many bigots in West Marin. "Those people in West Marin don't like Synanon in the same way some people don't tolerate blacks in their community," she told me.

I said I disagreed but didn't argue the point. By now I was beginning to suspect *The Examiner* was looking for any excuse available not to cover an organization that had badly burned the newspaper once already. I felt that the resentment in West Marin toward Synanon focused not on the members' strange ways but on the organization's disregard for zoning and other laws. What I was hearing from the *Examiner* reporter sounded like the Synanon line as reported in *The Pacific Sun*. I thanked the reporter for her observations and hung up.

Besides the Cardineau beating, I was working on two other Synanon stories. Sunday's *Independent-Journal* had reported Synanon was returning its headquarters to West Marin after three years in Tulare County. I called a newspaper in that Central California county to find out what was known there about the move. Synanon had two facilities in Tulare. One was a resortlike retreat where Dederich and other top officers of Synanon lived. The other included an airstrip and building complex of living and working quarters built by Synanon amid many disputes. Tulare supervisors had ruled the airstrip lacked necessary permits and could not be used. Synanon had responded with a suit against Tulare County, a number of Tulare County officials, and a Tulare County newspaper that had editorialized about Synanon activities there. Citing county "hostility," Synanon had decided its headquarters should be in a friendlier location—West Marin.

An editor at *The Visalia Times-Delta*, the newspaper being sued, was cordial when I called but provided little new information. His newsroom, the editor said, was under orders from management to go light on Synanon now that a suit had been filed.

That made three news organizations that had been scared off the story by Synanon, I realized. I felt more annoyed than threatened. The press should not let itself be intimidated—to me that was the first ethic of journalism. I had learned that in college twelve years before and had never doubted it.

But to the editor I was sympathetic; in fact, I felt a bit sorry for him; I think he wanted to cover the story. I cut the conversation short, however, since the call was long distance. Normally, *The Light* would call no farther than a neighboring county for news. Cathy and I were so narrowly in the black, we could not afford much of a long-distance phone bill.

But I decided to violate our phone policy one more time. *The Independent-Journal* had mentioned a Tulare County supervisor named Fred Batkin, who had been repeatedly harassed by Synanon members because of the airstrip dispute. Synanon had outfitted a van with a camera crew and filmed Supervisor Batkin at meetings, around his house, wherever he went. As a takeoff on Batman's "batmobile," Synanon had dubbed the camera van the "Batkinmobile."

Batkin was in a meeting when I called, and his secretary said she would have him call back. Half the promises for call-backs a reporter receives are never honored, and I was dubious. But an hour later, the supervisor was on the phone. I can do a longer interview than I planned, I laughed to myself—Batkin's paying for the call!

The supervisor was in high spirits. How was Tulare County reacting to word that Synanon was moving out of its headquarters? "There was a sigh of relief by the board and the people in the mountains . . . around Synanon," answered Batkin. I could tell from his voice that the supervisor was smiling. Batkin noted that Synanon's 360-acre airstrip and building complex had been listed with a real estate broker. The supervisor hoped some businessmen would make an offer on the property.

I wrote a brief story on the return of Synanon's headquarters to West Marin and then began working on my fourth consecutive Synanon editorial. The grand juror on Friday had mentioned that another member of the jury had once done Synanon some favors. At my request, the stop-in juror had agreed to get the second juror to call *The Light*. He did, and I used my interview with him as the core of our March 30 editorial.

The editorial observed that West Marin residents, who believed the county had been lax in regulating Synanon, were "being written off as a bunch of rednecks" by some in East Marin. Helping foster that impression, I wrote, had been Synanon coverage in the East Marin press—puff pieces on Synanon's giveaway, playing down Synanon's problems. I attributed such coverage to fear of legal reprisals.

"At the same time," I commented, "Synanon has encouraged mistrust of the grand jury report, claiming they are victims of a grand jury campaign of persecution. That claim is ironic given information *The Light* received this week from one grand juror. The grand juror, who asked that his name be withheld, told us he previously arranged for a $3 million paint factory to be donated to Synanon by Dutch Boy Paints." I quoted the juror as saying "I did all the legwork" in getting Dutch Boy Paints to donate the factory building, which Synanon used for storage and living quarters. "Yet he agreed to release the grand jury report since he had now received new information."

On Tuesday, I waited until *The Independent-Journal* was almost at its noon deadline before calling the main office of the sheriff's department about the Cardineau beating. My earlier concern was over what Sheriff Mountanos would do once he realized I knew about the incident and the fact that one of his Synanon deputies was there. I feared that Mountanos, in an attempt to put as good a face as possible on the situation, would issue a press release. By waiting until noon Tuesday, I was crowding my own deadline, but if Mountanos chose to put out a release, *The I-J* could not run it until Wednesday afternoon. By noon Wednesday, *The Light* would be on the streets.

And I was a bit leery about writing the Cardineau story from merely the deputy's report. Should a lawsuit result, I wanted to be able to show we had checked our information several places.

My first call was to Captain Sid Stinson, the number three man in the sheriff's department. I wanted Stinson on record as providing the Cardineau information, so as not to burn the two West Marin officers who had tipped me. I also wanted to know what the sheriff's office was doing with the report.

Captain Stinson seemed surprised by my call but didn't ask how I came to know about the beating. "We've sent an initial report to the DA," said the captain. "Some deputies are going to Synanon today to question a number of people." There would be no arrests until the sheriff's office investigation was completed, he added. "We had all the suspects in the office yesterday," he noted, "but they wouldn't talk."

"I understand that Buddy Jones was involved," I ventured.

"Buddy and Art were in here with the rest," said Stinson, "but they made no statements on the advice of their counsel."

The divining rod in my brain took a dip. "Art?" I asked. "You mean Art Warfield?" Art Warfield was the second Synanon member deputized by Mountanos.

"Yeah," said Captain Stinson.

I suppressed my surprise in hopes Stinson would keep talking. "Mountanos has them both working with the dicks, doesn't he?" I asked.

"Oh," replied Stinson, "he can't have them in there since all this happened."

Both Synanon deputies were involved! I wanted a last bit of

confirmation. "Cardineau mentioned both Jones and Warfield?" I asked.

"He said they saw him getting pulled from the car," replied Stinson, "but didn't see him getting hit."

Stinson had a few more things to say: Synanon had "guaranteed not to move any of the suspects to other facilities while the case is being investigated. . . . We need to get two more things for the DA before he decides if he'll file charges. I'm hoping [Detective Sergeant] Jim Riddell will finish up this week."

My next call was to District Attorney Bruce Bales. "I've just been talking with Captain Stinson in the sheriff's department about the Cardineau beating at Synanon," I said. "Are you going to file any charges?"

"My deputy, Michael Gridley, is handling the case," answered Bales carefully. "We haven't made any decision." He sounded uninterested in the matter. Before the beating, Bales had been quoted in *The Independent-Journal* as having no intention of investigating Synanon as the grand jury had recommended. Either he was still uninterested in Synanon, I speculated, or he was trying to play down what had happened.

According to the deputy's report, Synanon had tape-recorded the interrogation of Cardineau. I followed up: had District Attorney Bales heard the tape? "Synanon refused to turn it over," Bales replied. He added that Synanon would not allow any of the suspects to be interviewed.

Bales is absolutely gutless, I thought to myself. But to him I asked, "What charges are you considering filing?"

Bales said, "Battery and false imprisonment." He added he might have a decision to announce by next week.

So there was the story. I had confirmed it with the DA and sheriff's brass.

One problem remained, however—there had been no arrests. Most of my information had come from the deputy's report, and I feared police reports were not absolutely privileged—unless there was an arrest. I couldn't wait for an arrest, since *The Independent-Journal* would undoubtedly scoop us if I delayed. I had put too much work into the story to let another paper pick it up routinely and break it.

Cathy and I suspected we had escaped a libel suit from Synanon so far because our editorials were aimed more at county government for not regulating Synanon than at Synanon itself. We doubted any jury would find against us if our "crime" had been to say government wasn't doing its job and should be.

Tuesday afternoon's *Independent-Journal* arrived, and we scanned it quickly. No Cardineau story. I called Cathy at the college. If Thursday's *Light* broke the story, it would be eleven days after the fact. The delay worried Cathy. "What if the other papers know something we don't?" she asked. I doubted other papers knew of the beating, but had worries of my own. The way Bales had talked, I was not at all certain he would file charges.

Adding to our concern was a visit the previous week from a prominent man in town who was known to be a friend of Synanon. "It's your newspaper," the man had said, "but if I were you I'd go easy on Synanon. They'll sue you right out of town if you're not careful."

Cathy had been indignant: "If it's a legitimate news story, we're going to cover it! We're not going to print anything that's false, and they can't win a libel suit unless we do."

"I think we just got a threat," observed Cathy once the man was out the door. "But I still think we ought to stay with the story."

Now it was Tuesday. The man's warning and the comments from other news organizations had convinced us a lawsuit was inevitable. "If you want," I told Cathy, "I'll call Ladd Bedford." Bedford had been in my eating club, a fraternity-like organization, at Stanford. He was now a lawyer with an office in nearby Novato. Cathy agreed to my plan; I called him and arranged for us to see him early that evening.

"Along with the Cardineau story, let's have him read over our libel insurance policy," Cathy suggested.

When we got to the law office, Bedford looked through the insurance policy first. "It'll hold up," he said. His evaluation of the Cardineau beating story was barely more expansive: "Looks okay to me."

Bedford invited us over for dinner, and we accepted. After dinner, while we were taking a dip in the attorney's hot tub, Cathy remarked how pleasant it was to be away from West Marin and Synanon: "This constant worrying about what Synanon may or may not do is really wearing me down."

Her worry and mine concerned getting enmeshed in the hassle of a lawsuit. Our lives were harried enough already. There was never any doubt in our minds that we could win such a suit, and now Bedford had said our insurance was good for the legal costs. We saw a lawsuit as more an emotional than a financial threat.

On Wednesday, March 29, 1978, *The Light* hit the streets with the top headline on page 1 announcing: BEATING PROBED AT SYNANON. For effect, the next article down the page was: SYNANON RETURNS, the story about foundation headquarters moving back to West Marin from Tulare County.

In general, it was a good issue. It carried a lengthy feature with pictures on a commercial fisherman's life; there were a couple of bizarre crime stories, several long environmental stories, and the usual political briar patches. But all Cathy and I could think about were the two Synanon stories and the Synanon editorial. "Well, we've done it now," said Cathy.

Libel suits in California are usually heralded by a demand for retraction; if the demand is ignored, the plaintiff has a right to ask for punitive as well as actual damages. The demand must be made, however, no more than twenty days after publication. For three weeks, we waited in vain for the letter that would announce Synanon was suing.

CHAPTER

4

THE INVESTIGATION BEGINS

Publication of the Cardineau beating story immediately changed the mood in *The Light*'s newsroom. Synanon was no longer merely a civic problem, it was also a potential threat to the newspaper itself. Cathy, Keith, and I saw the threat entirely as the likelihood of a libel suit; we did not assume we were in any physical danger.

Synanon by now had lawsuits pending against four larger news media: a $76-million suit against *Time* over the December 26, 1977, "kooky cult" story; a $42-million suit against ABC Television over the coverage its San Francisco affiliate, KGO-TV, had given Synanon's gun buy; a $15-million suit against *The Visalia Times-Delta* over a critical editorial; and a $40-million suit against the Hearst Corporation stemming from two 1972 articles in Hearst's *San Francisco Examiner*.

Hearst in 1976 had paid Synanon $600,000 in an out-of-court settlement of the first of two lawsuits springing from the 1972 articles, which described Synanon as "the racket of the century." Synanon claimed this was the largest libel settlement in history and had the fact recorded in the *Guinness Book of Records*.

The Hearst side of the case was severely weakened by the reputation of *The Examiner*'s main reporter on the 1972 stories, Bob Patterson. Patterson had been in and out of jail on bad-check charges and was later fired when he filed reports from "inside" Red China although he had gotten only to Hong Kong.

The second Synanon lawsuit against Hearst resulted from the publishers' efforts to defend themselves against the first lawsuit. Synanon claimed two men working for Hearst's attorneys stole some tape recordings from Synanon.

The Hearst corporation might have been able to defend itself despite the burglary and Patterson's reputation, but it also had harassment from Synanon's lawyers to contend with. Synanon lawyers were masters of wearing down opponents with endless depositions. No judge is present during normal depositions, which are frequently taken in the law offices of one side or the other. The scope of permissible questioning is immense, making it easy to ask witnesses about events only vaguely related to the litigation. As a tool of harassment, Synanon lawyers found depositions to be unnervingly effective.

One *Examiner* reporter, John Todd, was deposed for a day and a half in 1973 even though he had been on the East Coast when the Synanon articles were written and published. He later told me of being among seventeen *Examiner* employees subpoenaed at one time for a deposition at Synanon's Oakland facility. Todd noted that Synanon lawyers usually took at least a full day deposing each witness, meaning that the other sixteen merely sat around at *Examiner* expense. And although *The Examiner* is a large newspaper, having seventeen employees out of the office simultaneously severely hindered its operations.

Finally, at the insistence of *Examiner* attorneys, the depositions were moved to the *Examiner* building, but as a condition for the transfer Synanon insisted no one could smoke in the presence of its members. Given the number of cigarettes normally smoked by a typical reporter, Todd pointed out, many were frazzled by the end of their deposition. Todd recalled being warned by *Examiner* attorneys that the most "tricky" questions would come only after he was worn down.

One of the dozens of Hearst corporation employees deposed was an *Examiner* proofreader, Yvonne Rawstron, who happened to be a former Synanon member. The questioning she was subjected to by Synanon attorney Dan Garrett typified the use of depositions for harassment.

Mrs. Rawstron knew Synanon founder Dederich well enough to consider him crudely offensive, and in response to a question from Garrett sneered that Dederich "is an ill-mannered, boorish Midwestern creep." Garrett immediately demanded that she "describe what it was that he did that was ill-mannered, boorish, creepy, or Midwestern." Mrs. Rawstron replied, "He farted, belched, and drooled."

To her chagrin, Mrs. Rawstron then found herself having to answer question after question about Dederich's farting. "Did you hear it, smell it, or did somebody else say something?" attorney Garrett wanted to know. Each time she tried to drop the topic, Garrett had another question. How many times did she recall Dederich farting? At what distance from him were the farts obvious? At one point, she snapped in frustration, "For Christ sake, if you hear somebody fart, it registers!" But still the questions continued.

Similar tactics were used on *Examiner* executives. Garrett harangued Randolph Hearst in the publisher's office and then back at Synanon played a tape recording of Hearst's discomfort for the amusement of Synanon members.

Eventually the strategy worked. Hearst settled the suit. Two years later, Hearst offered the second settlement.

The settlement made other news media leery of critical stories on Synanon and made Synanon more aggressive in filing suits against the media. As we had previously, Cathy, Keith, and I discussed the implications of a Synanon lawsuit against *The Light*. There was no soul-searching at this point—only our combined acknowledgment that we couldn't be beaten on the facts, only by the costs. Our libel insurance, we reasoned, might cover us for one case, but our insurance company would then probably cancel further coverage. Synanon could then file a second suit, as it had against *The Examiner*. However, we refused to dwell on the possibility. I ended the discussion by quipping, "It'll be interesting to see if we're still in business at this time next year." Cathy and Keith smiled uncomfortably.

But Cathy and I thought we had one advantage—our small size. Synanon could present themselves as a small, charitable drug rehabilitation center under attack from giant corporations such as Hearst, Time-Life, and ABC, and possibly find a sympathetic jury. Against a "mom and pop" newspaper, our attorney Ladd Bedford had pointed out, the roles would be reversed. We figured Synanon attorneys would realize that fact.

The Light's newsroom, meanwhile, was taking on the character of a wartime command post. Or so we joked to each other. We had begun to hide important Synanon documents. Phones were ringing continually as neighbors of Synanon called with tips. We had begun to ask for identification from strangers who arrived to talk about Synanon. Dominating our own conversations were guns.

On April 11, Marin County supervisors would hold a hearing on the grand jury report, and three of the supervisors had said their major concern was Synanon's gun and ammunition purchase. *The Light* would have one more issue before the hearing, and we decided to arm the supervisors and the public with all the information on Synanon we could amass in one week.

We had come to suspect earlier coverage of the weapons buy had not told the full story, thanks to a source I was cultivating in county government. At first gingerly and now more openly, I had begun to discuss Synanon matters with a little-known but well-placed official. From the official, I had found out about dissension in county departments and among county supervisors over whether anything should be done about Synanon.

At first, Keith and I had referred to the official as "Deep Throat," the name used by *Washington Post* reporters Bob Woodward and Carl Bernstein to refer to their anonymous Watergate source. "But we ought to have an original name," Cathy had objected. Since Woodward and Bernstein had borrowed "Deep Throat" from a pornographic movie title, I suggested calling the Marin County official "Green Door," taking the name from another porno film, *Behind the Green Door.*

It was Green Door who first questioned whether the well-publicized weapons buy in San Francisco had been the only purchase. "Where else has Synanon bought guns?" I asked.

Green Door didn't know, but in turn asked, "Where else does Synanon have facilities? That might be a good place to start looking."

I couldn't tell if this was a hint or Green Door's merely musing aloud. In any case, it wasn't much of a lead. "Who could I call?" I asked.

"I doubt if they'll tell you anything," answered Green Door, "but the U.S. Bureau of Alcohol, Tobacco and Firearms should know."

I called a supervisor in San Francisco's ATF office, a man named Bill Vizzard. Vizzard was aware of Synanon's San Francisco gun buy: "We looked into the situation and found no violation of federal law. . . . Synanon is entitled to buy guns until hell freezes over." Had there been any Synanon gun buys elsewhere—say, around Synanon headquarters in Tulare County? That would be handled out of ATF's Fresno office, Vizzard replied.

Were any other agencies looking into Synanon's arming itself? Vizzard didn't know, but added that ATF routinely passed on its information to the California attorney general's office. I called the ATF office in Fresno, but the agent there was more close mouthed than Vizzard. "We have no open investigation" was all he would say.

My next call was to the Law Enforcement Division of the attorney general's office; I asked an official there what he knew about any Synanon gun purchases besides the one in San Francisco. The official said he had been told by investigators there had been some purchases in Tulare County, but he didn't have any details. Could he get the details? "That's not public information," the official replied. Could he at least say what kinds of records were kept on gun purchases? When someone bought a handgun, the official explained, the purchase was recorded in quadruplicate. One copy stayed in the gun store; one went to the attorney general's office; one went to the police where the purchase was made; and if the buyer lived in a different jurisdiction, one copy went to his hometown police.

Badger, the town where Synanon was located in Tulare County, was not an incorporated city; law enforcement would be provided by the Tulare County sheriff's department, I reasoned. That department should have records of any Synanon gun buys around there. I called the Tulare sheriff's office.

A detective in the office said his only record was of the San Francisco gun buy. He had heard, however, from an attorney general's investigator that the state had "one hell of a list" of Synanon weapons. Then why wouldn't he have more records? "If the guns were bought by individual members and not by Synanon," the detective replied, "the records would be under their names—not under Synanon."

Synanon had around a thousand members. Checking all those names would be impossible, but I had one last idea: "What's the nearest city to Badger?" The detective said it was Porterville.

I thanked the detective, who then made me promise I wouldn't quote him by name: "I don't want to get sued, you know." My God, I mused to myself, Synanon's lawyers have scared even the cops.

I called Porterville police and—assuming the city was small—asked for the chief. Police Chief John Smith was friendly but had no information. "Synanon is sixty miles away," he noted. Had Smith heard any talk around town of Synanon members buying guns in Porterville? The chief hadn't. Who were the gun dealers in Porterville? Chief Smith named two stores. If the gun buys weren't there, where else might they have occurred? Smith listed major gun stores throughout Tulare County.

I took down the names and gave the list to Keith. While Keith started calling names on the list, I called the two gun stores in Porterville. Neither reported selling any weapons to Synanon members. I was again beginning to worry about our mounting long-distance phone bill when I overheard Keith on the phone ask, "And when was that?"

At a gun store in Lindsay, Tulare County, an employee reported Synanon had kept an account there since 1976 and that "probably twenty-five" Synanon members had bought guns there in 1977. The store employee estimated 90 percent of the guns bought were handguns, including revolvers and automatics. The rest were shotguns.

The store employee said Synanon members had come in singly or in twos, threes, and fours. It was "very clear that they were Synanon people because of their dress and their appearance," he said. Beginning in 1975, male and female Synanon members were required to wear their hair in crew cuts, like Marine Corps recruits. Standard garb was overalls. In an era of long hair, Synanon members were conspicuous.

The gun store clerk told Keith, "There was nothing obvious, such as arming everybody; they just did it over a period of time, and they didn't buy that many guns from us." The employee suggested Keith call bigger gun dealers in Fresno and Bakersfield.

He also said various law enforcement agencies had made inquiries about Synanon members buying guns in his store. In fact, he added, when some Synanon members had applied to buy handguns, their applications had been turned down by some law enforcement agency; he wasn't sure whether the agency was state or federal. He also didn't know why the applications had been turned down, but noted that an application's being rejected usually meant the would-be buyer had been convicted of a felony.

Armed with Keith's information, I called Marin County Sheriff Louis Mountanos. Mountanos acted unconcerned: "The weapons are all in Tulare County. I know what they have out here—only a few."

I pointed out that the Marin sheriff's office should have a record of any gun purchase elsewhere made by a local Synanon member. How many guns had Synanon deputy Art Warfield bought? Not many, replied Mountanos. How many? "Seven," said the sheriff. Would he mind checking? Mountanos put down the phone, and I could hear him on an intercom: "Clem, check how many guns Art Warfield has bought."

"And how many for Buddy Jones?" I quickly added when Mountanos picked up the phone again.

"Check Buddy Jones too, Clem," the sheriff said.

I didn't want to alarm Mountanos into silence, so while Sergeant Ed Klementovich checked gun records, I chatted with Mountanos about the San Francisco gun buy. He had obviously worked out a spiel on that topic. "There's quite a list—the types of weapons and number of rounds of ammunition," observed the sheriff. But, he added, Synanon would have no valid "purpose" for bringing the weaponry into Marin County. Then why wasn't the sheriff more concerned? "They're in Tulare County," he answered. "There are agencies that have the complete information. They also have the bigger picture."

Sergeant Klementovich apparently came in with his gun records. "Just like I told you," said the sheriff, "twelve guns." Mountanos went on to say Warfield had bought eleven guns for himself and two for Buddy Jones.

This is insane, I thought with annoyance. One moment

Mountanos tells me flatly it's seven; then he says it's twelve; the next moment it's thirteen.

"What kind of guns?" I asked.

Mountanos replied, ".38-caliber handguns and .45-caliber." Warfield had picked up the arsenal bought in San Francisco. Mountanos now revealed that Warfield, the reserve deputy from Synanon, had bought other guns in Santa Monica. Suddenly the sheriff was talking rapidly: "There's no justifiable reason or purpose for any person or persons to have any large amount of weapons or ammunition in Marin County. If that ever happens, the welcome mat will be taken in."

I now had enough for a story on Synanon's smaller gun buys, but wanted more information on the large buy in San Francisco. I called Green Door, who seemed pleased that I had made good on his suggestion and now revealed that Supervisor Denis Rice had a list of weapons bought in San Francisco. After a couple of calls, I reached Rice, and he read the list over the phone: 380,000 rounds of ammunition, including almost everything from .22-caliber to armor-piercing bullets; six .22 rifles; twenty-four Colt .45 automatic pistols; three lightweight Colt pistols; fifty-seven shotguns; twelve Ruger Mini-14s; ten .22 Ruger automatics; and seven .308 Remington bolt-action rifles. Rice said he had heard that NATO forces routinely trained with the Mini-14s.

I took the list over to the West Marin sheriff's substation and found a couple of deputies who I knew were skeptical of Mountanos's friendship with Synanon. The two were interested in seeing what kind of arsenal Synanon had amassed; when they saw the list, they were impressed. Remarked one of the deputies, "That's the kind of weapons purchase the Philippines government might make."

While I typed my story on the Synanon arsenal, Keith called the superintendent of the Shoreline School District about Synanon's threat to enroll its children in local schools. Synanon had no permit to operate a school, and grand jurors had urged the county to "immediately" require Synanon to get a permit. Synanon's response was to threaten the local school district: "If we are forced to close our schools, we will have no recourse but to place the burden of educating our 300 school-age children, some of them vicious juvenile delinquents, on the Marin County school district and the Marin taxpayer."

Public schools in California are largely financed by property taxes, and Synanon, as a nonprofit charity, claimed exemption from paying property taxes. The entire school district contained only 913 students; an additional 300 from Synanon would swell that total by a third without providing the district with additional property taxes. Worse yet, Tomales Elementary School, the one school in particular that most Synanon children would attend, would have its enrollment doubled.

District Superintendent Ken Barnes told Keith a large influx of Synanon children would require the district to hire new teachers, change school bus routes, buy new desks, chairs, and textbooks, and possibly acquire new classrooms. Synanon could then withdraw the students, Barnes warned, leaving the district to pay for the new materials and unable to immediately lay off the new teachers.

The Synanon threat was dramatic, but Keith also uncovered some weaknesses in it. The previous fall, in an affidavit, Synanon had claimed 113 elementary students, 22 high school students, and 82 in vocational and rehabilitation programs—a total of 217, not 300. Moreover, many of the 217 had parents living outside Marin County and so would not be entitled to attend Shoreline District schools. Synanon, however, was making the most of its threat. Superintendent Barnes reported that Synanon attorney Howard Garfield had called the previous week to ask about the procedures for transferring Synanon students into the district.

By now I was working on a third Synanon story for the April 6, 1978, issue—an analysis of Synanon's finances. In their report, grand jurors had said, "Top executives (at Synanon) receive substantial salaries, large retirement bonuses, and other executive benefits." The information was new to me, and I thought *The Light* ought to check the claim.

The public generally assumes that some agency somewhere makes certain that organizations calling themselves charities are, in fact, charities, that the money they get is used solely for charitable purposes. In California, the Charitable Trust Division of the attorney general's office is supposed to be that agency. I called the division and asked about its financial records on Synanon. "Oh, those figures," said the woman who had answered. "Auditor Larry Micheli gives them out." I realized my call was not the first.

The most recent financial records Micheli had on Synanon were for the organization's fiscal year ending August 31, 1977. As Micheli read the figures over the phone, a new vision of Synanon began to emerge for me. I called a banker friend to make sure my impressions were accurate. They were, and I wrote:

> A balance sheet filed with the State Attorney General reveals Synanon is by far the largest corporation headquartered in West Marin.
>
> Figures filed last August show Synanon's assets to be about $20 million with founder Charles Dederich receiving an annual salary for the past couple of years of about $75,000. Dederich last year also was granted a $500,000 retirement bonus. His salary in the earlier years of Synanon was minimal.
>
> According to the Attorney General's office, the top-paid officials at Synanon received these salaries from September, 1976, to September, 1977:
>
> Charles Dederich, $75,000 ($76,227 the year before); Charles Dederich, Jr., vice president, $30,000; Cecilia (Jady) Dederich, vice president, $15,000; William Dederich, director, $50,000.

Dan Sorkin, director, $20,000; Ronald Cook, vice president, $30,000; Dan Garrett Jr., vice president, $50,000; Frank McFarlin, vice president, $20,000; Howard M. Garfield, secretary, $20,000.

Liz Missakian, president, $816; David W. Ross, controller, $780; David J. Binns, treasurer, $878; Harvey Hecht, director, $786; Art Warfield, director, $2,000.

The nonprofit corporation listed its total assets at $19,622,834. Synanon's income for 1976–77 totaled $13,776,108, according to the Attorney General's office."

One of the first things that struck me in the financial report was that Art Warfield was a director of the Synanon corporation. Warfield's name kept coming up in the oddest places. He was a reserve deputy, a fact grand jurors disapproved of. He had been present at Cardineau's abduction. He had picked up the large Synanon gun purchase in San Francisco and made smaller gun purchases for Synanon. Now he was revealed to be a low-paid but fairly high-ranking officer of Synanon. Twice I had met Warfield briefly: once while he was on duty at the sheriff's substation, once on a visit to Synanon. Warfield was a handsome black man with the typical close-cropped Synanon haircut. He supposedly was a former New York policeman who had quit the force when he started using heroin. He seemed a friendly enough fellow.

The other item in the financial report that struck me was the level of salaries being paid to members of the Dederich family—$170,000 in 1976–77, not counting Dederich's $500,000 "pre-retirement bonus." This was my first realization that to a large extent Synanon was a family corporation. Simultaneously, I began to wonder about its tax-exempt status.

Still working on the upcoming April 6, 1978, issue, I called District Attorney Bruce Bales Tuesday morning to find out what charges, if any, he planned to file in the Cardineau case. Bales said he still hadn't decided and to call back in the afternoon. That meant calling back after deadline, but I felt it was worthwhile to hold space for the story. When I called back in the afternoon, Bales passed word through a secretary that he couldn't give an answer yet but to call again in half an hour. I waited forty minutes and called a third time.

When I had talked to Bales a week earlier about the Cardineau case, he had not seemed terribly interested. But when Bales came on the phone this time, he was very interested. "I'm going to file against four defendants," he said emphatically. "The charge is 236-PC, false imprisonment, a felony." The DA said he was charging Philip Black, Harvey Litwin, Christopher Benton, and Floyd Egan each on one count.

A week ago, Bales had said he was *considering* charges of false imprisonment and battery. Why wasn't he charging the four with battery as well? "This is a better charge," answered Bales. "This is false imprisonment with violence. He [Cardineau] was removed forcibly from his car, forcibly detained, and handcuffed." Bales added that Synanon attorneys had said the four would surrender themselves Friday; they were due in court at 1:30 P.M.

That made four Synanon stories for the April 6 paper, and I still had an editorial to write. Green Door had heard that Supervisor Denis Rice would propose requiring Synanon to get use permits for activities at two of its West Marin ranches. The third facility already had a permit. With use permits counties grant permission to carry out certain activities on a parcel of land. Unlike zoning—which merely says that a parcel is suitable for residence, agriculture, or whatever—use permits in California govern specific uses such as schools, garages, and junkyards. Moreover, local governments in issuing use permits can attach conditions to the use—something they can't do with zoning.

I liked Supervisor Rice's proposal. Through use permits, the county might be able to control the size of Synanon's population, the number of weapons, and the provisions for children. And so my editorial called for the county to secure use permits.

My final research for the April 6 paper was a check of the grand jury documents at the civic center. With the help of the clerk of the grand jury, I at last found the *Time* magazine and *Los Angeles Times* stories, which had first hit hard at the problems in Synanon. I also discovered an amazing advertisement that Synanon had run in *The Los Angeles Journal*, a paper primarily devoted to legal news and legal notices.

The ad made ideal material for my weekly anecdotal column, "Sparsely, Sage, and Timely." (The column's name came from the Simon and Garfunkle song "Scarborough Fair," which refers to "parsley, sage, rosemary, and thyme.") "Did you ever wonder how Synanon recruits lawyers for its huge legal staff?" I asked in my column. I then reprinted the ad:

> Exciting career opportunities for trial lawyers, legal generalists, new graduates, and disbarred lawyers at Synanon. Large varied practice: administrative, zoning and environmental law, civil rights, personal injury defense, contract litigation, corporate securities, libel and extraordinary writs. Current litigation includes $76 million libel suit against Time Inc., and $40 million civil conspiracy suit against Hearst Corporation. Offices in San Francisco and Central California. Compensation includes room, board, complete health care, monthly stipend, and unique Synanon lifestyle. Disbarred lawyers will be considered for paralegal positions. Contact Adrian Williams, Synanon Legal Department, (415) 647-0440, or write 2240 24th Street San Francisco, CA 94107."

The lead story on page 1 of the April 6 *Light* unveiled some businessmen's plans to start a ferry system on Tomales Bay. I had written that story too. The Synanon gun story ran low on page 1. On one inside page were the three further Synanon stories: their finances, their threats against the school district, and the district attorney's filing charges. My column revealed Synanon's recruitment of lawyers, and the editorial advocated use permits for Synanon and urged West Marin residents to attend Tuesday's board of supervisors hearing on Synanon.

"Six Synanon pieces!" I exclaimed to Cathy as we pasted up the issue. "The volume alone ought to convince the supervisors there's a problem they better not duck."

Cathy too was impressed by the amount of research we had done. "I don't know what else we could have added," she agreed, standing back from the light table to survey page after page on Synanon.

CHAPTER 5

A HEARING ON FEAR

Marin County supervisors had set Tuesday, April 11, 1978, for their hearing on the grand jury's charges against Synanon. The grand jury report was now five weeks old. In the past, county supervisors had often discussed such reports and then forgotten them. Lest the hearing be merely a disturbance sparked by the jurors' report on its way to the county filing cabinet, we had urged the county in five consecutive editorials to take action.

But Cathy and I were having trouble telling if our editorials and news stories on Synanon were having any impact. Readers I met on the street, if they mentioned Synanon at all, usually approved of *The Light*'s Synanon coverage. However, there had been only one letter to the editor about Synanon, and even an announcement about repaving a county road would usually draw at least one letter. We had put whatever influence *The Light* had on the line, in saying there were a number of problems at Synanon, that the county should correct them, and that *Light* readers should attend Tuesday's hearing to demonstrate their concern.

What if no one showed up for the hearing? The possibility began to worry me. I asked the various readers who dropped by the newspaper office on Monday if they planned to attend the hearing. None did. With each demur, I got more and more depressed. I was embarrassed that *The Light*'s efforts seemed to be having so little impact. Worse yet, I reasoned that if West Marin residents appeared unconcerned about Synanon, county supervisors most probably would do nothing. Synanon would continue to break zoning laws. Synanon's harsh treatment of children—referred to in the grand jury report and detailed in *The Los Angeles Times*—would continue unregulated. And the sheriff—after a suitable delay—might well give Synanon deputies back their badges.

A Realtor friend, Cecil Asman, dropped by *The Light* that Monday to place an ad, and I repeated my usual question: was Asman going to the hearing? Asman doubted he would go. How did he feel about Synanon? Asman said he was annoyed that Synanon could avoid regulations other county residents had to obey. "You might tell the supervisors that," I replied. "It's beginning to sound like there won't be many people showing up to speak." Asman agreed to go although it meant he would have to change his plans for the next day. I suspected he had agreed to go more in the spirit of friendship than as a partisan for good government.

After Asman left, I began wondering if it was ethical for me so directly to influence events I was covering for *The Light*. I felt a reporter should try to keep an objective distance from the events he covers. But I realized I was also the editorial writer for the paper, and *Light* editorials had urged readers to speak up. If in an editorial I can tell people to do something, I reasoned, it's not unethical for me in person to tell them the same thing.

The problem, as I saw it, stemmed from *The Light*'s small size. On a larger paper, where editorial writers and reporters were different people, this conflict wouldn't arise. Since I was obviously not neutral, I finally concluded, the next best thing was to be fair and accurate. Cathy was having similar concerns. "When you go to that meeting tomorrow," she advised me, "you shouldn't say anything, no matter what happens." I agreed.

Cathy also found herself becoming emotionally involved in the Synanon story. Normally her involvement in covering the news was indirect: suggesting story ideas and helping me decide what topics should be covered. I was the editor, and Cathy left the day-to-day news operation up to me. She was the paper's business manager and made the day-to-day business decisions: when to take a debtor to small claims court, which creditors to pay promptly and which to let wait, how much money she and I could draw, and so forth. Such decisions bored me, and I was content to leave all but the biggest business decisions to her alone. Major decisions—when to buy new equipment, how much of a raise to give employees—we reached together.

The arrangement suited both our temperaments. Cathy was less gregarious. I would sometimes spend days cultivating a news source who had important information. Cathy had no patience with "wasting" so much time. I hated the endless arithmetic necessary for making business decisions. Cathy, who had entered college as a math major, plunged into the books with the enthusiasm of a Monopoly player. There were also practical reasons for our division of labor, for Cathy continued to teach at Santa Rosa Junior College Monday through Wednesday—the main news-gathering and production days at *The Light*.

As Cathy drove the thirty-five miles to the college one morning shortly before the supervisors' hearings, she passed a large bus with a logo on its side: SYNANON, THE PEOPLE BUSINESS. It was an innocent enough vehicle, but in the wake of the Cardineau beating even the mere sight of the Synanon logo seemed ominous to Cathy. Driving alone on a country road, it occurred to her that she was glad she was unrecognizable in her twelve-year-old Toyota and not driving my Fiesta, which was bright yellow with personalized license plates reading LIGHT.

Her first class that day was a seminar with three of the students who put out the campus newspaper, *The Oak Leaf*. The students were writing a handbook to establish style and policy for their paper. The topic this day was the handbook's section on libel laws.

Since *The Light* might soon be hit with a libel suit, Cathy realized that day's seminar would be more than an academic discussion. She admitted to the students she was "under a lot of pressure" and explained that *The Light* "might get a harassment libel suit."

Cathy's students knew about *The Light*, since she often drew examples from our experiences to illustrate lessons for her classes. The students were unfamiliar, however, with our stories and editorials on Synanon. Now curious, they asked about our coverage, and Cathy described the Cardineau beating story, the grand jury report, and other news media's relations with Synanon.

Cathy admitted the college was becoming her "haven" from the pressures of dealing with Synanon. Her students, however, thought it was "neat" that their teacher was a crusading journalist. "We're proud of you," one said. Another asked that she begin bringing copies of *The Light* to class. It was the most enthusiastic support either of us had received so far for our Synanon coverage, and by the end of the seminar, Cathy's tension had mostly disappeared.

I, on the other hand, found little to buoy my spirits. In fact, by the time I left the newspaper office Monday evening before the hearing, I was intensely depressed. "We've done everything we can," Cathy tried to reassure me over dinner. "If the readers don't care, that's ultimately their problem—not yours or mine." She may have been right, but her observation gave me little satisfaction, and I lay awake much of the night, churning with frustration.

Why weren't more people concerned? I had exhausted myself digging up information. Keith too had uncovered some good stuff. I was terribly disappointed our articles hadn't had more impact on the readers I'd talked with. What the hell was wrong with them? What the hell was wrong with me?

Tuesday morning, Cathy returned to the college, and I drove alone over the coast range to the supervisors' hearing in San Rafael. I was still upset as I parked outside the civic center Frank Lloyd Wright had designed for Marin County. Running across a hillside like a train, the building looks like some sort of "city of tomorrow" pictured on the cover of a 1950s science fiction book. County workers dubbed it "Big Pink" (from the title of a Bob Dylan album) because of its pink exterior under a brilliant blue roof.

I took the elevator to the board of supervisors' chambers on the third floor. Inside the chambers, a knot of people was beginning to swell to small-crowd size. I recognized several ranchers from Marshall. My God, I thought with relief, some people are going to show up. Spotting a reporter I didn't recognize, I introduced myself. She turned out to be Narda Zacchino from *The Los Angeles Times*. A dozen reporters from around the San Francisco Bay area were also finding seats—some at the press table, others, like me, in the audience. Wondering if there was anyone present from Synanon, I scanned the room and spotted one shaved head.

The supervisors began taking their high-backed black-leather seats above the audience, and I was delighted to see that several were reading last week's *Light*. But when the hearing got under way, a split among board members was soon obvious. Supervisor Arnold Baptiste, who had voted against holding the meeting, was now chairing it. After declaring the hearing open, Baptiste turned to Supervisor Barbara Boxer and sarcastically commented, "This is your show." Boxer bristled.

Baptiste asked the lone Synanon member in the audience if

he wished to say anything. The member identified himself as Doug Hurt and read a six-page letter from the Synanon legal department accusing the Marin County Grand Jury of "racism" and "religious prejudice. . . . The grand jury report is not worthy of a point-by-point response."

Supervisor Denis Rice had immediate questions for Hurt. Was there a school at Synanon? Was there a hospital? "I am not officially a spokesman for Synanon," Hurt replied. "I am not authorized to answer any questions."

Then it was time for West Marin residents to speak. Rancher Alvin Gambonini described Synanon members trying to drag him from his car one night in June, 1975, while he and his family were parked on their own property bordering on Synanon. Gambonini said he had been punched in the face repeatedly.

"I'm a little bit scared about Synanon having all those guns in Marshall," said a jeweler, David Clarkson. Similar concern came from Wick Ahrens, who said he lived on a neighboring ranch to Synanon. Sheep rancher Dick Respini said a burglar carrying a Synanon posse badge had been caught in his house and that the burglar had been armed with two knives. Respini added that he might not be still alive if the burglar had been armed with a gun.

"I share my neighbors' concern about the violence," said a sculptor from Marshall, Al Clarke. Synanon's huge gun purchase, he figured, "must be scare tactics to the neighbors, the press, and even the supervisors." A commercial fisherman, Roger Wishard, added, "Everyone is afraid. We're all small people out there. . . . I'm not [down] on Synanon. The people are fine. We just don't understand why this threat, why this force."

By now there was standing room only in the supervisors' chambers, but John Vertigan, former owner of Marshall's tavern, said, "There would be more from West Marin today were there not intimidations by lawsuits." Supervisor Bob

Roumiguiere agreed, saying he had received calls complaining about Synanon from people who indicated they were too scared to attend the hearing.

Roumiguiere's outspokenness surprised the audience and fellow supervisors alike. Traditionally he had allied himself often with Supervisors Baptiste and Giacomini against Supervisors Rice and Boxer. But suddenly he was taking up Rice and Boxer's case emphatically. If Synanon refused to cooperate with county government and continued to threaten its West Marin neighbors, Roumiguiere added, "We'll have to take what steps are necessary to get them out of Marin County."

West Marin's supervisor, Gary Giacomini, five weeks before had attacked the grand jury's report as "rank hearsay, triple removed." Now he seemed to be having second thoughts. Synanon, he said, should have sent someone to the hearing who could speak for the organization. "It's a tragedy that Synanon isn't here," the supervisor remarked while directing his gaze at Hurt. "Synanon has to be treated like anyone else in the county. There's no excuse for not being here."

While all this was going on, I was hastily jotting notes on what each speaker said. Since I didn't know many of the speakers from the audience, after some sat down I scurried over to get their names and have them spelled. As much as possible I tried to remain inconspicuous, but since I was also jumping up to take photos whenever speakers used the microphone at the front of the audience, my presence was fairly obvious. A woman asked me if I was from Synanon and looked greatly relieved when I said I was from *The Light.*

Although the hearing had been scheduled five weeks earlier, I began to notice that only a few people in county government were prepared to discuss Synanon. Again I was irritated that county government was still not taking seriously the problems at Synanon. As the meeting progressed, some of the supervisors continued to read *The Light*'s articles on Synanon. A county staffer from the Department of Health and Social

Services told the board her department was arranging with Synanon to have the county child-abuse unit conduct an inspection. County Counsel Doug Maloney then contradicted her. "As of yesterday," he reported, "they [Synanon] said we will have to get a search warrant."

One county official was prepared: Supervisor Boxer. I discovered that, like me, she had feared no one from West Marin would show up. She, therefore, had arranged for a videotape of KGO-TV's report on the Synanon gun buy to be shown to the board. On the news clip, a KGO reporter noted the station could find no one to talk on camera about his fear of Synanon, although several West Marin residents, the reporter said, had privately expressed fears.

Synanon for weeks had belittled the grand jury's call for an investigation of child abuse at Synanon, citing the jurors' admission that they had insufficient direct evidence to charge "offenders." To demonstrate that grand jurors had at least some evidence of child abuse, Supervisor Boxer read a declaration from a Los Angeles court case. The declaration had been written by a fifteen-year-old girl, Julie Moncharsh, who had twice run away from Synanon facilities in West Marin.

"I was always being hit," the girl had written. "If I didn't run in 'basic training,' I was hit. If I did an exercise wrong or changed my sheets wrong, I was hit. Once I was taken in front of a classroom with another girl and hit."

The girl noted that she ran away to the nearby town of Petaluma in January, 1976, but police there returned her to Synanon. "When I returned, I was given a 'contract' for trying to escape. I was made to wear large gas station attendant's clothes and made to eat standing up and given only three hours' sleep. I was not allowed showers, and I was made to work cleaning up pig feces with carrot sticks, putting the feces in cups."

Also talking about children's problems at Synanon was rancher Gambonini. He told the supervisors that children running away from Synanon had arrived at his home at all hours. He estimated there had been "about thirty in the last three years." Other accounts of runaways came from some of Gambonini's neighbors.

The West Marin residents who spoke had criticisms to level at county government as well as at Synanon. Marshall resident Roger Wishard noted his neighbors were "afraid to call the sheriff" about troubles with Synanon, worried that the sheriff's office "may be in cahoots with Synanon."

Several of the supervisors didn't like Sheriff Mountanos; for years he and the board had feuded over the budget for the sheriff's department. The supervisors now were glad to be able to focus anti-county resentment on the sheriff. Supervisor Giacomini called on Mountanos to make permanent his dismissal of the two Synanon deputies. Deputies, "like Caesar's wife, must be above suspicion," Giacomini declared. He also directed county staff to determine by the following Tuesday what use permits Synanon needed. Aha! I noted to myself. Giacomini must have read last week's editorial. Giacomini's directive was supported by the rest of the board. Even Supervisor Baptiste, who had voted against holding the hearing, called Giacomini's approach "reasonable."

As the meeting came to an end, I was buoyant. The public *had* paid attention; the supervisors *would* take action. Supervisor Boxer spotted me. "Congratulations," she said happily. "If it weren't for you, this wouldn't have happened."

I went out into the hall and was stopped again, this time by a group of people, most of whom I didn't recognize. It was the grand jury, and they too were happy. They felt vindicated, and I deserved much of the credit, one told me. I would have enjoyed staying longer for the compliments, but it was almost deadline. I excused myself and ran down to my car.

The road over the coast range back to Point Reyes Station is narrow and winding; I usually drive it too fast. This time I backed off slightly on the accelerator. I didn't want to concentrate that hard on driving. I had spent an almost sleepless night expecting to be humiliated by the hearing. For a moment as I drove back to the paper, my eyes teared up in relief. Then I found myself shouting: "We did it!" "We did it!"

Back at *The Light*, calmer but still jubilant, I began to figure out how to write up the meeting. There was too much material for one story, I decided. The lead story (later headlined: SUPES GET TOUGH WITH SYNANON) would cover the board's directives to staff and most of the public comment. A second story would focus on the child-abuse issue and Synanon's refusing entrance to the inspection team. A third would cover discussion of the sheriff's relations with Synanon.

And then I remembered a comment by *The Los Angeles Times* reporter, Narda Zacchino, that she was looking into the campaign nomination papers filed by Mountanos with the county elections clerk. There must be some Synanon signatures on those papers, I surmised. Narda had given me the phone number of where she was staying, and I called. "I want to follow through on this Mountanos thing," I told her. "But since I heard about it from you, I don't want to steal your story. Is there a problem if we run it in tomorrow's paper?" Narda said there wasn't; she was merely going to tag the information onto her hearing story.

"To hell with the deadline," I said to myself. "We'll just work late tonight." Then I realized there was no one to research and write the Mountanos story. Keith, the news editor, had his own stories to write. Cathy was teaching. And I had already assigned myself three Synanon stories and an editorial.

I called a former reporter for *The Independent-Journal*, Karen Peterson, who lived in West Marin. She was about to take a sick cat to the veterinarian but was enthusiastic. As soon as she had dropped off her cat, Karen promised, she would drive to the civic center.

Three hours later, she came back with her story—an even more interesting one than I had anticipated. A Synanon member, Karen reported, had solicited signatures on nomination papers for Sheriff Mountanos's reelection. Who was the member? "Art Warfield," Karen replied. I observed that Warfield "certainly does get around." There were about ninety signatures on the nomination papers. Karen said she was able to recognize those of Synanon members by their addresses: 6055 Marshall-Petaluma Rd. or 18500 State Route 1, Marshall. She had checked other candidates' nomination papers; none had any mass support from Synanon.

Karen had also learned that two Synanon members, Jack Harrison and Carolyn O'Connell, had picked up from the county the documents necessary to run as write-in candidates for the local Democratic Central Committee. No one else had filed for the seats, she pointed out, and if the pair ran uncontested, they would need only a vote apiece to be elected.

The central committee is a minor body that gets out the vote for party candidates and helps with fund-raising. Two Synanon members showing interest in running for office, however, was significant since Synanon had previously declined to be openly active in Marin County politics. Karen called the committee chairman and asked what he thought of Synanon's possibly winning two seats. The chairman liked the idea: "Synanon is interested in the county . . . and wants to be good neighbors."

Karen's story on Synanon's entrance into county politics was the last article written for the April 13, 1978, issue. The article noted Mountanos's support from Synanon and discussed the central committee race. She also pointed out, "There are 500 registered voters at Synanon, making it the largest precinct in the county."

CHAPTER 6

SYNANON AND THE PRESS

The board of supervisors' hearing on Synanon and the issue of *The Light* that covered it seemed to Cathy and me the climax of a month and a half of intense work. But in politics, a climactic event is usually the start of another series of events. The supervisors' hearing, we soon discovered, was more foreplay than climax.

Before the week was over, Marin News Service had called to say it had been too cautious. It would now cover Synanon news for *The Light*. A little-known candidate for sheriff issued news releases lambasting Sheriff Mountanos's handling of problems at Synanon. The challenger was Al Howenstein, a captain on the small San Anselmo police force. I didn't think Howenstein had much of a chance to beat Mountanos, but I was glad to see Synanon become an issue in the sheriff's race.

Howenstein's making an issue of Synanon meant that in Marin County, *The Light* would not be solely responsible for keeping the Synanon story alive. Cathy several times had warned me that I was in danger of looking like a "screamer" since no other newspaper in the San Francisco Bay area was taking the story as seriously. "If readers think you're obsessed," said Cathy, "they'll ignore your stories."

As Cathy saw it, *The Light* should start paying more attention to other topics and running Synanon stories much less often. I, however, was beginning to be fascinated by this strange institution the grand jury had left on our doorstep. Moreover, I had now done enough research on Synanon to believe the situation there was far worse than most people realized.

At home, I admitted to Cathy that my pride was also involved. I wanted to show that, unlike neighboring newspapers, *The Light* had recognized the significance of the grand jury's findings. I did not want *The Light*'s previous coverage written off as "much ado about nothing." Irritated by Cathy's lesser interest in the story, I would argue, "At least *The LA Times* also thinks it's an important story." Cathy finally responded, "At the very least then, we ought to start running Synanon stories below the fold when they are on page 1, and more often run them inside." I reluctantly agreed.

Part of what kept me convinced that Synanon deserved more coverage were repeated hints—often from county staffers—that staff in various state agencies were concerned about possible child abuse, MediCal fraud, and financial irregularities at Synanon. If their concerns were made public, I reasoned, there would be more public pressure for solutions. Moreover, if I could document official concern, I could show that *The Light* was not imagining wrongdoing where none existed.

The problem was locating those staffers in government who were probing Synanon. My source in county government, Green Door, was familiar with several state agencies; I called to find out what he knew. Green Door, as it turned out, had heard a rumor that the California Department of Health was preparing to go to court seeking an inspection warrant to go into Synanon. Green Door also reminded me that an investigation of Synanon's finances was under way in the attorney general's Charitable Trust Division.

It was one of my last calls to Green Door for information. The main help he could give me was to direct me to sources of information. With his tips on the health department and Charitable Trust Division, he had literally exhausted his stock of sources. I knew that he, along with a number of other state and county people, believed that Synanon was outfoxing government and resented it; that accounted for his cooperation. I suspected that he enjoyed providing tips the way children enjoy directing the searcher in a game by yelling: "Warmer . . . colder."

Working from one of the tips Green Door gave me, I called Deputy Attorney General Jim Schwartz in the Charitable Trust Division's San Francisco office. "We are doing an audit," Schwartz confirmed, and added, "We will not release any information." What if the audit turned up irregularities? "We would simply move to correct the problem," answered Schwartz. I told Schwartz I thought the public had the right to know if a charity was mishandling charitable funds. Only if a lawsuit was necessary to force Synanon to change its practices, Schwartz said curtly, would the results of the audit "become a matter of public record." The deputy attorney general clearly resented the questions. I, in turn, told Schwartz he seemed to be forgetting his "obligation to the public" and hung up.

My next series of calls was to the health department, where I happily found a more helpful group of officials. An official who asked that his name be withheld—a request I was getting used to—reported an initial investigation had already been completed. The investigation, he said, was to determine whether Synanon needed licensing as a care facility. Results of the investigation had been turned over to the attorney general's office, since the AG's lawyers represented the health department when it needed to go to court, the official added.

His explanation seemed to confirm Green Door's information that the health department would seek an inspection warrant. I called the health department's lawyer in the AG's office, Tom Warriner. Did the health department hope to get an inspection warrant? "That's not an illogical assumption," Warriner replied.

The Synanon story was getting bigger. Two state agencies as well as a variety of county departments were now involved. In reaction to this closer scrutiny, Synanon began to step up its public relations activities to counter what it called bureaucratic "harassment."

Synanon up to now had been taking a stick to its critics. Dederich had threatened to investigate health department officials if they persisted in bothering Synanon. Suits had been filed against critics in the media. And Synanon members had harassed grand jurors in their homes. Now, without abandoning the stick, Synanon laid on the carrot.

Synanon had already tried to win support from other organizations with its two-day giveaway of surplus property in March. For some time Synanon had held a barbecue and open house for the public on Saturdays. As problems within the organization received more and more publicity, Synanon began to promote the barbecues. "Come and see for yourself," proclaimed Synanon.

County supervisors had been told, "Everyone is invited." The same public invitation had been repeated in an *Independent-Journal* article. I called Synanon to see if I could attend; I was not eager to show up only to get into an angry confrontation. A woman in Synanon's public relations office said she didn't know if I was included in the public invitation. She promised to have her boss call back. When he didn't, I called again. This time the woman reported, "I have been instructed to tell you you are not welcome at the barbecue."

I was all the more disappointed when *The Light*'s advertising manager at the time, Darlene Leighton, returned from

Petaluma, a city of thirty thousand some twenty miles from Point Reyes Station. Darlene had gotten into a conversation about Synanon with a merchant who said he had been invited to the barbecue. The Synanon member who had invited him had said the barbecue would be a chance to hear Synanon's side of the "dispute" with *Time*, ABC, and *The Point Reyes Light*. So Synanon *was* taking us seriously! Flattered, I said to Darlene, "At least we're in good company."

The more Cathy and I thought about it, the more puzzling Synanon's relations with the news media seemed. The foundation had sued ABC and its San Francisco station, KGO, over coverage of the weapons purchase. *Time* magazine had been sued over its somewhat sarcastic article calling Synanon a "kooky cult." But *The Los Angeles Times*, which in October, 1977, had launched the current critical reporting on Synanon, had not been sued. Nor had *The Light*. We couldn't find a pattern to the lawsuits.

At the same time, we resented and were puzzled by the East Marin press's continuing defense, even promotion, of Synanon. San Rafael's *Independent-Journal* had been welcomed at Synanon's barbecues and ran a large photo of one. (In the background of the picture was a Synanon banner proclaiming: TIME AND KGO TELL LIES.)

On April 13, *The San Francisco Chronicle* wrote in an editorial, "Marin County's supervisors are quite right to tell Synanon . . . to get rid of its weapons depot and act like a peaceful, law-abiding resident if it expects to remain in West Marin. . . . Synanon should discontinue its highhanded and thoughtless approach to the community."

Two days later, *The Independent-Journal* countered with an editorial of its own: SYNANON STANCE MAY BE MISUNDERSTOOD. The *I-J* editorial declared, "Synanon members are fiercely dedicated to helping others; they are friendly people, and probably in a ratio favorable to 'the outside' law abiding. . . . So why the mounting criticism? For starters, Synanon members—living in a county where 'being different' is always accepted and generally praised—*are very different*. . . . At this point it appears the immediate need is for Marin 'straights' to visit Synanon in a friendly spirit, seeking to relate to the needs, attitudes, and ambitions of its members."

I was offended by the editorial. In Marin County, the word *straight* usually means "not hippie," and the editorial seemed to imply that criticism of Synanon was coming from "hippies" such as myself or other West Marin residents. The message apparently was that straights should see for themselves what was going on and should pay little attention to what we hippies were complaining about. Recalling the *Examiner* reporter who compared anti-Synanon feelings in West Marin to anti-black prejudice, I griped to Cathy, "One moment we're being written off as rednecks. The next moment we're being written off as hippies."

In other circumstances, we would have been pleased if East Marin papers such as *The Independent-Journal* and *The Pacific Sun* ignored West Marin news; it would make *The Light* all the more in demand. Now we found the week's *Pacific Sun* attacks on the grand jury and *Independent-Journal* defense of Synanon frustrating. Most county staff and officials lived in East Marin, where *The Light* was not sold, so government people got most of their county news from the East Marin press. No wonder they previously had felt little urgency in correcting wrongdoing at Synanon—they weren't hearing about it.

Cathy and I tried to figure out *The Sun*'s and *I-J*'s pro-Synanon stance. Did the two papers owe Synanon a favor? Were they stupid? Were they somehow allied with the county officials who had spoken out against the grand jury report? I shared my musings with a reporter from another newspaper and learned a couple of rumors.

One was that *I-J* reporter George Nevin had an unusual incentive to maintain good rapport with Synanon: he was supposedly negotiating to do an interview for *Playboy* magazine with Synanon founder Charles Dederich. Nevin had written numerous stories for *The I-J* about people and events at Synanon. The articles were fascinating, but I thought they uncritically reflected Synanon's point of view. In fact, Synanon sometimes reproduced Nevin's articles for distribution by Synanon's public relations office.

I called Nevin. Was he negotiating a *Playboy* interview with Dederich? The *I-J* reporter said he had contacted *Playboy*, but "they weren't interested." Dederich wasn't enough of a national figure, Nevin candidly explained.

It seemed to me that Nevin had done nothing unethical. Part of a reporter's job is to establish rapport with sources—even unsavory ones. The worst Nevin could be accused of, I concluded, was being insufficiently skeptical. Nevin was personable and said to be the "fair-haired boy" of *I-J* management. I too liked him, but wished *The Independent-Journal* didn't view Synanon through Nevin's eyes.

The second rumor I had picked up was that *The Sun*'s assistant publisher, Hut Landon, had a mother living in Synanon. Landon had written the article GRAND JURY STUBS ITS TOE ON SYNANON, which misrepresented the roles within the sheriff's office of the two reserve deputies from Synanon. When I called, Landon confirmed that his mother was a Synanon resident. That was one reason Synanon was willing to talk to him, Landon added. Might the relationship bias his reporting? Landon didn't think so. Would Landon ever write anything unflattering about Synanon? Landon doubted he would, but said someone else at *The Sun* might.

The revelations about Nevin and Landon were somewhat reassuring. There was no conspiracy. No payoff. I was more critical of Landon's situation than Nevin's but even Landon seemed more naive than sinister. Had Tuesday's board of supervisors' hearing not gone so well, I might have felt less charitable. As it was, it had been a pretty good week.

And then the week got better. Cathy took her students to the annual convention of California's Journalism Association of Community Colleges. Part of the convention was a presentation of awards to campus newspapers. Cathy's students had entered several categories but were pessimistic about getting any awards; Santa Rosa Junior College that year had been reclassified a "large" college. The college's paper, *The Oak Leaf*, was now competing against student papers from the huge junior colleges in Southern California. As awards were announced, the pessimism seemed justified. Reporting, cartooning, and photography awards all went to students from large schools. Announced last were the most prestigious prizes—those for general excellence. As Cathy's students waited for it all to be over, the master of ceremonies declared *The Oak Leaf* to be the best large-college tabloid in California. Cathy was still ebullient and couldn't stop talking about the award when she came home two days later.

I insisted *The Light* carry a story on *The Oak Leaf*'s award. The triumph was completely independent of me, and in our marriage, that was important. As partners in publishing *The Light*, we competed intensely with other newspapers. As husband and wife, we competed with each other, although not always consciously. Cathy resented it when I got sole credit for *The Light*'s accomplishments. In covering *The Oak Leaf*'s "general excellence" award, I hoped to somewhat even the balance.

Back at work Monday, April 17, I put out calls on a number of Synanon stories and waited for call-backs. Sheriff Louis Mountanos denied charges from challenger Al Howenstein that the sheriff's office wasn't adequately policing Synanon. Jack Harrison, the Democratic Central Committee candidate from Synanon, returned a call to say he was running strictly because he wanted to help the Democratic Party. Carolyn O'Connell, the other candidate from Synanon, was dropping out of the race.

I hadn't really expected Harrison to return my call and was not as prepared as I could have been to interview him; later I thought of all the questions I should have asked. Since February I had periodically called Synanon for a comment on stories coming up on the organization. For a while, I was told that someone from Synanon would call back. Twice Synanon had waited to return my call until *The Light* was on the newsstands. Then call-backs stopped altogether. Eventually I had Keith call Synanon to see if he would fare any better. After that week's paper was out, Synanon's public relations officer, Mike Kaiser, called Keith to say Synanon would not return calls to anyone at *The Light*.

When Harrison returned my call, I wondered if it signaled a change in policy. "You're the first Synanon member to return a call in months," I told Harrison. The candidate said it was no wonder since *The Light*'s coverage of Synanon had been so "one-sided." What did Synanon expect if it didn't return the newspaper's calls, I countered.

Harrison was guarded in what he could say but discussed his background in Southern California Democratic politics. When the interview was over, I told Harrison I would like a chance to talk with him at more length in the future. "I can assure you it won't be a setup," I said.

"It's interesting you'd say that," Harrison replied.

"I said it only because you seemed so skeptical," I parried.

I often worked on several stories at the same time. Because a source might take hours—or even days—to return a call and because some calls were never returned, it was impractical to wait until one story was finished before beginning on another. One of those who did return a call that Monday was Don Gutoff, director of Marin County's planning department. I had called him wondering how long the momentum of the previous week's county hearing would last.

The supervisors had instructed Gutoff to determine what use permits Synanon needed. Gutoff was also to decide what conditions should be placed on those permits to control problems ranging from child abuse to weapons. The planning director had until the next day, Tuesday, to prepare his answer.

How was his preparation going? Gutoff admitted with frustration he was having to look into everything from how Synanon should operate its schools to "whether filing a shear pin will turn an M-14 into a machine gun." Gutoff said he would rather skip the use permits altogether and instead have Synanon itself draft a master plan for the county to approve. Synanon would also prefer that approach, I noted, since it essentially regulated new activities but not existing ones. The county could demand that Synanon complete the masterplan within three months, Gutoff ventured. I pointed out the county had given Synanon just such a demand three years before, and nothing had ever come of it.

What did the county plan to do about Synanon's $9-million-a-year Advertising Gifts and Premiums business being operated in agricultural zoning? (ADGAP was a pen, pencil, and knickknack distributorship with sales teams operating out of Synanon. Hundreds of businesses around the United States bought from ADGAP ballpoint pens and so forth embossed with their company logos.) Gutoff replied he didn't realize ADGAP was that big. The planning director added that he had been unable to get an appointment to look over Synanon's facilities until tomorrow. "But that's the day you're supposed to make your recommendations to the board," I pointed out. Gutoff realized this but reiterated that Synanon had said it could not find time for him until Tuesday. Since Synanon's "observer" Doug Hurt, had tape-recorded the board meeting, the foundation obviously knew the county's timetable and was trying to slow it down. The tactic was working.

Realizing that nothing would happen, I let the now-emboldened Marin News Service cover Tuesday's board meeting for *The Light.* As expected, the supervisors postponed action another week. However, one revelation was made during the meeting: the county public works department on three occasions had issued building permits at Synanon even though the county planning department had not issued the prerequisite use permits. The planning department was unhappy about the public works department's actions.

I used my interview with Planning Director Gutoff in an editorial for the April 20 paper. The editorial, headlined GUTOFF AND GOLIATH, contrasted Synanon's aggressiveness with the planning director's passivity. "If all this sounds like criticism of Gutoff, it shouldn't," the editorial commented.

> Rather it should be taken as a glimpse of the obstacles to adequately regulating Synanon. County government was established to perform various housekeeping duties for the public: maintaining roads, providing law enforcement, planning for orderly private development. It's the kind of work officials like Gutoff can do well.
>
> But along comes Synanon. It draws a population, in part, from the criminal justice systems of numerous states. It operates a $20 million nationwide corporation owning several businesses. It has a private legal staff bigger than many large law firms. And it is incredibly sophisticated in politics. The scope of the Synanon problem is immense. Gutoff and his department are outgunned.

The following week, Gutoff had his recommendations ready, and the supervisors voted to start procedures to rezone Synanon to agricultural/planned development. The only significant effect would be to control new construction. The supervisors also considered stopping Synanon from using its schools, airstrips, and medical facilities until they received permits. But neither this proposal nor the proposed rezoning fully satisfied board members. "The board isn't addressing the serious problems of Synanon," said Supervisor Gary Giacomini. "The schools aren't the serious issue. . . . Guns are."

In an attempt to do better, the supervisors invited Synanon to send representatives to the board's next meeting, May 2. It was to be the fourth consecutive board meeting that would be largely devoted to Synanon. Since our weekly deadline and the supervisors' meetings coincided, I had let the MNS cover the last two board meetings. However, since the May 2 meeting promised to be more significant than the last two, I went.

As with the first hearing, a crowd of West Marin residents showed up. This time several major ranchers were in the group. The delegation from the press was also bigger. *NBC Nightly News* sent a producer from New York and a camera crew. The one group not represented was Synanon.

In the absence of anyone from Synanon, the supervisors merely took testimony from the West Marin residents. Most—like Supervisor Giacomini the week before—said the county still hadn't taken control of the Synanon situation. "In my daily activities, I must conform and help other people conform to a myriad of ordinances," said Realtor Cecil Asman. "I don't want to be a second-class citizen and have Synanon be a first-class citizen."

Toby Giacomini, the owner of a Point Reyes Station trucking company, complained, "Those people up there can do anything they want." His nephew, Robert Giacomini, a rancher, added, "We want to see Synanon treated exactly the same as everyone else. . . . There seem to be two sets of laws in this county. We just feel Synanon has put a snow job on the county for the last umpteen years. We're fed up."

Supervisor Bob Roumiguiere agreed: "We certainly have been able to act very strongly with individuals but have been less successful with Synanon."

Lively as the morning hearing was, it was overshadowed by what followed that afternoon. After the hearing, NBC producer Patricia Lynch took a camera crew to property next to Synanon to film a report on conflict between Synanon and its neighbors. Suddenly Lynch discovered she and her crew were themselves in a conflict with Synanon. Ten Synanon trucks converged on the camera crew and its van.

Synanon members parked the trucks so as to blockade the camera crew's exit, and raised the trucks' hoods. "There must be a Bermuda Triangle here," mocked a Synanon member, "because our engines are all out." About fifty Synanon members, ranging from children to adults in their forties, circled the camera crew. Producer Lynch and her crew tried to interview some of the circling crowd, but word was passed from one Synanon member to another: "Don't talk to them."

After about ten minutes of harassment, the NBC crew escaped by driving across a pasture. Meanwhile, rancher Alvin Gambonini, who had seen the blockade, had called the sheriff's office. *The Light*'s news editor, Keith Ervin, arrived just behind the deputies and photographed producer Lynch filing a report with officers. While this was going on, Synanon brought out over one hundred reinforcements to chant protests about news media coverage of Synanon.

The protest was still under way when the NBC camera crew arrived at *The Light*'s office. Producer Lynch was furious. She filmed an interview with me about Synanon's power to avoid regulation in Marin County, but the footage was never used.

The NBC crew was still in Marin County a week later, when the supervisors held their fifth hearing on Synanon. This time, Synanon sent a formal delegation. Supervisor Giacomini had urged his West Marin constituents to also attend, and the biggest crowd yet was on hand.

Synanon sent as its main spokesman a dapper (aside from his prisonlike haircut) lawyer, Howard Garfield. His presentation lasted two hours, including a slide show of Synanon activities and buildings. Garfield had arrived prepared to take the offensive, and the opening speech he read was delivered angrily.

"It seems to us these procedures serve some ulterior purpose," he snarled, in apparent reference to the upcoming election. "The real issue is not Synanon's lawlessness," he said, but "prejudice." Since 1973 Synanon residents had been shot at, insulted, and forced off county roads, Garfield claimed. "We are victims of a rising tide of terrorism. . . . It is sadly ironic that our attempts to protect ourselves have generated so much fear among our neighbors." The attorney said Synanon had kept the sheriff informed about the whereabouts of its weapons and would not bring them into Marin County "unless we are forced to do so to protect ourselves. We hope that circumstances will not force us to use our arms." For the moment, Garfield implied, the bulk of the weapons would remain in Tulare County.

Supervisor Roumiguiere responded to Garfield, "Your presentation came across to me as if you have a persecution complex."

Garfield's speech was followed by an address from another Synanon member, Leon Levy. Levy told how brutal and sordid the outside world had been for him and how much better his life was inside Synanon, which he described as a "loving" environment.

Then it was time for the West Marin audience to speak, and several residents lined up to use the microphone. The Synanon contingent immediately hurried from the room, ignoring a request from Supervisor Roumiguiere that they remain. Supervisor Giacomini rushed out of the room and persuaded them to return. "Synanon takes two hours to explain all their friendly and good deeds. After saying all that, the moment residents of West Marin stand up, they walk out," angrily observed rancher Bob Giacomini, a second cousin to the supervisor.

Other West Marin residents had complaints of their own. Sandra Chatham of Marshall told of a Synanon runaway breaking into her house. She said she came home to find the Synanon man asleep in her bed, wearing clothes he had found in her house. In fact, refugees from Synanon were a major problem for the community. Those escaping Synanon found themselves miles from any town or public transportation. Often they were afraid to be seen along the road, fearing other Synanon members would catch them and take them back. Rancher Gambonini earlier had complained about another runaway who had broken into the rancher's house and stolen a pickup truck.

Another rancher, Al Poncia of Tomales, told the supervisors he had seen conflicts between Synanon members and townspeople where "if someone had been armed on either side, someone could have been killed."

The supervisors wanted the Synanon contingent to remain not only so it could hear the complaints of its neighbors but also so the board could ask questions about Synanon. Synanon had no permits for an airstrip or a medical and/or health clinic. Were there such facilities at Synanon? "There is no health clinic," said attorney Garfield emphatically. "There is no airstrip!"

Supervisor Denis Rice, who was also a lawyer, noted that Synanon had paid founder Dederich and seven other top officers $795,000 the year before. "Would that pose in your mind," Rice asked in his lawyerly way, "whether that is a business rather than a charitable organization?"

Garfield responded that $500,000 of that was Dederich's "pre-retirement bonus" and said, "It is the duty of organizations like Synanon to provide for the retirement of employees." Garfield said Dederich had paid more than half the $500,000 in state and federal income taxes, although he could have saved money by taking the bonus in other ways. "As a proud American . . . he insisted on paying the maximum taxes he possibly could," Garfield claimed. The audience snickered. It was an incredible assertion, especially in light of Synanon's continual claim that it should pay no income or property taxes. In fact,

Synanon was suing the state for taxing Synanon's airplanes and boats. If Dederich was insisting on paying taxes, it was certainly in contrast with the attitude of his organization.

Supervisor Giacomini asked Garfield for a commitment that Synanon would "give away" its weapons (to whom was not specified). "I don't have the power or authority to make a response," Garfield responded. He promised to relay the request to Synanon's board of directors.

It was now obvious that Garfield had not come to the meeting ready to make any compromises. The supervisors had to content themselves with reiterating their commitment to correct zoning problems at Synanon and to investigate child-abuse allegations. They again, however, formally asked Synanon to get rid of its arsenal.

Once more a meeting on Synanon concluded with the supervisors in frustration. Throughout the five hearings, the board's concern about Synanon had steadily grown. Synanon apparently didn't care. Rather than making a pretense of cooperating with the board, Synanon instead had sent a spokesman who angrily denounced it. In my article for *The Light*, I summed up the meeting: "When it was all over, the supervisors had stuck to their guns, and Synanon still had theirs."

CHAPTER

7

A SOCIOLOGIST'S THEORY

The Light's coverage of Synanon in the spring of 1978 attracted little public attention outside of West Marin. But West Marin readers—particularly those living near Synanon—read our articles and editorials intently. A few residents of the Marshall area had previously tried without success to get other news media to investigate Synanon. After he was beaten in June, 1975, Alvin Gambonini, the rancher whose property bordered on Synanon's, tried to get several papers in Marin and Sonoma counties interested in Synanon wrongdoing. All turned him down, apparently writing him off as the bitter victim of a simple assault.

In the two and a half years Cathy and I had owned *The Light*, no one had asked us to look into Synanon, perhaps thinking we were too small to matter. Now that we had demonstrated our concern about Synanon, we suddenly began to hear from Synanon's neighbors. Gambonini sent *The Independent-Journal* a letter to the editor contrasting *The I-J*'s supportive coverage of Synanon to our probing coverage. Others encouraged us more cautiously; a few offered confidential tips. After one of the supervisors' hearings, a workman from Marshall pulled me aside to say "a friend" had some documents I might be interested in. I suggested the friend bring them by *The Light*. Returning from lunch a few days later, I found the "documents" lying on my desk with a message saying they had been found at the scene of a motorcycle accident. The documents seemed to be a diary lost by a Synanon member. Included in it were notes taken at a Synanon meeting; the notes described how Synanon's private police force was organized and deployed.

I was less than enthusiastic about receiving the diary. Some of it was intimately personal, and I felt guilty skimming through it. I was also worried that the diary might have been planted by Synanon. One of the alleged "causes of action" in Synanon's suit against *The Examiner* was that the newspaper had received some tape recordings allegedly stolen from Synanon by an ex-member.

Cathy and I agreed we could not use the diary for any news stories. But what to do with it? Cathy noted that the sheriff's office was the normal place to take found property, so I called a deputy at the West Marin sheriff's substation and described the diary. "I want to get rid of it," I told the deputy. The deputy, however, replied that the diary should be in the hands of the attorney general, since it indicated paramilitary activity at Synanon. I called a deputy attorney general in San Francisco, who said he would arrange to have the diary picked up. An hour later, I got a call from the Federal Bureau of Investigation. An FBI agent said he was on his way to Point Reyes Station to get the diary. The FBI! I felt a momentary flush of excitement. Were *they* interested in Synanon?

A short while later a young man in a denim leisure suit arrived. I gave him the diary and asked how the FBI was involved with Synanon. The agent was friendly but evasive, saying only that the FBI was aware of Synanon's large weapons purchase. Call the bureau, he suggested, if anything else like the diary came my way. I was noncommittal.

In the next few weeks, more documents were passed along

to me, often by people who had picked them up from Synanon's public relations department on tours of the foundation. Only one pamphlet was at all startling; it gave Synanon's rationale for creating a private police force: "If trouble should occur, we're prepared to handle it. We don't need to call the police to handle our problems. We're proud to be joining the ranks of citizens everywhere who believe that the answer to keeping crime out of our neighborhoods is a good self-defense program." The rest of the material, while not very newsworthy, contained considerable information on the history of the Synanon corporation.

Another person to contact *The Light* during the supervisors' hearings was a professor of sociology at the University of California at Berkeley, Dr. Richard Ofshe. I was out the first time Dr. Ofshe called. Before I had time to call him back, he called again. Ofshe said he owned a weekend home in Dillon Beach on the West Marin coast and was a subscriber to *The Light*. He had been following with interest our Synanon coverage, since he had spent over a year doing research on Synanon during 1972–73. Much of his research, Ofshe added, had been done inside two of Synanon's three West Marin facilities.

The professor offered to share any information he had on Synanon, but was more interested in what might come of the board of supervisors' hearings. Did I think the board was serious about dealing with the problems at Synanon? I acknowledged that the supervisors so far had been mainly grandstanding for the voters, but added that at least two supervisors, Barbara Boxer and Denis Rice, seemed sincerely upset by what was coming to light. The other three supervisors, I noted, seemed to be coming around to that position.

Ofshe related that he too was worried by developments at Synanon—particularly the violence. When he had done his research inside Synanon five years ago, Ofshe explained, the organization absolutely forbade physical violence. There had been considerable verbal violence in the group encounter sessions Synanon called "games," but while one could shout at others in a game, he could not so much as rise from his chair.

Ofshe said that more recently he had begun hearing from acquaintances in West Marin about violence involving Synanon members. At first he had suspected the accounts were exaggerated. He remembered from his experiences at Synanon that the organization and its members could be arrogant in dealing with outsiders—but violent? Never. However, he had asked a deputy sheriff living in Dillon Beach, Steve Kane, if there was anything to the stories of violence. Kane said there was and described several reports that the sheriff's office had received.

An isolated violent incident could be dismissed as a momentary breakdown in Synanon discipline, Ofshe had reasoned, but repeated violence could reflect a change in Synanon policy. Ofshe told me he knew from his research that the Synanon organization exercised extreme control over Synanon members. If organization policy now included violence, Ofshe warned, a dangerous situation was developing in West Marin.

Ofshe asked if I could arrange a meeting between him and county supervisors so he could explain some of the tactics being used against the county by Synanon. The professor was familiar with the strategy Synanon had used against the city of Santa Monica nineteen years earlier. I knew a little about the incident from the tour I had taken of Synanon in 1975. Charlie Downs, Synanon's public relations director at the time, had recounted it as an example of the obstacles Synanon had overcome. Santa Monica conservatives were suspicious of an organization of addicts setting up shop in a former National Guard armory in their city. Synanon had been harassed with zoning laws, and eventually founder Charles Dederich was jailed for a zoning violation. But Synanon had turned the incident to its advantage. The foundation got widespread publicity and drew immediate sympathy from Southern

California liberals. Ever since then, Ofshe pointed out to me, Synanon had cried "prejudice" whenever it had been accused of breaking the law; he cited zoning disputes in Malibu; Westport, Connecticut; New York City; and San Francisco as examples.

There was something else Dr. Ofshe wanted to tell the supervisors. Synanon was less a commune or a rehabilitation center than a "company town," he insisted.

Up to this point, I had accepted the professor's interpretation of Synanon at face value. Now I began to argue with him. I could agree that Synanon overpaid its top officers and that nepotism was rampant; Dederich had his brother and two children in key positions. But I doubted Synanon was *primarily* a business. As I saw it, Synanon *operated* businesses but was basically a rehabilitation center. Synanon members I had talked to on my tour all told stories about the way Synanon had changed their lives.

Ofshe, however, countered that a lot of people now in Synanon went in "with no more problems than you or I have." Synanon, he said, had discovered that it could provide a luxurious life for its "elite" by taking advantage of the corporation's tax-exempt status. Ofshe insisted Dederich and his cronies "live in Synanon-provided housing, eat Synanon-provided food, ride in Synanon-provided cars, and fly in Synanon-provided airplanes. It's a lifestyle based on perks"—perquisites—"the non-cash benefits that come with a job. If you can get everything you want in perks, you don't need much cash." Ofshe said he had been predicting that Synanon would reduce its membership to "a few hundred people" and evolve into an "elite retreat." As such, he explained, Synanon would take advantage of the public by exploiting its dubious tax-exempt status, but would otherwise be harmless to the outside world. If Synanon were now turning to violence, however, there was a more serious problem, Ofshe stressed.

The professor said he feared that the board of supervisors

was not thinking beyond the immediate problem of guns and zoning violations. "They need to understand how Synanon works and come up with a comprehensive program for regulating it. Otherwise," he warned, "the county is going to have conflicts with Synanon again, and again, and again."

I was impressed by how much Ofshe knew about Synanon, but wondered if he wasn't making the facts fit his theories. However, enough of what he said made sense so that I agreed to help set up a meeting for him with the board of supervisors. In the meantime, Ofshe promised to send me copies of two scholarly papers he had published on Synanon.

Having agreed to arrange for a meeting, I wondered how to go about it. Normally I would have called West Marin's supervisor, Gary Giacomini, but I was unsure of Giacomini's true feelings on Synanon. He had talked tough and been critical of Synanon in hearings when West Marin voters were present, but he had also attacked the grand jury report as "rank hearsay, triple removed."

Supervisors Rice and Boxer already recognized that the Synanon problem was immense, and they would likely be receptive to a meeting. But if they appeared to be behind it, other supervisors with whom the two were frequently at odds would probably shun it. Supervisor Baptiste had voted against holding hearings on Synanon, so he was hardly the person to organize a briefing. That left Supervisor Bob Roumiguiere. Roumiguiere had been outspokenly critical of Synanon and was a close friend of Giacomini's. I gave him a call.

Roumiguiere said the meeting sounded worthwhile but that only two supervisors could attend without breaking the state's law banning secret board meetings. He suggested Giacomini be the second supervisor at the meeting, since Synanon was in his supervisorial district. Roumiguiere said he would set something up with Giacomini.

A week passed and no meeting was scheduled. Ofshe called

me to find out what was going on. He and I then called Roumiguiere at different times for another two weeks. I even tried going directly to Giacomini. The problem, we were repeatedly told by the supervisors, was finding time for a meeting. The meeting proposal was never rejected, but no meeting was ever held.

"What is going on?" I asked Cathy one evening in frustration. "Here is a Synanon expert offering to consult with the county at no charge. The supes say they're worried about Synanon but can't find time to meet with him."

"The supervisors are like firemen," she replied. "There are so many demands on them that they only have time to put out whatever fire is burning. Ofshe wants to get them involved in a long-term project. They don't want to spend that much time."

"If Synanon is committed to fighting the county, but the county isn't committed to fighting Synanon," I countered, "you know who's going to win."

Cathy agreed: "You may be right, but we're stuck with the reality of county government." Events later bore out Cathy's assessment of how local government works, but still, her comments were hardly consoling to me. She was ready to drop the topic. I wanted to *do* something.

Our cabinlike home sat on a slope overlooking some newer homes and older farmhouses. Green pastures spread south across the valley below to the wooded Inverness Ridge two miles away. To the northwest, a late spring sun was setting over Tomales Bay. Cathy had her back to me and through a window was watching clouds over the bay turn from pink to red. "You should see the sky," she murmured. I was busy dialing Richard Ofshe's phone number.

"Looks like we're not going to get a meeting," I told the professor. "Roumiguiere and Giacomini still can't get together on a time."

Ofshe wasn't surprised. "That's why I asked you earlier if the supervisors are serious about Synanon," he pointed out.

"Riddle me this," I demanded. "Why the runaround? Why are so many county officials pro-Synanon? Why are the two newspapers friendliest to Synanon both in Marin County? Riddle me that!"

"What do *you* think it all means?" Ofshe countered. I admitted confusion but said I was again beginning to wonder whether Synanon had some hold—financial or otherwise—on the power structure of Marin County.

"I doubt it," responded Ofshe. "Synanon's probably had a lot of reporters and county officials on the same public relations tour you took. I'll bet lots of those people just believe the hype. Whenever Synanon's caught breaking the law, the leaders claim that if they have, it's only in a technical sense. They pose as a small social program trying to do good but caught in red tape."

"What about the rumors that Dederich's gone crazy?" I interrupted. "Maybe that explains the recent lawbreaking, especially the violence."

Ofshe scoffed, "Almost everything that happens in Synanon is done for a reason. The organization controls people too much for members to start going off on their own and beating up people. That wouldn't happen more than once," Ofshe reasoned, "unless the corporation wants it to happen."

"Well, if Synanon does, Dederich *is* crazy," I persisted.

"Maybe not," said Ofshe. "What's happened to Synanon after these incidents? Almost nothing! The organization's learning it can get away with it. It's a bully-boy tactic to quiet troublemakers. Did you ever hear about the purple-pickup-truck incident in Tomales?"

"I think I know what you're talking about," I answered, "but it happened the spring before Cathy and I bought *The Light*, back in August of '75."

Ofshe recounted the story. In March, 1975, a Synanon member, Thomas Quinn, had been driving a motorcycle toward Synanon on the Marshall-Petaluma road when an oncoming purple pickup truck had swerved into his lane, in an attempt—Quinn assumed—to force him off the road or scare him. The pickup had returned to its own lane, however, before any collision and continued on its way. Quinn didn't see who the other driver was but tried briefly to turn around and catch up with the pickup. When he couldn't, he returned to Synanon and put out a call for other members to help find the culprit.

Synanon members then joined in a search that seemed more emotional than methodical. The purple pickup had been eastbound, but some Synanon members raced west into the town of Tomales, where they spotted a purple pickup truck parked in front of Diekmann's General Store. Synanon members parked behind the pickup, blocking its exit, and demanded to see the driver's license of its teenage driver, John Jensen. A member then phoned Synanon to find out what to do next. The call brought more Synanon members to Tomales, until there were about seventy in all. They told Jensen he could not leave until they found out who was responsible for frightening Quinn, the motorcyclist.

Townspeople began to gather in Jensen's defense, and an argument broke out between Rodgers Martin, a black artist living in Tomales, and a Synanon member, who punched Martin in the face without provocation, as several townspeople later reported to officers. The Synanon member, in turn, told deputies he was struck first.

The officers had trouble deciding who was to blame in the fight but reported that Synanon members "acted wrongfully in detaining the victim's [John Jensen's] vehicle in Tomales."

I knew enough of the story to realize Tomales residents were still indignant about Synanon members sweeping into town and trying to take the law into their own hands. Townspeople had complained about the incident during the board of supervisors' hearing.

But Ofshe had another story to tell that I had heard nothing about. In July, 1975, Synanon members had seized two men in a red pickup truck, taken them in handcuffs to a Synanon ranch, brought them before an angrily shouting crowd of Synanon members, and shaved off their hair. Synanon members accused the pair, Richard Marino and Calvin Smith, both of Sebastopol, of crossing the centerline on a curve and frightening two young bicyclists from Synanon.

After shaving Marino's and Smith's heads, Synanon called the sheriff's office and demanded that the pair be charged with assault with a deadly weapon (the pickup), resisting arrest, drunk driving, and possession of dangerous drugs. Deputies who picked up Marino and Smith at Synanon, however, found little merit to the accusations. Instead, a deputy warned Synanon members that *their* actions bordered on kidnapping and violation of civil liberties. Marino and Smith later filed suit against Synanon because of the incident.

Still another incident related by Ofshe involved two model airplane fliers on the Cabral ranch next to Synanon. Although the pair said they had the rancher's permission to fly model airplanes on his land, Synanon members accused them of trespassing. About ten Synanon members armed with clubs seized the men, Michael Clancy, thirty-four, of Daly City, and Ronald Pearson, twenty-six, of Novato, and took them to a Synanon building. While three Synanon members held each of them, other Synanon members emptied Clancy's and Pearson's pockets. They were then interrogated, with a videotape machine recording their answers.

Again Synanon eventually called the sheriff's office, and deputies arrived to question Clancy and Pearson. Midway through that questioning, however, a Synanon man announced that a foundation lawyer had just called and demanded "the guys get the fuck out of the building right away." After finishing their questioning in a patrol car, the deputies concluded that Clancy and Pearson should not be considered trespass suspects but victims of a "possible kidnapping." Synanon attorney Dan Garrett, however, later justified Synanon's action: "We'll do whatever outraged citizenry has to do with these punks when they get on our property or our neighbor's property!"

Ofshe had several more stories along these lines to tell, but I cut him off. My phone call to him had lasted two hours. Cathy had finished cooking dinner and had already begun eating. "I'm really getting tired of Synanon," said Cathy when I finally hung up.

"And I'm just getting my second wind," I replied. Cathy was feeling affectionate and trying to show it, but I wanted to relay the information from Ofshe.

"When we got back together," Cathy reminded me, "you agreed we would devote more time to each other and less to the paper. But for the past couple of months, all you've wanted to talk about is Synanon."

"Synanon isn't exactly an everyday news story," I shot back. "It's probably the most important story you or I have ever covered."

Cathy insisted that our marriage was important too, and I conceded the point begrudgingly. The argument, however, wouldn't die, and for the next several days we fought it off and on.

Meanwhile, I was becoming increasingly troubled by the accounts of Synanon violence described by Ofshe. Like Ofshe, I was beginning to see an ominous pattern. In an editorial, I had commented, "It seems unlikely Synanon would ever carry out any military action against anybody. . . . [But] Synanon members have already found themselves involved in small-scale violent clashes with outsiders. With so many weapons now available, the potential for tragic incidents is greatly increased."

County elections were coming up June 6, and as May drew to an end, a "candidates night" was scheduled in Point Reyes Station. Among the candidates agreeing to debate were Sheriff Louis Mountanos and challenger Al Howenstein. I hoped the debate would get into Synanon violence. I had already interviewed both candidates, and Howenstein had told me he believed there were more weapons in Synanon's West Marin facilities than Mountanos was saying. Howenstein claimed his information came from a confidential informant.

I sat quietly in the audience while the debate skirted the Synanon issue, and focused instead on the leadership—or lack of it, according to Howenstein—in the sheriff's office. During the question-and-answer session that followed, I noted that both candidates had been making contradictory statements about the extent of weapons at Synanon. Could they each provide evidence for their assertions? Howenstein said information available to him as a captain in the San Anselmo police department indicated that Synanon locally had once stored weapons openly but now the weapons were out of sight. Mountanos countered that weapons from the San Francisco gun buy had not been brought into Marin County and that if Howenstein had evidence to the contary, he should forward it to proper authorities (implying himself).

Score one for Mountanos, I said to myself. After the meeting, I told Howenstein I liked him as a candidate but thought Mountanos had won the debate. "If you're right about the guns," I advised, "you shouldn't let the sheriff get off so easy. You need to be more aggressive."

Because of Synanon, I decided I would vote for Howenstein, but the paper would make no endorsement. Mountanos was almost certain to win, and on matters other than Synanon he seemed to do a good job. The sheriff had given West Marin deputies considerable discretion in flexing with local lifestyles. The area's huge counterculture population was allowed to grow its own marijuana in peace and sunbathe in the nude, as long as both activities were kept discreet. Cathy and I, along with most *Light* readers, approved of such tolerance. At the same time, West Marin was enjoying a low crime rate. Major crimes were almost nonexistent, and deputies seemed to be holding their own against burglars. Mountanos's only serious problem was Synanon.

Synanon was becoming an octopus of a news story. Keeping track of all the tentacles left me with little time to cover other news. By May, Keith, the news editor, was handling almost all of *The Light*'s general news. I had the "Synanon beat." Synanon by now was a political issue and a law enforcement issue. Its $20 million in assets, its excessive payments to top officers, and its tax exemption made it a financial issue. The child-abuse reports and Synanon's authoritarian structure made it a social issue. And the zoning violations made it a land-use planning issue.

In the previous week's board of supervisors' hearing, Synanon attorney Howard Garfield had flatly said that at Synanon's West Marin facilities "there is no health clinic. There is no airstrip." Sitting in the audience listening to Garfield was county planning director Don Gutoff. Gutoff said nothing, but I learned after the meeting that the planning director had been taken on a tour of the Synanon health clinic a year earlier. Had Garfield also lied about the airstrip? I called the county Public Works Department to find out.

A county engineer, Irving Schwartz, refused to say on the record whether or not there was an airstrip, but read over the phone some correspondence between himself and Synanon. In a letter dated May 5, 1976, Schwartz had written to Synanon: "We have completed our review of your application for an excavating permit to grade an access road to the existing landing strip and to level the area at the end of the landing strip. In checking with our planning department, we have been informed we cannot issue an excavating permit at this time based on the current zoning. The aircraft landing strip would require a use permit."

On October 10, 1976, Synanon attorney Phillip Bourdette had written to Public Works Director Ray Foreaker: "In our discussion, you indicated that you felt that the road must have some justification other than to obtain access to the airstrip area." Bourdette acknowledged, "Our primary reason is to develop better access to the airstrip," but added there were additional reasons the road was needed.

During the second supervisors' hearing on Synanon, it had come out that the planning department was unhappy with the public works department for issuing building permits at Synanon in violation of zoning. I had learned from Green Door that within county government Foreaker was thought to be friendly toward Synanon. Later I learned that the public works director eventually had a falling out with Synanon—in part over Synanon's airstrip.

Suddenly Schwartz, who had been reading the correspondence over the phone, became impatient. "That's all I have time for now," he announced. "You'll have to come here and read the rest for yourself." I wondered if the engineer was really out of time or if one of his bosses had just walked into his office. I never found out, but I had enough for a story.

I was amazed that Synanon would try to get away with two such enormous lies: denying the existence of an airstrip and of a health clinic. Synanon leaders, Ofshe had claimed, were not above manipulating the membership, and lying was considered an acceptable part of the Synanon game. But lying to county supervisors in a public hearing was downright arrogant, I felt. The isolation in which Synanon members lived was becoming apparent. Garfield apparently was used to getting away with deceptions inside Synanon, where conflicting information was not available. Why didn't he realize the public and county government already knew about the airstrip and clinic? He must have forgotten that different tactics were necessary "off campus," I reasoned. The more I thought about it, the more I realized that almost all of Garfield's angry presentation to the board was characteristic of the Synanon game as Ofshe had been describing it.

Garfield's attack on the county had seemed absurd—that the county in challenging activities at Synanon was primarily motivated by prejudice against the "Synanon religion." That was how the Synanon game worked, Ofshe had insisted. The accuracy of an accusation against a game player didn't matter, the professor had said, only the vehemence. I began laughing out loud in the newsroom: "Synanon just gamed the board of supervisors!" Cathy was sitting at the next desk, and I remarked, "I think this Ofshe guy knows what he's talking about."

"Well, he sure requires some very long phone calls in which to say it," Cathy responded. But when Ofshe's papers on Synanon arrived in the mail, she also read them with interest.

Another tentacle of the Synanon story was the organization's relations with the press. I had written a news story describing *I-J* reporter George Nevin's rapport with Synanon and *Pacific Sun* assistant publisher Hut Landon's having a mother there. Cathy, however, had refused to let the story run, arguing it could be considered too self-serving as a news article. I later used the material in a column.

In the wake of the supervisors' hearings on Synanon, I received a call from Joanne Williams, editor of *The Sun*; she wanted some information on Synanon. Landon had been taken off the Synanon story, she said, and it had been assigned to her. *The Sun* was becoming more aggressive in covering Synanon, with the result that editor Williams was no longer welcome at Synanon's "public" barbecues. Laughingly, I commiserated with her. Clearly we were both on Synanon's enemies list. Secretly, I was delighted, *The Sun* had many times the circulation of *The Light*. If *The Sun* kept reporting the troubles at Synanon, the impact in East Marin might be significant.

Within a week of editor Williams's phone call, Synanon was in the news again. And this time, the organization's tactics raised eyebrows in East as well as West Marin. On May 23, 1978, a five-member state health department team armed with an inspection warrant tried to enter Synanon but was stopped at the gate.

The team was ushered to a building, where the five found themselves in front of a menacing crowd of Synanon members. Adding to the intimidation were video cameras, which were focused alternately on each of the five. Synanon spokesmen then told the team members they could go on Synanon property only under three conditions: that health department physicians not talk to Synanon physicians, that the inspection team stick together and not work as individuals, and that they interview no Synanon residents without a court reporter taking notes. The inspection team withdrew rather than abide by the conditions.

A health department spokesman, Bob Nance, told the press the state was surprised by Synanon's resistance. Health department lawyers had conferred by phone with Synanon lawyers until late the night before. Synanon's lawyers had "pledged full cooperation," Nance reported. He said the team was now meeting with the attorney general's office to decide the next move.

Nance did not explain what the inspection team hoped to find. However, the health department had indicated in a court filing, when it got the inspection warrant, that it believed Synanon's clinic needed licensing, as did its program for taking in troubled children.

The court filing proved to be at least as interesting as the frustrated inspection. Included in the filing was a sworn statement from a former Synanon member, Sheldon Ira Ross: "During my residency at Synanon in Marin County, I visited a large metal building, the interior of which was partioned into small medical-examination rooms and doctors' offices. When residents became ill, they would go to the . . . building, which was referred to as an infirmary, for medical treatment. Several of the young male residents received vasectomies on the premises from Synanon doctors." Ross said three of his friends, including one who was eighteen years old, were among those receiving vasectomies at Synanon.

It would later come out that the vasectomies were given not to just a few men but to hundreds of Synanon members, many of whom were far from enthusiastic about the surgery. The fact that an eighteen-year-old had been rendered sterile for life startled me. It seemed cruel. In fact, much of what I recently had found out about Synanon seemed cruel.

Another declaration included in the court filing also pointed to the existence of a clinic and reminded me of the grand jury's concern that Synanon might be defrauding the federally financed state MediCal program for the needy. State health inspector Christopher Brett declared that Synanon had received over $40,000 in MediCal payments between January, 1975, and October, 1977. "I am advised that in Marin County, Synanon maintains a clinic or hospital where patients are kept overnight," noted Brett. He added that state law required such medical facilities to get state licensing.

Also requiring licensing, said Brett, were community-care facilities that provided residential care for children, the handicapped, or incompetent people. "We have received information from persons resident at the facility to the effect that minor children are cared for at Synanon facilities in Marin County," the health inspector declared. "These children are cared for separately from their parents. We believe Synanon has solicited children from various states to be cared for at their facility. This information comes to us from the states of Michigan and Wyoming."

As the health department had prepared to seek an inspection warrant, it had received an angry letter from Synanon attorney Phil Bourdette, included in the filing. Wrote Bourdette: "This, of course, must be another of your continuing acts of harassment against Synanon Foundation Inc. It does not seem to matter what we do to inform you that Synanon is not subject to licensing by your bureaucracy."

The following week, the state attorney general's office went back to court, seeking an order requiring Synanon to cooperate with the inspection. Synanon countered with a motion calling the inspection proposal "unconstitutional." A judge said he would rule on the matter in two weeks.

Meanwhile, in another Marin County courtroom, Judge

Gary Thomas reduced from felonies to misdemeanors the charges against the four Synanon members accused of beating and imprisoning ex-member Tom Cardineau in March. Judge Thomas reduced the charges, he said, because Cardineau had suffered only cuts and bruises and was not requiring ongoing medical care. "Remind me not to vote for Judge Thomas," I growled.

"Umm," muttered Cathy. She was reading the mail; in it was a card from Richard Ofshe. "We've been invited to a party at his Berkeley home." I wanted to talk with Ofshe again, and we sent a note back that we would attend.

The party was a catered affair, with guests drinking white wine on Ofshe's deck overlooking the Berkeley hills. His modern house was decorated with large dramatic pictures. The furnishings implied that professors at the University of California were paid well. Ofshe's taste obviously ran to antiques, and we later learned he was a frequenter of flea markets.

Cathy and I got into conversations with visiting professors from Europe, graduate students from Iowa, almost everyone but Ofshe. The topic was invariably Synanon. Ofshe, swarthy and bearded at thirty-seven, sometimes lurked outside the circle of conversation but never took part. Our only exchange with the professor was to say "thanks" when we left.

The next morning, however, Ofshe called me at *The Light.* "It's Richard," he began. "I was listening to what you had to say yesterday about Synanon. You may be the only other person anywhere who has the same concern I have about Synanon. Why don't you and Cathy and I write a book?"

"A book?" No one had ever asked me to collaborate on a book before. I was flattered but puzzled.

"For years," said Richard, "I've watched Synanon outmaneuver one regulatory agency after another. We could use Marin County as the classic example. With what I know about Synanon and what you know about Marin County politics, it would be great."

Richard envisioned a book geared to academics and government officials. He hoped it would provide the information necessary for government to neutralize Synanon's tactics. He noted that other organizations were beginning to use the same strategies—that the problem went beyond Synanon.

I was intrigued by the proposal. When I told Cathy about it, she wasn't. We had now been back together six months, and our second honeymoon was over. "I have enough to do teaching at the college and running the business side of *The Light*," she insisted. "And I'm no longer that involved in covering Synanon. It's gotten to be your story."

"I wish you'd reconsider," I told her. "I'm going to do it, and it would be better for both of us to be in it together."

Cathy finally relented. "But I want you to know," she said, "that I'm going to be pressuring for us to get interested in some other things besides Synanon. I'd like us to spend *some* time just having fun together, and I don't like the way it's dominating our lives."

CHAPTER 8

"BOMBS COULD BE THROWN"

The June 6, 1978, county elections beheaded Marin County's criminal justice system. Unexpectedly, challenger Al Howenstein easily defeated Sheriff Louis Mountanos. Superior Court Judge Charles Read Best was unseated by a municipal court judge, Peter Allen Smith. And Deputy District Attorney Jerry Herman ousted his boss, District Attorney Bruce Bales.

Cathy and I were amazed by Howenstein's victory, even though we had voted for him. No one in county political circles had given Howenstein a chance. Our friend Lieutenant Art Disterheft had considered running for sheriff, but dropped the idea when Mountanos decided to run again. "I could have won," grumbled Art the day after the election. But he was starting to build a house and added that being sheriff would have "messed up" his construction schedule.

In West Marin, which voted heavily for Howenstein, several people told me they voted against Mountanos only because of his ties with Synanon. Why East Marin voted for Howenstein was less obvious. Howenstein had campaigned in East Marin as a progressive who would modernize an out-of-date sheriff's department.

I was also pleased with Herman's winning the DA race. Art had worked in Herman's campaign, and Cathy and I were particularly unhappy with Bales's irresolute handling of the Cardineau case when it was first brought to him. The one worry we had about Herman was that he appeared to be on good terms with one of Synanon's chief lawyers, Phil Bourdette. When we interviewed Herman during the campaign, he admitted receiving a couple of small campaign donations from Synanon members. I, however, trusted Art's evaluation of Herman and voted for him. Cathy remained skeptical and voted for a third candidate.

The results of the criminal justice races were so surprising that few people paid any attention to the Democratic Central Committee race, where Synanon's Jack Harrison was elected with only ninety-three write-in votes.

The election came at the busiest time of the year for *The Light*. Every June, the West Marin Junior Livestock Show was held in Point Reyes Station. The livestock show was for 4-H and Future Farmers of America (FFA) youngsters. The same weekend, popularly dubbed "Western Weekend," a two-hour parade traveled down the town's three-block-long main street. Friday and Saturday evenings, Point Reyes Station's two bars, the Old Western Saloon and the Two Ball Inn, hired country-and-western bands. The Lions Club also threw a dance, with gambling at dice games in the back room. For ranch hands who seldom got into town, Western Weekend was a two-day drunk reminiscent of the fiestas Mexicans had held in California a hundred and fifty years earlier. By late Sunday, the gutters along main street literally flowed with beer.

Each year *The Light* held a beard-growing contest on the eve of Western Weekend. *The Light* also came out with a second issue on the Friday of Western Weekend—the only time of the year when there were two issues in one week. The special issue not only provided readers with a program of weekend events, it also allowed the paper to sell a significant amount of extra advertising. For *The Light*'s small staff, producing two issues within a week required an exhausting effort.

In the middle of Western Weekend's hustle and macho merriment, I suddenly found myself having to deal with a shift in the Synanon story—it was moving out of town. In San Francisco, police and sheriff's deputies acting under a Los Angeles court order helped a black woman from Canada, Ernestine White, remove three grandchildren from Synanon.

The woman's attorney was then a little-known lawyer in private practice from Pacific Palisades, Paul Morantz; four months later he would become a central target of Synanon. Already he had fought Synanon in three civil cases. At Morantz's request, a Los Angeles court had instructed Marin and San Francisco authorities "to take all actions necessary" to help Mrs. White pick up her three grandchildren: Otis Butler, seventeen, Niama Butler, sixteen, and Joe Butler, thirteen.

Synanon did not want to give up the children, and the children did not want to leave. For two hours, police and deputies negotiated at Synanon's facility in the old Dutch Boy paint factory for their release. Finally Synanon acknowledged it had no choice, and turned the children over to the authorities.

In frustration, Synanon members mounted a letter-writing campaign attacking San Francisco police and deputies, accusing officers of trying to intimidate Synanon. *San Francisco Chronicle* columnist Herb Caen took their side and in print accused officers of overreacting.

Months later, Synanon's treatment of Joey Butler would be cited in court as one of the most flagrant examples of child abuse within the foundation. Shortly after their release, the three Butler children were taken by Mrs. White to Ted Patrick, the nationally known deprogrammer of cult members. Following deprogramming, Joey Butler began to talk about his experiences inside Synanon—including a vicious beating by a Synanon man.

The next out-of-town installment in the Synanon story came in the second week of June, when NBC aired its series on the foundation. Synanon's blockading of the NBC camera crew a month earlier had created intense interest in the NBC series among West Marin residents. Cathy, Richard, and I were particularly looking forward to it. We hoped that NBC, with its prestige and its millions of viewers, could do what we had been so far unable to do: force state government to act.

Since I had been interviewed for the series, Cathy and I called relatives around the country, telling them to watch for the broadcasts. I was disappointed and a little embarrassed when nothing from my interview was used. But I consoled myself that at least a headline identified as coming from *The Light* was flashed on the screen: SYNANON RESISTS CHILD ABUSE PROBE. Cathy, however, was pleased that the interview had been omitted. She had said nothing when it was filmed, but now revealed she had worried for a month that the interview would focus Synanon hostility on me.

We had expected the NBC series to say what we already knew about Synanon, and when NBC broke new information, we felt scooped. Especially newsworthy was their revelation that Synanon had contacted an accounting firm, asking how to convert some of its assets into diamonds without paying taxes and how to convert other assets of the charity into foreign currency. The accounting firm, worried about the legality of all this, had notified the Internal Revenue Service.

NBC aired footage of Synanon members interrupting an ABC stockholders' meeting. These members had taken the floor to warn ABC executives and their families that they might be in danger because its KGO affiliate's unflattering coverage of Synanon. A Time-Life stockholders' meeting was also interrupted by Synanon members for a similar message.

NBC showed a previously taped interview with Synanon founder Dederich, in which he cautioned: "Bombs could be thrown into odd places . . . into the homes of some of the clowns who occupy high places in the *Time* organization. That's too bad. That's too bad." When the interviewer noted that Dederich's statements would be taken as a threat, the Synanon founder replied he himself would not "initiate" any bombing but could not be responsible if it occurred without his authorization. Dederich commented he was just being "decent" in giving *Time* "a warning."

The NBC series had been scheduled to run for three nights, but Synanon activities then under way in Washington, D.C., brought Synanon back onto the *Nightly News* for a fourth broadcast. During the spring of 1978, Synanon had contracted to buy the Boston House, a large apartment building on Massachusetts Avenue, Washington's embassy row. Synanon moved about seventy-five members into the building and converted the seventh and eighth floors into offices and a dining room. At the same time, Synanon began pressuring other tenants in the building to leave.

Synanon's conversion of the building appeared to violate Washington zoning laws, and Boston House tenants appealed to Washington authorities for help. NBC was present with a camera crew when Washington officials tried to inspect the Synanon floors and were rebuffed.

A *Washington Post* photographer, Douglas Chevalier, who tried to take a picture of Dederich and attorney Howard Garfield, was chased down the street by the two men, Dederich brandishing a cane. Unknown to Dederich and Garfield, plainclothes police were watching the attack and interceded. The next day, police drafted arrest warrants for Dederich and Garfield plus an unnamed Synanon member who had threatened Boston House tenant Arthur Greles.

The day the arrest warrants were announced, Pat Lynch, who had produced the Synanon series for NBC, called me with the news. She also gave me the phone number of the police officer investigating the case. I called the number, but he was off duty, returning Sunday. I said I would call back.

That afternoon, there was to be a fund-raising cocktail party for Barry Keene, a Democrat running for the state senate. The party was to be held in East Marin at a mansion on the slopes of Mount Tamalpais. When I heard that Governor Jerry Brown would also be there, I decided to attend.

It was a lavish affair. Guests drank white wine and cocktails on the lawn as maids scurried about with silver trays of hors d'oeuvres. I spotted Supervisor Barbara Boxer and pulled her aside. "I've got a tidbit for you," I whispered in her ear. "Washington police have issued arrest warrants for Dederich and Garfield." Boxer made a little jump and clapped her hands. I quickly explained the circumstances, and when the tête-à-tête ended moments later, Supervisor Boxer was beaming.

Sunday, I went down to the newspaper office, which was normally closed on the weekend, and again called Washington. This time the officer was there. He confirmed what Pat Lynch had told me, but beyond that was guarded. He seemed to suspect that I might be calling from Synanon, rather than a tiny weekly on the California coast. How much did he know about Synanon, I asked. "Not a hell of a lot," the officer replied. I briefly summarized the grand jury's findings for him and offered to send a copy of the grand jury report. "I'd appreciate it if you'd do that," the officer said. I promised I would, and urged him to let me know if anything came of the arrest warrants.

The next morning, I arranged to have the clerk of the grand jury send Washington police a copy of the Synanon report. I had always prided myself on being able to establish rapport with policemen, and counted on such rapport to surreptitiously get me stories from time to time. But to do the same thing with transcontinental phone calls seemed to me an almost hopeless undertaking. Having the grand jury report sent to the officer was a small ploy to cultivate a source, but I doubted it would work.

A few days later, I discovered I was wrong. "You have a

call from an officer ———————— in Washington," said *The Light*'s receptionist, Gayanne, poking her head around the oak filing cabinet next to my desk. The officer was calling with a tip. I was incredulous—and appreciative. "If you can leave me out of it," he said, "I'll let you know what happened here today." I promised him anonymity, and the officer then described a meeting earlier that day in the office of federal prosecutor James Owens.

An attorney for Synanon had told Owens that twenty-five of the seventy-five Synanon members living in the Boston House had already left Washington and that the rest would be gone by the end of the month. The attorney noted that the three who were cited in the arrest warrants had left the District of Columbia. The officer added that since charges against the three were merely misdemeanors, they could not be extradited back to Washington. Prosecutor Owens had agreed to let the warrants expire in thirty days if Synanon completed its withdrawal from the capital and if there were no further problems.

The officer added, however, that Synanon members had begun denouncing Washington police in letters to congressmen, claiming that they had prevented Dederich from getting medical assistance when he suffered a heart attack while attacking the *Post* photographer. The officer insisted the accusation was untrue, and I assured him the criticism was Synanon's standard operating procedure.

When I finally got off the phone, I was laughing with delight, and boasted to Cathy, "*The Light* has managed to cultivate a source inside the Washington police department. For a little country weekly on the other side of the continent, that ain't half bad!"

Our coverage of events in Washington and San Francisco was a break with *Light* policy. As long as Cathy and I had owned the newspaper, we had refused to carry even countywide news. "We're too small to report on anything but West

Marin news," Cathy told those occasional callers who wanted *The Light* to cover something happening outside our sphere. My usual line was that "if a tidal wave hit San Rafael [the Marin county seat], the only way you'd learn about it in *The Light* would be if someone from West Marin happened to be over there shopping and drowned. We leave it to the dailies to cover state and countywide news."

It was a practical policy. *The Light* seldom had space for all the local stories we wrote; expanding coverage would only crowd out local news. Moreover, phoning East Marin was a toll call. We were then netting $13,000 a year from *The Light*, including profits and both our salaries. Long-distance calls meant cutting into that meager income. By now, Cathy was complaining every month about our rising phone bill. I rationalized, "It's our contribution to solving a community problem."

Synanon, I pointed out, was a nationwide—even international—organization headquartered in West Marin. Besides facilities throughout California, Synanon had at various times had centers in New York, Michigan, Puerto Rico, Pennsylvania, and Texas, as well as Germany, Malaysia, and Italy. We had to know what was happening with Synanon elsewhere to understand what was happening here, I insisted. Cathy accepted the argument but urged me to be restrained in my phoning.

Among the calls contributing to *The Light*'s rising phone bill were those we returned to NBC producer Pat Lynch. Following the NBC series, those with tips on Synanon saw her as the major journalist interested in exposing the foundation. She began receiving calls from all over the United States. NBC executives, however, considered Synanon primarily a "regional" story, since its large facilities were concentrated in California. The network was unwilling to cover Synanon night after night, Lynch explained. It was ironic, I mused. We worried about our Synanon coverage ranging all over the country, while NBC viewed it as having only regional interest. But producer Lynch also pointed out that newspapers, unlike television, can do regular follow-ups. With nothing else to do with the tips she received, she began passing some of them along to *The Light.*

I think Lynch was as disappointed as Cathy and I were when California authorities failed to react to the NBC series. The only official we saw showing any interest was Sheriff-elect Al Howenstein. In July, he accompanied Cathy and me to NBC's San Francisco affiliate, KRON-TV, for a rescreening of the series, and we all took notes. Afterward, Cathy gloomily confessed to Howenstein: "You're about the only official who seems to care."

Meanwhile, back in West Marin, Cathy, Richard, and I had begun a summer of meetings "to work on the book." Often we would get together for dinner and talk late into the night. The discussions were often really debates as we argued the significance of various happenings at Synanon. Our get-togethers frequently were at Richard's new home in Marshall, which he had bought when he sold his cottage in Dillon Beach. The new home sat on pilings over the edge of Tomales Bay. While we argued theories of what lay behind Synanon's violence, pelicans would dive for fish outside the window; an occasional seal would surface to survey this almost-deserted stretch of bay.

For three months we talked much and wrote little. Cathy began to ask, "When are we going to stop this endless talking and get to work?" It wasn't until much later that she and I realized that over the summer Richard had inadvertently given us a cram course in sociology.

CHAPTER 9

THE EDUCATION OF DAVE AND CATHY

I would find it difficult to say whether Richard joined our investigation of Synanon or we joined his. When we all began to meet weekly to discuss Synanon during the summer of 1978, Cathy and I had been gathering information on the foundation for three months; Richard had been studying it six years.

Our teaming up was—as far as we knew—unprecedented: a professor in a prestigious department of a prestigious university and two publishers of an obscure country weekly. We often laughed about how absurdly disparate the members of our team were, but some of Richard's colleagues at the University of California were not amused.

Richard's entire career, however, was marked by nontraditional pursuits. Born in the Bronx in 1941 to Russian Jewish parents, Richard grew up in a lower-middle-class family. His father designed half-size dresses for older women, developing a new line each year. The family moved to a small apartment in Queens, where Richard attended Jamaica High. In the 1950s Jamaica High enrolled about five thousand students, but Richard was recognized as bright and put in a special program that included only about fifty other gifted students.

The Ofshe family could not afford to send Richard to a private college, so he lived at home and attended Queens College. It was not a happy existence for him. "I never had a room to myself until I was twenty-two," Richard once told me. Sharing a room with his brother and financially excluded from the *good* schools, Richard felt oppressed by circumstances. He lost interest in his classes and concentrated on becoming a skillful bridge player. When he received his degree in psychology in 1963, he was an undistinguished C student.

Graduation, however, revived Richard's interest in accomplishing something for himself. He "talked" the sociology department at Queens College into letting him work there on a master's degree, meanwhile supporting himself by delivering laundry in the evenings. A year and a half later, Queens College gave Richard the first master's degree in a newly expanded sociology program. Richard applied to Stanford University to work on a doctorate in sociology, and Stanford—pointing out that it was "against its better judgment," he recalls—accepted him. But without a scholarship. Without money, he could not afford to go. Richard had already drafted a letter to Stanford saying he would be unable to attend when a student who had been given a fellowship in sociology decided to go elsewhere. Stanford passed the fellowship along to Richard, but, mindful of his undergraduate record, warned him the money might end in a year.

Richard, however, had found his interest: the study of power and decision-making in small groups. His research so impressed the sociology department that within his first year at Stanford the department recommended him for a second fellowship, this one from the National Institutes of Mental Health.

It took Richard only three years to complete his doctorate, and he was immediately hired by the University of California, which was then trying to modernize its sociology department. For a former C student at Queens College, it was an almost unbelievably prestigious appointment.

During his first couple of years at the University of California, Richard did conventional academic research and in 1969 published, with his wife, *Utility and Choice in Social Interaction*, a mathematical explanation of how small groups of people make decisions. Six months later, in the spring of 1970, his department recommended him for tenure. When he was promoted from assistant to associate professor the following year, Richard became one of the youngest tenured professors at Cal.

He had escaped the world represented by that cramped apartment in Queens. He was self-confident. When a fire razed the house he had bought in the Berkeley hills, Richard himself designed the dramatic home that replaced it. He could now afford to shape his own life.

When Cathy and I met Richard in the spring of 1978, our lives had been moving in opposite directions from his for a decade. We had both grown up in urban homes but after ten years in small towns were becoming countrified. The radio in my Ford was usually tuned to a country music station; the radio in Richard's old Porsche was usually tuned to jazz. Cathy complained about my looking too thin, while Richard worried about putting on weight. The press described Cathy and me as "plain" and "rangy," respectively. Richard, with his swarthy complexion, thick black hair, and salt-and-pepper beard, was dashing.

Cathy and I had been married ten years. Richard, who had been divorced for years before we met him, had lots of women friends—invariably professionals, and often beautiful. At dinnertime, it was common for Cathy and me to unscrew the cap from a bottle of Italian Swiss Colony. Richard usually uncorked his wine twenty minutes before the meal to allow it time to breathe.

In fact, it was Richard's love of the good life that indirectly brought about his first contact with Synanon. In April, 1971, Richard bought for a mere $12,500 a weekend cottage in Dillon Beach, the most remote town covered by *The Light.* Two neighbors who became his friends were Paula and Dr. Steve Obrebski. Dr. Obrebski, a marine biologist at the Pacific Marine Station in Dillon Beach, was asked by Synanon for advice in setting up a laboratory for the foundation's sewage-treatment system. On one of his visits to Synanon, Obrebski took Richard along.

This was the summer of 1972, and Richard already knew a little about Synanon. A couple of his students had written papers on Synanon, and one had joined a Synanon game club in Oakland. Among the courses Richard taught was one on the history of utopian experiments. When Obrebski reported being told by a Synanon member, "We'll take over the world," Richard became intrigued by this would-be utopia.

On that first visit to Synanon with Obrebski, Richard was taken on a trail-bike tour of ranching facilities by an eighteen-year-old member, Steve Meyers. Meyers, recalls Richard, revealed some "strange attitudes." As they talked during the tour, Meyers told Richard the world outside of Synanon was almost universally evil; the only good place to live was Synanon. "By the end of the day," Richard remembers, "I had the impression, 'This is a very odd place.' "

Meyers introduced Richard to the ranch's director, Jarrie Tent, and Richard asked if he could come back to do research. After some discussion, she agreed. Over the next year, Richard paid more than fifty visits to the ranch and other Synanon facilities in Oakland, San Francisco, and Santa Monica.

In 1972, Synanon welcomed middle-class professionals, hoping to recruit them. Richard also was following three other researchers, who had previously visited Synanon and then gone home to write glowing books: Daniel Casriel, *So Fair a House* (1963); Lewis Yablonsky, *The Tunnel Back* (1965); and Guy Endore, *Synanon* (1968).

There was an important difference, however, between the

way these researchers studied Synanon and the way Richard went about it. The earlier researchers had access to founder Charles Dederich and other Synanon officers. Because they spent much of their time with Synanon leaders, these early researchers saw the organization from the top looking down. And they liked what they saw. Richard started at the other end of the organization. The first Synanon game he played was with workers in a mailroom. Looking up at the organization from the bottom, he was less enthusiastic than his research predecessors.

Rather than enjoying the camaraderie and courtship of Synanon management, Richard tried to keep "a very low profile." He would wander onto a Synanon facility and usually hang out in the dining room, where there was always someone to talk to. On Friday nights, he would join Synanon members in their famous encounter sessions, the games. In urban Synanon facilities, hundreds of visitors took part in Synanon game clubs, but in West Marin, Richard was the only outsider. "I was facetiously introduced as *the* game club," he laughs. "I was the only member."

"It was clear the less I was noticed, the longer I would have in the organization," Richard later explained to Cathy and me. "I stayed at the lowest levels as long as possible." As a result, Richard played games with members who were merely "*conducting business* with each other," he told us. From this, he discovered an unreported aspect to the game. Heretofore the game had been recognized by researchers only as a procedure for curing addicts, but Richard discovered the game could also be a tool for enforcing business policy.

Cathy and I had never witnessed a Synanon game, so early in our association with Richard, we began peppering him with questions about this much vaunted Synanon activity. In *The Light*, we had described Synanon games as "no-holds-barred encounter sessions," but Richard insisted the intent behind the game was much less benign than that description implied. Games in Synanon were usually "played" by fifteen or so members sitting in a circle. They were aggressive, Richard explained, because they usually proceeded on the basis of "indictments." One player pointed out the defects or mistakes of another, and then other players joined what regularly was an angry attack. Unless the accused could quickly talk his way out of the indictment, he faced a snarling pack of game players denouncing him. "It is difficult to make you understand how emotionally devastating that can be," Richard emphasized. "It's a tidal wave of hatred. The first time it hits you, it absolutely destroys you."

Unable to withstand the emotional assault, the target usually had little choice but to admit wrongdoing and promise to mend his ways. Since there was no requirement that either attackers or defenders speak the truth, an inexperienced game player often found himself confessing to fictitious misdeeds to stop the attack. As a device to make addicts give up the behavior that originally got them into trouble, the game was powerful—at least as long as they were being routinely subjected to it.

On a day-to-day basis, a member's life in Synanon could be pleasant. Members spent well-ordered days working and living among friends. So when in a game a misbehaving member found himself in sudden disrepute, his easiest means of regaining friendship and support was to promise to start behaving.

To a large degree, however, the anger voiced in a game was a pretense, and in time Synanon members learned to receive the onslaught without feeling devastated. They also learned that an attack in a game might be suggestive of punishment to come when the game was over. Wrongdoing exposed in a game could result in the culprit's being demoted to less pleasant work, being reassigned to less comfortable housing, or being shunned by other members, Richard noted.

Moreover, Richard added, there was a saying within Synanon: "The game remembers." Misdeeds a person might admit in one game could be brought up in future games—even years later—to fuel an attack against him. Other game players could humiliate a target by demanding he recount his "dirty, rotten story." In Synanon jargon, this became his "jacket," which would stay with him until he left the foundation. An ex-member told us some months later of being jacketed as a "fuck-up" because he had once forgotten to set the brakes on a truck and it rolled downhill, causing minor damage. Years later, other game players would browbeat him with the incident when they wanted to claim some recent misstep was part of a long pattern of "fuck-ups."

Those who came to Synanon with drug problems were labeled "dope fiends" as long as they were in the organization. Richard pointed out that by constantly reminding members of their previous troubles, Synanon was able to make many members doubt they could survive if they left Synanon.

But we had been told by Synanon members—and later would be told by ex-members—that they often thoroughly enjoyed playing the game. We asked Richard how this could be so, if the game was as devastating as he described. He explained that games were also a forum to discuss personal problems: "people share experience in sensitive ways." It could be an opportunity for other game players to express their concern. And, Richard said, games could be used to show support for members who were doing what Synanon wanted them to do.

And even the attacks members received were not uniformly threatening, Richard pointed out. "A good game player can distinguish when he's being merely fucked with from when it truly matters," he explained. "When you're vulnerable, the attack is incredibly important. At other times it can be sportive."

"As a sport, it sounds more vicious than fun," I remonstrated.

"After a while," Richard replied, "members get used to it.

Being called an 'asshole' or a 'cocksucker' gets to be as everyday an experience as having someone say, 'How are you?' Members become skilled at verbal gymnastics; they have to in order to defend themselves. They learn to be aggressively articulate." This was one of the reasons, explained Richard, "that outsiders often regard Synanon members as arrogant, nasty, or aggressive."

"There were always a few guys when I was in college," I observed, "who were masters of put-downs. I'd watch them sparring over lunch, and while I might have admired their rhetorical skill, I always thought it revealed something unpleasant about them."

"Well," remarked Richard, "if I were to put a value judgment on the way the game is used, I'd call it loathsome."

Cathy demanded to know why anyone would stay in Synanon, given the way members were sometimes treated.

"Most of the time," Richard answered, "life in Synanon is very pleasant." If someone joined Synanon as a "square" (without drug or criminal problems) or if one was a rehabilitated "dope fiend," he didn't have to do the menial work that people must do on the outside, Richard added. "You walk into the dining room, and your food is waiting for you. There are people to do the laundry. You don't have to mess with your kids; Synanon takes care of them for you. And since the Synanon school was touted as being progressive, you could even rationalize that your kids were better off."

The menial work, he noted, was done by newcomers who came in as "dope fiends" or "character disorders." And these people were continually promised better jobs as soon as they demonstrated responsibility. They were usually assigned jobs within their first forty-eight hours in Synanon, and kitchen work was a typical job.

In the early days of Synanon, when most members came in as "dope fiends," their families would sometimes follow them in later. From the late 1960s on, when more "squares" than "dope fiends" became members, it was not uncommon for whole families to move in together, Richard noted. Even so, Synanon usually had more men than women—often about a 60–40 split, according to Synanon documents.

Unlike the "dope fiends," who entered Synanon with minimal status in the organization, middle-class "squares" had status even as newcomers. Instead of doing menial work as the "dope fiend" newcomers did, "square" newcomers often continued in the same kinds of jobs that they had held on the outside. Later, they frequently were transferred into other work. Richard explained that Synanon told "dope fiends" their work in Synanon would teach them responsibility and so was part of their rehabilitation. "Squares" were told their work was a contribution to the common good.

Cathy and I, however, still had only a vague impression of what Synanon was all about. We knew it had started in Santa Monica as a rehabilitation program for drug addicts and to a lesser degree alcoholics. It had bought its first property in West Marin in 1964 and was now a wealthy tax-exempt corporation. But we couldn't understand why the "squares" would enter a rehabilitation program. We could accept Richard's explanation as to why Synanon members often appeared arrogant, but we could see no reason for the violence. Richard had called the violence a "bully-boy tactic," but that seemed more a description than an explanation.

Richard had an explanation, but not one we could absorb at a single sitting. For one, Richard's theory of Synanon was largely (but not fully) developed when we met him. There was still much research to be done, and we were all doing it together. For another, after eight years in newspapering, Cathy and I had learned to question all but the most obvious explanations. We were not about to accept Richard's theories as fact merely because he believed them.

Throughout the summer of 1978, we met once or twice a week with Richard in West Marin. When he was in Berkeley, we talked with him almost daily by phone. Later we were to refer to this period as "the education of Dave and Cathy." But ultimately the three of us were a research team and not a seminar. Since Richard didn't have any rank to pull on us, it was lucky he liked the seemingly endless debates as to how one argument or another best fit the facts. By summer's end, Richard finally had what he wanted: people with whom he could talk about Synanon, who knew enough of the facts and were sufficiently involved so that they, too, could fit pieces of the puzzle together.

Central to understanding Synanon, we came to realize, was understanding how it had evolved. Synanon was the creation of an alcoholic, Charles E. Dederich, born March 22, 1913, in Toledo, Ohio. A Notre Dame and then Toledo University dropout, he had worked many years in a minor white-collar job for Gulf Oil in Ohio. When a marriage failed, he drifted to Southern California and tried another marriage; it too failed. Dederich by then was a confirmed alcoholic.

Before kicking him out of the house, Dederich's second wife, Ruth Jason Dederich, had gotten him to join Alcoholics Anonymous. After some initial backsliding, Dederich in 1956 went on the wagon, and he stayed there for the next twenty-two years. He became an AA speaker and toured California. "I was a salesman and a fair-to-middling standup comic," he recollected for *People* magazine in 1976. "I had a speaking engagement every night somewhere in California. I would talk about my adventures with Demon Rum." The experience taught Dederich how to attract and hold an audience. He began to see himself as a leader.

In early 1958, he gathered around him a group of alcoholics who met weekly in his Santa Monica apartment. The group went with Dederich to the weekly AA meetings, but as "Dederich's faction." In July, Dederich, who was living on a $33-a-week unemployment check, rented a nearby storefront and announced establishment of the "Tender Loving Care

Club." The following month, he pulled his faction out of the AA chapter.

Shortly before the split, a heroin addict was introduced to Dederich's group by one of the alcoholics. The addict hung around for a few months, taking part in the club's bull sessions, and stayed off narcotics. Dederich later said that by the end of July, "I knew I had something that would work on addicts."

Other addicts joined the club until they outnumbered alcoholics. From their weekly bull sessions, the Synanon game was born. Dederich later claimed that the word *Synanon* was created by an addict who accidentally blended the words *seminar* and *symposium.*

There were some significant differences between Dederich's club and the AA chapter from which it had broken. A number of members moved into the club's storefront, some sleeping on mattresses on the floor. The club provided their food. Unlike AA members, those belonging to Dederich's club depended on the organization to manage all aspects of their lives. The club also had special significance for Dederich: through it he was building a career for himself. Since he took responsibility for soliciting the contributions of food and money on which the club depended, he was unquestionably in charge.

Difficult as it was to get people to contribute, it was even more difficult at first to keep the club together; in those early days he did not have the near-absolute power over his followers that came later. "Sex was all over the place," he later told researcher Daniel Casriel. "In a way I felt I was merchandising. I had to allow them to have something quickly that they could understand and stay with. I tried to allow them to have fun in any manner as long as they didn't get drunk, shoot dope, or hurt anybody."

When some of the "alkies" complained about the way their social club was evolving without their having any say, Dederich responded, "No, it's my club," reported researcher Lewis Yablonsky, and "chucked the alcoholics out."

In September, 1958, Dederich incorporated his club formally. Incorporation required a board of directors who would theoretically control the organization. Dederich later explained to Casriel how he avoided this potential threat to his power: "I needed [as directors] dummies that I could control . . . and I didn't want to put on somebody that would be frightened or rebel over what I would do."

Synanon had about forty members when it was incorporated, and the organization immediately began to draw favorable publicity. Some Synanon members appeared on the Paul Coates television show out of Los Angeles and told stories of horrible drug addiction before coming to Synanon. *The Santa Monica Evening Outlook* followed with favorable human-interest coverage. (Years later, the paper reversed itself and published some very unfavorable stories on Synanon.)

Richard pointed out to us that no one ever had demonstrated with statistics that Synanon was unusually successful in curing addicts. For one thing, Synanon never kept any records on what happened to addicts after they left. For another, apparently Dederich and other Synanon spokesmen were loose with figures when asked by researchers and reporters about the organization's "cure rate." Sometimes the figure for staying clean was reported as 80 percent—in contrast to federal hospitals, which could claim only a 10 percent cure rate. At other times, Synanon's success rate was given as 40 to 45 percent. Richard did his own analysis from what statistics were available. His conclusions did not establish any rate of success but suggested that Synanon's reputation of having a cure rate of 40 to 90 percent an extreme exaggeration. Moreover, his research revealed some interesting patterns.

In 1961, Dederich quoted statistics that implied a 40 percent success rate for the first 176 addicts who had entered Synanon and stayed.* But Richard also noticed that the men in this

---

* Dederich said that of the 176 addicts who by then had stayed in Synanon five days or more, he could list 70 who were drug-free. Al Greenstein,

early group averaged thirty-three to thirty-four years old. Those who entered Synanon the following year (1961–62) were typically five to six years younger still.* Synanon members who for years to come were trotted out to tell the press about their addiction and cure were often from that first group—the older members.

For Richard, their age was important. He pointed out that, contrary to popular opinion, a heroin addict is not automatically trapped for life by addiction to narcotics unless rescued by a cure. Many people simply get too old to continue living with the strain an addict's lifestyle requires. Addicts seemingly outgrow addiction, in some numbers. "From a study† of heroin users returning from Vietnam," said Richard, "we know that people often stop using heroin when their situation changes—as in leaving Vietnam or entering Synanon."

And, Richard claimed, Synanon's success rate of 40 percent evaporated when the average age of incoming addicts dropped to the mid-twenties. America's main "heroin problem," he explained, was concentrated among people in their mid-twenties, and it was not surprising that the bulk of the addicts who entered Synanon after its first two years were in that age group. How much success did Synanon have with these younger people? "Not much," Richard told us. The most telling statistic on them, he noted, was that 90 percent left before completing *any* rehabilitation program.

Richard reached this conclusion in the late 1970s, but some earlier drug experts were also skeptical about Synanon's success rate. In 1964, a New Jersey Drug Study Commission opted not to give Synanon any funding after reviewing rehabilitation statistics supplied by the foundation.‡

"Simplicity Marks Synanon Method," *Santa Monica Evening Outlook*, May 1, 1961.

* Daniel Casriel, *So Fair a House* (1963).

† Lee Robbins, *The Vietnam Drug User Returns*, U.S. Government Printing Office: Special Action Office for Drug Abuse Prevention, 1973.

‡ The figures showed that of 1,180 addicts who by then had entered Syna-

Richard's conclusion that Synanon had a success rate of 10 to 15 percent seemed significant to me, but equally important seemed the fact that 90 percent of newcomers quit within a year. This figure was reported by former Synanon president Liz Missakian, testifying in a 1979 child-custody case. Richard called the constant turnover of members "a revolving door. . . . But that explains how Synanon can claim twenty thousand people entered Synanon during its first twenty years." At its high point in 1972, Synanon had only 1,700 members, and by the summer of 1978, it was down to about 1,000 members. I knew those statistics since Synanon had given them to the county planning department.

Richard, in turn, was most interested in those former addicts who stayed on as employees of Synanon. He noted that Dederich had told researcher Yablonsky, "I, of course, want our best graduates to work for Synanon, and we try to make working for Synanon attractive. In this respect, we operate much like any other corporation; we want to hold our very best executive staff."

"It sounds as if Dederich was less interested in curing addicts than in building an organization," I commented.

Richard looked pleased: "That is one possible interpretation," he said approvingly.

But the news media for years paid more attention to testi-

---

non, 717 had left as treatment failures after an average stay of only forty-one days. Twenty-six had completed the program and graduated back into the outside world. Another small group had finished treatment but stayed on as low-paid staff; from other sources, Richard estimated there were about 50 in this group. Failures, graduates, and staff together totaled about 793. Subtracting 793 from 1,180, he got 387—the number still in treatment. What their success or failure might be was unknown, since they typically had been in Synanon less than a year. What was known, he pointed out, was that of the 793 addicts who had begun and ended treatment, only 76 had demonstrated long-term abstention—about 10 percent. Synanon has said only 10 percent of newcomers stay a year or more. If 10 percent of the 387 in treatment completed rehabilitation, that would add less than 5 percent to the overall cure rate. Synanon would have a cure rate of under 15 percent—similar to that of federal hospital programs.

monials from former addicts in Synanon than to Synanon's statistics. Synanon sought out publicity as a means of attracting contributions and members, and throughout the 1960s Synanon received much favorable coverage. Dederich and Synanon were glorified in a 1965 movie, *Synanon*, starring Chuck Connors, Edmond O'Brien, and Richard Conte. *Life* magazine did a lengthy article on Dederich. Other favorable stories appeared in such magazines as *Time* and *The Saturday Evening Post*. The coverage convinced Americans that Synanon was doing "what no one else could do: cure drug addicts," and numerous other therapeutic communities were patterned after Synanon.

Then, in the late sixties, Richard told us, Synanon went through a major transformation. In 1966, Synanon began operating game clubs so nonaddicts outside Synanon could play the famous game. Three clubs were opened in California, one in Detroit, and one in New York City. By 1968, some 3,400 outsiders were playing the Synanon game.

It was a time when the human potential movement was coming into flower, Richard reminded us. I could remember middle-class sophisticates getting in touch with themselves, taking part in sensitivity training, and flocking down the coast to Big Sur to take off their clothes and encounter each other nude at Esalen. Dederich, explained Richard, chose to change with the times.

The game clubs, he said, were Synanon's answer to the human potential movement. And they were cheaper. At one time, outsiders could play the game for a penny a month. But there was a hook inside this low-cost bait. The game clubs were Synanon recruitment centers, and Synanon now wanted to recruit members of the middle class.

In 1968, Synanon formally abandoned the idea of returning cured addicts to the outside world. Three years later Dederich explained, "We once had the idea of 'graduate.' This was a sop to social workers and professionals who wanted me to say we were producing 'graduates.' I have always wanted to say to them, 'A person with this fatal disease will have to live here all of his life.' I know damn well if they go out of Synanon, they are dead."* Richard pointed out that Dederich's statement amounted to an admission that Synanon's supposed cure would not have a lasting effect for many addicts once they left the Synanon environment.

With the abolition of graduation, Synanon I (in Synanon's terminology) ended. Synanon I had been a therapeutic community. Synanon II was an alternate-lifestyle community. It was also a cradle-to-grave utopian society. Rehabilitation of addicts continued on a small scale—probably, said Richard, because Synanon needed the program to continue to attract contributions and to maintain its tax-exempt charitable status. But many people who moved into Synanon did so because they were told, "Synanon is a better way to live."

Moreover, Synanon promised career opportunities to middle-class recruits. "This is your chance to get in on the ground floor of a dynamic, growing *corporation*," many were told. Synanon by now was operating several businesses, ranging from a gas station to the million-dollar Advertising Gifts and Premiums business.

Also helping Synanon recruit the middle class was the fact that in the late 1960s American education seemed to many parents stifling and irrelevant. To recruits with children, Synanon offered a progressive school run by recently recruited progressive teachers.

"The recruitment was subtle," noted Richard, who had watched Synanon members plot their strategies for recruiting various game-club members. Game players were invited to Synanon for meals and to visit other facilities. More and more potential recruits found their time being spent inside Synanon. As the recruits developed new friends at Synanon, they had less time for old friends. Easiest of all to recruit, said Richard,

* Edward M. Brecher, *Licit and Illicit Drugs*. Boston: Little, Brown, 1972.

were people desperately looking for friends. "Typically," he noted, "these were people new to a community, people just out of a job, or people who had recently been separated from a spouse." Synanon members would show intense interest in these people, and, as Richard described it, "People were 'love-bombed' right in."

Moreover, he noted, Synanon did not wait for recruits to make up their own minds about joining. Instead, they were manipulated to join Synanon in stages. Typically, said Richard, Synanon members would point out to game-club participants that club dues covered only a small part of the clubs' costs; one way to repay Synanon for the benefits they were receiving would be to contribute some of their skills to Synanon. A doctor might help out in a Synanon clinic, just on a part-time basis at first; an architect might design a building for Synanon. Later the request would be raised to cash contributions, and still later it became pressure to move in. At each stage, explained Richard, a game player who balked was given a choice: he could demonstrate his "commitment" to Synanon or he could "not come back." Many dropped out at each stage; others were processed into Synanon.

I knew considerably less about Synanon's development than Richard did, but, working with documents Synanon had given the county for planning purposes, I too could chart some of Synanon's evolution. The documents revealed Synanon's spread across the United States and into Europe and Asia. By the mid-1970s, Synanon had opened facilities in Santa Monica, San Diego, San Francisco, Marshall, Oakland, Badger (Central Callifornia), Detroit, New York City, Tannersville (New York), Seattle, Washington, D.C., Chicago, Puerto Rico, Berlin, and Malaysia. In the late 1970s, Synanon added facilities in New Jersey, the Catskills of New York, Pennsylvania, Oregon, and Italy.

A number of the facilities were only temporary, serving as bases for Synanon sales teams. Synanon's main money-maker, its Advertising Gifts and Premiums business, was growing rapidly. In the decade from 1968 to 1978, ADGAP's gross sales climbed from $1.2 million annually to $9.58 million.

As Richard saw it, the ADGAP business—not the rehabilitation work of Synanon—had held the Dederich family's attention in recent years. The ADGAP operation was a distributorship of pens, pencils, key chains, playing cards, and other knickknacks. Customers ranged from local automobile dealerships to the biggest corporations in America, including General Motors, Control Data, IBM, and Bank of America. Sales teams, experienced in penetrating an executive's protective shield of secretaries, would approach corporate officers directly. The sales teams, mostly made up of former addicts and often including attractive women, would tell painful stories of personal degradation before coming to Synanon. Company executives were usually sympathetic but would brace themselves to be hit for a handout. Instead, they would be told that their company could help other unfortunates get off drugs merely by buying supplies from Synanon, and *at competitive prices*. It was an effective sales pitch. Back in Marshall, other Synanon members would arrange with suppliers such as the Sheaffer pen company to stamp the customer's logo on the products and ship them out.

Another sales team, which I had observed during my 1975 tour of Synanon, worked at a bank of phones with long-distance WATS lines, attempting to make follow-up sales from Marshall. Most of ADGAP's dramatic growth came under the supervision of William Dederich, brother of the founder, although the business was in operation before he entered Synanon.

But the deemphasis on rehabilitating addicts, the influx of nonaddicted members, and the growth of ADGAP began to cause tax problems for the foundation. In the early 1970s, the Internal Revenue Service began arguing that ADGAP was an "unrelated business" to the charity and should pay income taxes. One way I knew of Synanon's tax problems was from an auditor's report on Synanon that had been filed with the county tax assessor.

In 1975, Synanon attempted to protect its tax exemption by declaring that a major purpose of the foundation was to operate a Synanon "church," and by 1977 Synanon lawyers were referring to the "cult" at Synanon.

Synanon by the mid-1970s was becoming so wealthy, Richard pointed out, that the Dederich family began to more openly reveal the benefits of running Synanon. Founder Dederich began building a resortlike retreat for his family, all of whom had been brought into the foundation's administration, and other Synanon executives in the Sierra foothill community of Badger. It was a lavish facility with saunas, hot tubs, riding stables, and teams of servants. The servants, however, drawn from Synanon's membership, were not allowed to live at "the Home Place," as it was called. They were housed at a barren airstrip Synanon built, forty minutes away by car.

Until the mid-1970s, the three of us learned from Synanon's filings with the state attorney general, Dederich had drawn little out of the charity in cash, relying on Synanon perks for a high standard of living. But in 1975–76, Dederich's official salary shot up from $2,500 per year to $75,000. His brother's salary was set at $50,000, his twenty-five-year-old daughter's at $15,000, and her older half-brother's at $30,000. All this, of course, was in addition to their getting room, board, clothing, recreation, and travel free from Synanon coffers.

Richard insisted that the transformation of Synanon that occurred in the mid-1970s was as significant as the evolution from Synanon I to Synanon II in 1968. Although it wasn't called that, Richard claimed that what we were observing in the summer of 1978 was Synanon III: the corporate cult.

What was the significance of this latest transformation, Cathy wanted to know. Did it mean anything beyond the fact that Synanon was now wealthier, was having tax problems, and had decided to call itself a church?

Richard believed the change was more than cosmetic. When the transformation of Synanon I, the therapeutic community, into Synanon II, the alternate-lifestyle community, occurred, Dederich had been very direct in forcing acceptance of his new direction for Synanon, Richard noted. The "dope fiends" were told, "If you aren't able to take part in the new Synanon, get out!" The transformation into "Synanon III," Richard said, involved another "squeeze."

Coinciding with Synanon's evolution into a cult were increasing demands on the membership. Richard reeled off a list. In 1975, male and female members were required to shave off their hair. Next, some members were selected to undergo military or police-type training. In early 1977, all men in Synanon for longer than five years were required to undergo vasectomies and all pregnant women received abortions. (In the summer of 1978, Cathy, Richard, and I had heard a little about this. Throughout the following twelve months, we were to get more and more information on how grisly much of this surgery was.) The ultimate demand came in late 1977, when virtually all Synanon couples—married or not—were required to "change partners." One effect of these escalating demands, Richard noted, was to drive out all but those most committed to Synanon in its new cult form. Between 1972 and 1978, Synanon's population dropped by 41 percent, to 996.

As we talked for hours on end about what was happening and had happened in Synanon, the three of us reached a general consensus on how Synanon had evolved. One thing we never did agree on, however, was the character of Charles E. Dederich, "Mr. Synanon," as *Life* magazine called him. In some respects, we had too little information on him; in other respects, too much. None of us had ever met him, although we had met many other Synanon leaders. But since Synanon members in games sooner or later discussed every personal matter from their diets to their sexual problems, and since the topics of game discussions circulated throughout Synanon, an incredible amount of information on Dederich was available to us from ex-members. Moreover, Dederich—like former president Nixon—wanted his utterances preserved for posterity. So—like Nixon—he tape-recorded hundreds of hours of his daily conversations. Not surprisingly, those tape recordings—like Nixon's—eventually got into the hands of law enforcement and helped lead to his undoing.

Later in 1978, when we were to see transcriptions of some of Dederich's sadistic rhetoric, I developed a hearty contempt for the cult leader. He seemed to delight in being coarse and vicious. But all three of us also heard at one time or another an ex-member describe how "charming" Dederich could be. One of Synanon's former presidents, Jack Hurst, once told me Dederich was "the funniest man I ever knew."

Dederich reminded me of a barroom loudmouth. "That's just a pose," Richard insisted. "Behind the scenes, he can be reasonable." Cathy vacillated. She saw Dederich as either a genius, as evidenced by the wealthy organization he had put together, or a madman, as evidenced by Synanon's violence. "He's not crazy," Richard said over and over again. "He's not a genius, but he's a schemer."

"Well, would you call him charismatic?" Cathy wanted to know.

"He's not a charismatic leader in the way the word is usually used," Richard replied. Synanon members were impressed by Dederich, Richard argued, because of his power over their lives. "Of course, they're always being told of their great debt to Dederich, but they also know they can be tossed out of Synanon if they cross him."

Dederich was hardly a typical spellbinder when he spoke publicly; sometimes he would stumble along, speaking before he had thought through a sentence, necessitating a change of direction in mid-utterance. But he sometimes revealed "a way with words," Richard admitted. On that we all agreed. On occasion Dederich could turn a phrase, and one of his bons mots became known nationally: "Today is the first day of the rest of your life."

CHAPTER 10

DESPAIR

As I look back on 1978, August was the cruelest month. My depression was almost suicidal. Cathy and I were later to be praised by the California Press Association as "fearless, crusading editors," but in August of 1978 both of us were tired, beaten, and trying to sound retreat. Our personal lives, *The Light*, our editorial crusade on Synanon—all seemed disasters.

For as long as Cathy and I had been journalists we had held without question a somewhat idealized view of a newspaper's role in watching out for its community. If a newspaper discovered a civic problem, it should report on it. By bringing the problem to public and official attention, the newspaper would prompt government to act; the problem would get solved. That was how society was supposed to work and, in fact, often did work. While reporting for two other papers, I had instigated exposés of illegal real estate developments. Both exposés had sparked prosecution of the developers. We, as journalists, did our jobs; then the government took its turn.

With Synanon, the arrangement wasn't working. For six months, *The Light* had been publishing reports of wrongdoing at the foundation. In editorial after editorial, we had demanded that state and county government end the abuses. Both governments had tried, and both gave up when Synanon outmaneuvered them.

Following five public hearings on Synanon in the spring of 1978, Marin County supervisors had voted to begin rezoning Synanon's three properties in West Marin and to require Synanon to draft a master plan for any future development. Supervisor Denis Rice's proposal to control weapons and other problems through use permits, which *The Light* had endorsed, was dropped. Synanon did draft a master plan and accompanying environmental report, but they were so vaguely written as to be meaningless. Synanon agreed to rezoning of its two inland ranches totaling almost 3,300 acres, but insisted its 64-acre facility on Tomales Bay should not be rezoned. When the county nonetheless rezoned the bay facility to provide for development controls, Synanon angrily withdrew its master plan. Since the rezoning of all three properties would affect only future building on them, the county action solved no present problems.

Also coming to naught were county attempts to investigate child abuse at Synanon. When Synanon in April said it would not admit a county child-abuse team without a search warrant, county supervisors directed County Counsel Doug Maloney to arrange for an investigation. Maloney, however, had done nothing. When I called him in late July to ask why, he told me the county had not "developed" enough information to get a search warrant. Another county staffer blamed the inaction on a lack of eyewitnesses to any child abuse.

I called several other county staffers and officials. Most were surprised to learn the matter had been dropped. Supervisor Barbara Boxer said she had assumed Maloney was still preparing for a child-abuse investigation.

Throughout the summer, I had also been following legal wranglings between Synanon and the state health department in the wake of the department's unsuccessful attempt to inspect Synanon in May. The inspection was supposed to have been a prelude to the state's demanding that Synanon get licensing as a "community care facility." The inspection had been attempted following pressure from grand jurors concerned about possible child abuse and MediCal fraud at Synanon.

After Synanon obstructed the health inspection, the attorney general's office asked a Marin County superior court to order Synanon to allow an unhampered inspection. Synanon, in turn, asked the court to throw out the health department's original inspection warrant, requested the right to question under oath the department's investigator, Chris Brett, and sought a look at the department's investigative files on Synanon.

In July, the court ruled that the state did not have to turn over the files but said Synanon could question Brett. Brett was questioned during a two-day deposition in August but refused to answer questions concerning "privileged information." Synanon then announced it would seek a court ruling on whether Brett had to answer those questions. The attorney general prepared to fight the Synanon request but anticipated new legal objections from Synanon, entailing still more court hearings.

Synanon clearly knew how to endlessly tie up an adversary with litigation, and the state clearly had no heart for the fight. The health department never made any decision to drop the matter, but the attorney general's office did, without telling anyone. One day when I called to find out if the attorney general's office had made any progress, I was told the deputy attorney general on the case had been reassigned to other litigation. When I mentioned this to a health department/social services official some weeks later, she was surprised to learn her department no longer had a lawyer working on their case. It was a near-exact repeat of what had happened in Marin County; in legal confrontation, Synanon knew how to outlast government.

By now, *The Light* was the only news medium still grinding out Synanon stories. Reporters for KGO-TV and *The Los Angeles Times*, two media that had earlier led the way on Synanon coverage, now informed me that they were dropping the story for the time being. They explained it had become too much of a hassle to get stories past their companies' lawyers.

"We're the only ones left on the story," I dejectedly told Cathy.

"We might let it go for a while, too," she replied. "We're not getting anywhere with it. The horse may not be dead, but I'm tired of beating it. I keep hearing comments around town that we're obsessed with Synanon. If something happens, we ought to cover it, but there's no point in trying to drag the story out week after week."

Criticism of our Synanon coverage was not the only problem at *The Light*. Keith Ervin, our first-rate news editor, had fallen in love with a woman in Seattle and was preparing to move. He was also expecting to move up to a higher salary on a daily newspaper there. Cathy and I hated to lose Keith. His impending departure meant I would have to break in another beginning reporter—the only kind *The Light* could afford—and have to take on again many of the mundane jobs in the newsroom that I had bequeathed to Keith.

At home, Cathy and I quarreled often. She wanted me to spend less time at the office and on endless discussions of Synanon. I, in turn, found that Keith's impending departure meant I had to spend more time at the paper. And I was finding *The Light* less pleasant. The quality of *The Light*'s news coverage, I realized, would take an immediate drop when Keith left. Helping out a new reporter, I would have less time for the in-depth articles I enjoyed writing.

Journalists expect to take a certain amount of flak from readers, and so the scattered criticism we were receiving regarding Synanon was not devastating. But I found it one more irritant. By now I was convinced that Synanon was not only deceiving the public, it was a very dangerous presence in the community. But we simply could not get government sufficiently concerned to impose a solution; that was devastating and demoralizing to me.

If we couldn't accomplish anything with our major story, doing a good job with our minor stories began to seem less important to me. "I'm ready to sell *The Light*," I announced to Cathy one night. "I want to do something else."

"All right," she answered, showing no emotion. "It's your decision. You're the one who has to be down there every day." I suspected she was feeling more upset than she was revealing, but I also knew she had become as frustrated as I.

Financially, it was a good decision. As a reporter on one of the Bay area's dailies, I could probably make as much as *The Light* netted for both Cathy and me. *The Light* had grown to where we could probably get over $100,000 for it. I no longer would have to be custodian, repairman, and bill collector as well as editor/publisher. Cathy could stop being business manager and bookkeeper. We would have more time for each other. And making Synanon obey the law would no longer be our responsibility.

We knew that whoever bought *The Light* would have to be an experienced newspaperman. Several of *The Light*'s previous owners hadn't been, and they had all foundered. With this in mind, I contacted the assistant publisher at a neighboring county weekly about buying our newspaper. I respected his abilities and several times had asked him for advice. He, in turn, had told me he envied the independence Cathy and I had as owners. But, perhaps because he knew the newspaper business so well, he wasn't interested in buying *The Light*. He wasn't ready for the long hours at low pay *The Light* guaranteed.

His rejection further dejected me. I suspected other knowledgeable newspapermen would react the same way. I was aware, however, of several weeklies that had recently been sold to newspaper chains—and at high prices. Through a mutual friend, I had twice met a representative of one large chain. If Cathy and I ever decided to sell, he had urged, we should let him know. I called, and he promised the head of his chain would get in touch with me. A few days later, a letter from the company president arrived.

The president offered to meet with me, and asked for financial information on *The Light.* I consulted with Cathy and wrote him back, enclosing the figures. For weeks, we heard nothing more. When he finally wrote again, he said *The Light* was too small; his company wasn't interested.

I felt inspected, rejected, and dejected. Nothing was going right. I took the afternoon off and drove into San Francisco near Union Street, to bar-hop. It was mid-afternoon, and the bars were almost deserted. I was lonely and wanted to talk to someone. Finally, a fellow on a nearby bar stool fell into conversation with me. By now, I was a little tipsy, and we chatted convivially about photography, which he apparently knew something about. He bought us both drinks. Then I bought a round. The bartender who served us seemed obviously gay and, moreover, seemed to be an acquaintance of my companion. Slowly, it dawned on me my new friend was trying to pick me up. The attempt wasn't offensive—just depressing. I made a show of looking at my watch and then excused myself. After a hamburger and several cups of coffee at a diner a few blocks away, I drove back to Point Reyes Station. "What can I do?" I asked myself aloud. "What can I do?" No answer came, and I turned on the radio to drown out the broken record in my head.

After a few more days of gloom, it occurred to me there were other newspaper chains, including some that concentrated on small papers. Cathy and I were considering contacting one of them when a new consideration intervened. CBS had aired a documentary narrated by Hughes Rudd concerning the effects of chain ownership on American newspapers. Some mediocre newspapers had been improved when chains bought them, Rudd noted, but chain ownership could also make a newspaper less sensitive to its community. Cathy and I discussed *The Light*'s intense involvement in community affairs and began to wonder if selling our paper to a chain wouldn't be doing West Marin a disservice. Another escape seemed to be blocked.

Richard knew of our frustration but not of our plans to sell *The Light*. "Wait till the book comes out," he tried to reassure us. "Then government will have to deal with Synanon." He could be right, Cathy and I admitted to ourselves. But after our impotence with *The Light*, we weren't convinced. Sooner or later, we knew, we would have to tell Richard we were selling out. But we were embarrassed about giving up, and continued to hold off telling him.

CHAPTER

11

IS ANYONE LISTENING?

"Pomegranates," said Cathy. "I've got some pomegranates for dessert. If you have any advice on how to eat them, I'd welcome it."

I thought I remembered scenes of ancient Romans eating pomegranate seeds from silver bowls held by servants. I gave Cathy a small ceramic bowl and took one for myself. Side by side in the kitchen, we shucked pomegranate seeds. Cathy thought their color was dramatic.

"Somewhere we have two silver bowls we got as wedding presents," I observed. "How would you like to eat your pomegranate seeds from a silver bowl?"

Cathy shook her head. "It just wouldn't be the same without servants."

By now it was apparent that our efforts to unload *The Light* were meeting with no greater success than our efforts to use it to bring Synanon to justice. The fall semester at Santa Rosa Junior College was about to begin, and Cathy would soon be away from *The Light* three days a week. There were too many other activities to be taken care of to think about selling *The Light* at this time. At first I had accepted the situation with resignation, but once I had realized I was going to be editing

The Light for the foreseeable future, I began to get interested in West Marin doings again. I nosed around. Preparations were under way for the quadricentennial celebration the next June of Sir Francis Drake's landing in Drake's Bay. A San Francisco exporter, Jung T. Wang, was planning to raise elk commercially in Tomales and sell powdered elkhorn in the Orient as medicine; the humane society was irate. Covering West Marin news could still be interesting, I told myself, even if the Synanon story was getting us nowhere.

I had taken Cathy's advice and relegated Synanon to merely another story we were following. We would stay with it, but with a lessened emotional commitment. Our commitment, instead, would be to each other. "You might enjoy working at *The Light* even more," Cathy suggested. "if it were your job and not your life." I thought about her suggestion for quite a while and finally agreed. *The Light* could cover community affairs and sometimes try to shape them with editorials, but it could not control them. Synanon was defeating state and county government; it was not defeating us, I reassured myself.

To reduce Synanon's domination of our lives, Cathy and I made an agreement. On days she taught, I would fill her in on Synanon developments at the beginning of the evening. Then one of us would say, "Okay, no more Synanon for tonight." For the most part, we honored the agreement.

Synanon had dominated our attention for so long that after reaching the agreement with Cathy, I felt all at sea for a while. Appropriately, I took up sailing. Nine months earlier, Cathy and I had bought in on two friends' dilapidated sailboat. Our $500 investment was used to buy repair materials, and I had spent several weekends working with them to make the ancient craft seaworthy.

In September, we launched the rebuilt *Alberta*, an eighteen-foot plywood sloop. For the next few months, I set aside time to sail at least one day a week. For a whole day, my mind would be on tides and wind and how the sails were set. Except when sailing past the Synanon facility overlooking Marconi Cove, I could forget about that frustrating organization. Cathy came along about half the time; our relationship was still mending, and too much togetherness quickly strained it. By being careful, however, we began to have fun together on occasional outings.

At *The Light*, we were enjoying our fall tradition: the annual *Light* contest for Heavy Zucchini. Children from all over West Marin brought in the heaviest zucchini from their family garden. We photographed the youngsters with their squash, gave the winner $15, and ran all the pictures in the paper. For such a simple idea, it was incredibly popular; dozens of children took part.

We were also continuing to carry a Synanon story almost every week, although usually in the back of the paper. Because we had never dropped the story, we still got tips from time to time. One of the tips we got in September, 1978, was from NBC producer Pat Lynch. She had heard a rumor that attorney Howard Garfield had quit Synanon. If the rumor was true, it would make a major story. Garfield had been the fiery Synanon spokesman before the board of supervisors. He appeared to be one of Charles Dederich's closest advisers and was his almost constant companion.

But getting Synanon to admit Garfield's defection, if it was real, would be a difficult task. Pat Lynch had suggested calling attorney Paul Morantz in Los Angeles for information, since he was in the middle of a lawsuit against Synanon. Morantz told me he had heard the same rumor. Garfield, Dederich, and other Synanon leaders had traveled to Rome in August. Dederich had been drunk much of the time, said Morantz. *Drunk?* I asked Morantz to repeat himself. Alcohol—like drugs—was absolutely forbidden to Synanon members. But Morantz insisted that was how he had heard the story.

Dederich, who had reformed from alcoholism twenty-two

years earlier, had alternately raged and been extremely depressed in his drunkenness, according to the story Morantz had heard. Garfield supposedly had become repulsed. First, the violence back home; now Dederich's return to alcoholism; there was even talk among a couple of people in the party of possible group sex. Garfield had flown back to the United States, said his good-byes to other Synanon members, and quit.

Unfortunately, all of Morantz's information was second- or thirdhand; how to verify it? Morantz gave me phone numbers of several ex-members living in California. I called a couple of them. They both said Garfield had quit and was keeping out of sight. They knew people who had seen him, but they hadn't. There still wasn't enough for *The Light* to go on.

My next call was to Deputy Attorney General Jim Schwartz in San Francisco. He and I had had an unfriendly conversation the last time I had called him about regulation of Synanon, but he seemed to be in contact with the organization. Schwartz was more helpful this time and confirmed that Synanon had told him the week before that Garfield was "on leave."

That was only a partial confirmation, but hearing it from Schwartz gave me an idea. Rather than trying to call Synanon and getting the usual lack of response from their public relations department, I should try the legal department directly. Or should I? It might work better, I reasoned, if someone else called, someone with a different reason for calling. My eventual solution was to have a friend, who ran a process-serving business for lawyers, call and ask for Garfield. A process server makes a living getting past obstacles to locate people, and my friend was a pro. When told by a legal secretary that Garfield wasn't in, my friend demanded to know when he would be. The secretary couldn't say. My friend identified himself as a process-service operator and said Garfield had wanted to hire the service. When or where could

Garfield be reached? Finally, the secretary acknowledged that Garfield was "no longer" with Synanon.

We had our confirmation. Garfield, Synanon's top lawyer, confidant of Dederich, executive secretary of Synanon's board of directors, had quit! I went bellowing around the newsroom and into the back shop, where the two production workers—somewhat used to my eruptions—listened in bemusement. They didn't care that much about Synanon.

I made a few more calls to get whatever information I could; one of them was to the former president of Synanon's board of directors, Jack Hurst. Hurst was living in Marin County and running the Marin Community Workshop, a center for handicapped children. I had gotten his phone number from one of the ex-members I had called in Southern California.

Hurst also was aware that Garfield had left and was in contact with some members still in Synanon. He repeated that Garfield had left because of Dederich's behavior in Rome. But he added that Synanon members were being told Garfield had been talked into leaving by his fiancée, Liza Cameron, also a Synanon member.

The call to Hurst was made on Friday, September 8, and his added information only seemed to reaffirm how nicely the story was falling together for the following week's paper. The Garfield defection would be our first major scoop in several months. When I picked up Saturday's *Independent-Journal*, however, my excitement ended abruptly. Looking at me from page 1 was Howard Garfield's smiling face.

Had we been scooped? Above the photo of Garfield was a headline: SYNANON PUSHING 'MISSIONARY' ROLE. The article by George Nevin said:

> Synanon's leaders are traveling the length and breadth of America and the world, seeking sites for new centers where the social and political climate might be right for establishing arms of the rehabilitation foundation.

> They're moving in the name of religious expansion. They call themselves missionaries and they're looking for people who wish to join the religion without becoming full-time residents of Synanon.

The article quoted Garfield as saying many people doubted Synanon was a religion, but he blamed the doubts on a very limited view of religion.

The article didn't say Garfield was among the Synanon leaders "traveling" as "missionaries" for Synanon, but that might explain his absence. On the other hand, the article also did not say when Nevin had talked with Garfield, only that it had been "a recent interview." How long ago was "recent"?

I had planned the Garfield defection to be the lead story on page 1, but with this new uncertainty I readied another story to take its place in case we had to kill our scoop. I waited until *The Independent-Journal* was almost at its noon deadline Tuesday (and so could not use my call to scoop us) and then phoned and asked for Nevin. He was on vacation. I asked the city editor when Nevin had written the story, explaining we were about to run a story on Garfield and believed Garfield was no longer at Synanon's local facilities. We needed to know if their information contradicted ours, I said, because Synanon was "so quick to sue newspapers." *The I-J*'s city editor laughed; he understood our concern, and added that Nevin had done the interview several weeks ago. The story was okay!

I made a couple of pro forma calls to Synanon's public relations and legal departments and said I had heard that Garfield had quit. Did Synanon have any comments? As usual, I was told that someone might call me back; as usual, no one did.

We ran the story under the headline: MYSTERIOUS SYNANON EXIT. The article noted: "Synanon members have offered conflicting versions of why Garfield left. By one account, Garfield was upset by partying he witnessed among Synanon members in Europe. Another account is that he left at the urging of a girlfriend."

The September 14, 1978, issue of *The Light* was a near sellout. West Marin residents remembered Garfield well from the supervisors' hearings. What his defection signified was unclear, but it hinted that something important was under way within Synanon. I was pleased with my efforts in digging out a difficult story. We were back in the battle, and when a letter arrived from a former newspaper publisher who said he might be interested in buying *The Light*, I never wrote back.

The next week brought more Synanon surprises. The first surprise, which again reached me as a rumor, was that *The San Francisco Examiner* had agreed to an out-of-court settlement of Synanon's second lawsuit. I traced the rumor to an alternative weekly newspaper in San Francisco, *The Bay Guardian*, which had long been feuding with *The Examiner*. *The Guardian*, it turned out, had run a small piece on the settlement: an unbelievable $2 million. *The Examiner*'s attorneys, in defending the paper against a Synanon libel suit, had hired two men who then allegedly burglarized tape recordings from Synanon. In 1976, *The Examiner* had paid Synanon $600,000 to settle the libel suit, only to have Synanon start pressing the second lawsuit, a conspiracy suit. With *The Examiner* now settling the conspiracy suit for $2 million, Synanon had picked up a whopping $2.6 million from Hearst, the parent corporation, in two years.

I called *The Examiner* for confirmation and was referred to their attorneys. They in turn referred me to another law firm, which said the information was accurate. Synanon had now collected $2.6 million from the Hearst corporation in two years. "*The Examiner*'s getting to be easy pickings for Synanon," I later muttered to Cathy. "No wonder they're leaving the story alone."

I was more upset by the second surprise. Municipal Court

Judge David Baty, whom I knew slightly because he lived in Point Reyes Station, had passed sentence on three of the four Synanon members who beat ex-member Tom Cardineau in March. For agreeing to plead no contest, the three—Harvey Litwin, Philip Black, and Floyd Egan—were sentenced to twenty hours' work apiece in a county firehouse and put on three years' probation. The fourth defendant, Christopher Benton, would plead no contest two weeks later; he was fined $375 and placed on three years' probation.

When I called Judge Baty for an explanation, he told me, "I didn't think jail was indicated in the case." The four, he theorized, "probably overreacted to the trespasser." He added that his sentencing was influenced by Judge Gary Thomas, who had earlier reduced the charges from felony false imprisonment to misdemeanor battery.

Outside of Synanon, the sentences were unpopular. Deputy Attorney General Ed Hill, who had earlier represented the state against Synanon, called the sentences "A very minor penalty." Marin County Deputy DA Michael Gridley, who had prosecuted the case, concurred: "I can't disagree. . . . What makes me uncomfortable is no jail time. In my view, this is the kind of case that can *use* [benefit from] a deterrent effect."

The issue of *The Light* that covered the story was dated September 21, and Gridley's comments were later echoed in various forms by several people I was to interview about new events that took place that same day. Different people have different theories about which event led to the undoing of Synanon. In my opinion, the pivotal one was the near-fatal beating of an ex-member of Synanon, Phil Ritter, in Berkeley on September 21, 1978.

Cathy and I were home Saturday, September 23, when the phone rang. It was Jack Hurst, the former Synanon president, calling; his voice was shaking with anger. He had just returned from a Berkeley hospital where his longtime friend Phil Ritter was being treated for massive head wounds. Hurst wanted to talk.

Ritter, Hurst said, was a thirty-four-year-old accountant and mechanic who had been supervisor of transportation for Synanon. Ritter had left Synanon in early 1977 when Synanon management decreed that all men who stayed in Synanon more than five years had to get vasectomies. Ritter had been horrified by the mass sterilization program and had fled one night to the Marin County sheriff's department and asked deputies and the district attorney's office to intervene. The DA's office, however, had claimed the county did not have jurisdiction.

Ritter's wife, Lynn, remained in Synanon with their infant daughter. After much legal wrangling, Ritter had gotten custody of the daughter, only to have Lynn and a companion from Synanon steal back the child while on a supposed visit. Ritter hired an attorney, and a court hearing was less than a week away when Ritter came home from work the afternoon of September 21.

Hurst's account—later confirmed by Berkeley police—was that Ritter was getting out of his car when two men clubbed him from behind, knocking him to the ground, and then continued to club him as he lay injured on the sidewalk.

A neighbor heard Ritter's screams and rushed out as the assailants drove off in a red Toyota. The neighbor took down the getaway car's license number, but when police checked it, the number did not fit a red Toyota. Police did, however, find a Toyota registered to Synanon with a license number that nearly matched the number reported by the neighbor.

Ritter's skull was broken in the attack, and brain fluid leaking into his spinal column caused him to develop spinal meningitis. He went into a coma for a week, but just when death seemed imminent, he recovered.

I put the story together with calls to Berkeley police, ex-members of Synanon, the neighbor, Ritter's family, and his roommate. My father, who lived in Berkeley, pointed out there had been no report on the attack in *The Berkeley Indpendent & Gazette*. That daily was far enough away not to compete with *The Light*, and so I called its newsroom. My call was partly to see if *The Independent & Gazette* had any information I didn't, but also to let the paper know, if it didn't already, about the beating. It had been several months since any newspaper but *The Light* had shown much interest in Synanon, and I was eager to spark some.

The Independent & Gazette knew nothing about the attack on Ritter, but the city editor said he was definitely interested. He would have a reporter, Bob Kroll, call me back. When Kroll called, I gave him an account of the beating, told him about the grand jury report, and gave him a brief history of Synanon. We still beat his paper into print with the story, a fact we took great delight in, but Kroll came in with a comprehensive report on both the beating and Synanon. Over the next few months, Kroll did some of the most aggressive research and important reporting on Synanon that appeared anywhere.

Among the ex-members of Synanon I talked to while writing *The Light*'s story on the beating was Dr. Jerry Newmark, who headed an organization of ex-members called the Network of Friends. He saw a link between the light sentences handed out in the Cardineau case and the Ritter beating, which followed almost immediately. The sentencing was "sickening and disgusting," commented Newmark. "It's encouraging people that they can get away with this shit." Hurst concurred: "I'm shocked the courts let them off so lightly. . . . None of us are safe from this kind of treatment, from the beatings. . . . I'm fearful of my life." The two ex-members said they were raising funds from other ex-members to offer a reward for information on the Ritter assailants.

Several weeks would go by before any of us at *The Light*

realized the importance of Hurst's and Newmark's reactions. What we finally came to understand was that numerous ex-members of Synanon knew pieces of the Synanon-violence story. Newmark had made one unsuccessful attempt to interest authorities, but most had remained silent, fearing reprisals from Synanon. With the attacks on ex-members Cardineau and Ritter, any safety in silence suddenly disappeared. Many ex-members felt personally threatened. It was now to their advantage to have the world know what had been occurring within Synanon. If the public knew Synanon was capable of violence, attacks on ex-members would reverberate to Synanon. As a group, the ex-members had a well of information on violence, and over the next few weeks *The Light* began to pump it.

The severity of the attack on Ritter coupled with the meaningless sentences dealt out to the Cardineau assailants also alarmed Cathy, Richard, and me. "We have a major threat to public safety, and nobody in government seems to give a damn," I fumed.

Richard wanted us to write an editorial demanding that state and county authorities begin an immediate investigation. Cathy objected, "We've done that already. It won't do any good." In light of the Ritter beating, said Richard, an editorial would get more attention. Cathy noted that although Synanon was the obvious suspect, no one could say for sure that it was Synanon's work.

Cathy and Richard were becoming irritated with each other. She was sitting on the floor by our fireplace, her jaw muscles clenched. She seemed to resent Richard's intrusion into *The Light*'s editorial policy. Richard, on the couch, was speaking softly, as he often did when tense. Cathy frequently interrupted him, and Richard made a point of not objecting. He was in a difficult position: *The Light* was the one public voice available to him—but only if he could convince us, its sometimes obstinate owners, to use it. Richard more than we felt the potential danger of Synanon. Cathy and I recognized the threat without feeling it; as reporters, we were used to living with the risk of being assaulted. I had been threatened several times concerning other stories. And once, while I was a reporter in Sonora, a burly lumberjack had barged into *The Union Democrat* newsroom wanting to fight with me; I threatened to call the police, and the lumberjack backed off.

Rocking back and forth on a swivel chair in our living room, I let Richard and Cathy argue. I said little and occasionally would get up to stoke the fire in our Franklin stove. Without saying so, I agreed with Richard. The violence appeared to be escalating. *The Light* ought to comment. Richard thought that what he was asking us to write might put Cathy and me in danger. To be fair, Richard said, he would volunteer to sign the editorial with us. Cathy objected that editorials are statements of the *publishers'* opinions.

Cathy insisted we had to do something different. "The state and county are ignoring *The Light* as a Podunk newspaper," she grumbled. Richard countered that the problem with government; "the kind of thing that led to Judge Baty's wrist-slap of the Cardineau assailants, is that authorities see each incident as isolated. Synanon keeps getting away with this crap because there's no government agency anywhere keeping track of how much of it there is."

Attorney Paul Morantz in Los Angeles had won a $300,000 judgment that week for a couple suing Synanon. I had talked with Morantz by phone, and he was feeling the same frustration that we were—government was ignoring an extremely dangerous organization. I told Richard and Cathy about my conversation with Morantz.

Finally, I cast my vote for an editorial, but assured Cathy it would be written differently. She was right: past editorials hadn't worked. Perhaps, I mused, the problem was relying too much on cold logic. I tried one draft, threw it away, and tried another. Ritter at that moment was near death, and I felt we had to somehow make our warning be heard. The pressure was so intense that I kept hitting the wrong keys on my typewriter. What I finally produced was a blend of logic and rhetoric titled, IS ANYONE LISTENING? It asked:

> Is anybody out there? A number of West Marin people are learning what it feels like to be Alvin Gambonini—even if they don't know who he is.
>
> For those who don't know, Gambonini is a rancher who with his family lives next door to Synanon on the Marshall-Petaluma Rd. For years he had a story to tell, and no one listened.
>
> Gambonini tried to get help from county government after problems arose between him and Synanon. No one paid much attention. Three years ago, he was beaten by Synanon members; three were convicted, and no one listened.
>
> Last year, a Southern California woman announced she had been kidnapped by Synanon, brought to West Marin, and abused. No one here listened. Last week a Los Angeles Court judge awarded her $300,000 damages from Synanon because of the experience.
>
> As 1978 began, the press revealed Synanon had bought a large cache of weapons—including military types—and hundreds of thousands of rounds of ammunition. This time, officials listened. Then they forgot.
>
> In March, Synanon members dragged an ex-Synanon member from his car outside their Walker Creek ranch, handcuffed him, interrogated him, and then severely beat him. In West Marin, lots of people listened.
>
> At the county level, charges against the culprits were reduced from felonies to misdemeanors. And even when the three defendants pled no contest to charges stemming from the beating, they got off with no jail time and no fines. This time the criminal-justice system wasn't listening.
>
> In April, Marshall residents jammed the supervisors'

chambers saying they felt intimidated by Synanon. They told of Synanon runaways seeking asylum and of Synanon residents menacing townspeople. The supervisors listened. Their response was to rezone Synanon.

Twice—in March and August—county grand jurors called for investigation at Synanon of possible MediCal fraud, unlicensed operation of community care facilities, and child abuse.

Synanon listened. In April, the organization refused to admit a county child-abuse team. In May, Synanon obstructed a court-authorized state Health Department inspection. The state then went back to court; five months later, it's still there. We know that several judges have been hearing motions in the case. But there is more to listening than hearing.

What is so frustrating to many West Marin residents is that state and county government seem incapable of findind a pattern to these events.

Each case of violence by Synanon members is treated as unrelated to every other case. Marshall residents say they are intimidated; the county tries to solve the problems with better zoning.

West Marin residents have a significant problem with Synanon. But like rancher Gambonini we wonder: is anyone out there listening?*

---

* The editorial worked—but not in the way expected; government ignored this one too. But it made an impression on ex-members of Synanon who were beginning to realize they were in the best position to reveal wrongdoing inside Synanon. The editorial was photocopied numerous times and circulated among ex-members. As Cathy later observed, "It developed a cult following of former cult followers." In February, 1979, the California Newspaper Publishers Association judged it the best editorial written by a California weekly newspaper in 1978.

CHAPTER 12

REPORTING A "GOON SQUAD"

For the past several months, Richard had been telling us about Synanon's twenty-year fight with a host of regulatory agencies. Synanon had won almost every round, and in the fall of 1978 the significance of those victories became obvious not only to us but to the public as well.

As an organization taking in narcotics addicts, parolees, and juvenile delinquents while having a medical clinic, Synanon by rights should have been under the regulation of a host of government agencies. But, as Richard noted, Synanon had fought every attempt to impose outside authority over its internal affairs. Synanon's strategy, explained Richard, was "to avoid getting defined as anything that came under any agency's jurisdiction."

When Marin County objected to the housing complexes and other facilities Synanon was erecting in agricultural zoning, Synanon countered that the facility was an ecology and agricultural project. When the state Department of Industrial Relations questioned Synanon's failure to pay employees the minimum wage, Synanon responded it was a church and the workers were really "congregants." The pattern was repeated so often that Dederich developed a saying, "It's all done with words."

On those few occasions when the strategy didn't work, noted Richard, "Synanon's fall-back position was to resist." When zoning authorities objected to Synanon's opening a rehabilitation center in an expensive residential section of San Francisco, Synanon insisted that members/patients living there were really servants of the Synanon management residing in the building. After numerous hearings—at which Synanon posed as a small organization trying to do good but obstructed by bureaucratic nitpicking—Synanon was finally forced to abandon the building. But by that time it had found another home and had attracted much sympathetic news coverage. In fact, said Richard, Synanon seemed to welcome such fights as a means of getting publicity.

In many fights against external regulation, Richard pointed out, Synanon had enlisted the aid of friendly politicians. "The politicians were not paid off," he insisted, "only conned." Favorable news coverage was crucial to the "con." Synanon realized that testimonials made better newspaper copy than statistics. "That was great for Synanon," laughed Richard, "because the statistics were horrible but testimonials were easy to produce." Politicians shown the favorable publicity assumed Synanon was working miracles but caught in red tape. As a result, politicians such as California State Senator Nicholas Petris and Assemblyman Herschel Rosenthal at different times introduced legislation aimed at exempting Synanon from whatever regulations were then causing problems for the organization.

Why was Synanon so opposed to external regulation, I wanted to know. "It wouldn't matter," Richard replied, "if its prime goal was drug rehabilitation. But if the motivation was money, Synanon needed to remain flexible to launch off in new directions when they were financially advantageous." Outside regulation would have limited what management could do with Synanon members, especially those who were parolees or children.

Synanon's escaping almost all regulation, however, sometimes had tragic results. One of those tragedies had occurred in 1977 and in September, 1978, resulted in attorney Paul Morantz's winning a $300,000 judgment for the victim, Frances Winn. The judge who awarded the damages called Synanon's treatment of the victim "unpardonable" and accused Synanon of taking advantage of her disturbed mental condition. For Mrs. Winn, then twenty-five, the incident was a nightmare.

On June 6, 1977, Frances Winn was on the verge of a nervous breakdown. Her husband planned to take her to the Neuropsychiatric Institute at UCLA when he got off work, but during the day she became increasingly distraught. Having previously received birth control pills from the Venice (Los Angeles County) Family Planning Clinic, she went there and asked for tranquilizers. The clinic could not dispense them and instead referred her to Synanon's Santa Monica facility for counseling.

Once inside Synanon, she was not allowed to leave. The organization informed her husband by phone that his wife was now living in Synanon and that he would not be allowed to see her for ninety days. Nonetheless, Ed Winn made repeated attempts to visit her, only to be told she had now been transferred to Synanon facilities in West Marin, five hundred miles away.

Winn contacted several lawyers, all of whom told him it could take weeks to secure his wife's release. Morantz the previous year had made a name for himself by getting several skid-row derelicts out of a group of unscrupulous nursing homes. The nursing homes had shanghaied the derelicts from the gutter in order to collect government welfare payments.

When Winn learned of Morantz's expertise in getting people out of institutions, he called the attorney.

Morantz listened sympathetically, he later told us, but was sure it was all a mix-up. The lawyer called Synanon and asked to speak to "the administrator." Of course, he told us, laughing at his earlier naiveté, there was no "administrator" as such, since Synanon was not the kind of institution he was imagining. Morantz began looking for whatever county inspector had jurisdiction over Synanon, in order to get a licensing official to intervene. Incredibly, there was no such agency. Synanon had fought off all attempts to impose licensing. No agency had the power to force an inspection of Synanon facilities.

After nine days of private legal negotiation, Morantz secured Mrs. Winn's release. When she came out, her hair had been shaved off, she had been convinced by Synanon members that her husband wanted to divorce her, and she was more distraught than when she went in. The story she told of her experiences shocked Morantz and her husband.

As she related in a court statement:

> I wanted to leave. I was worried about my husband. I was told I could not leave, that it was too late to leave and that Synanon was now responsible for me. . . . I was told I could not speak to my husband or see him. . . . I kept asking the receptionist about my husband, and I was told that he came and left, had nothing to say to me, and wasn't interested in me anymore. My mental state was such that I could believe anything, become easily confused, and would follow orders. . . .
>
> I was put to work in the kitchen, and when I would stop working, they would say, 'You wanted to be here.' Often they would pull me around by the wrist, yelling at me.
>
> Finally, I was called into a room one day and told my

> husband was calling. It was suggested that I tell him I wanted to stay and not go home. I was told that in my state of mind I should stay. Another girl started talking about divorce proceedings, and I thought that was what my husband was calling for. . . . On the phone my husband said he had a lawyer and that they were going to get me back. After that, Synanon bused me home, but I was still scared and thought my husband was going to divorce me.

After hearing the story, Ed Winn had Morantz draw up a $5-million lawsuit, charging Synanon with kidnapping, wrongful imprisonment, brainwashing, and torture. It was fifteen months before the case went to trial, but during that time, Synanon attorneys so angered the judge in the case by disobeying court orders that he placed Synanon in default, and the only issue became the amount of money the Winns would collect.

After a doctor testified that Mrs. Winn had been subjected to "rape of the mind," the judge awarded the Winns $300,000.

The Light had covered the ruling in the same issue that carried the Ritter beating story and the "Is Anyone Listening?" editorial. In hopes of getting more information from Jack Hurst, the former Synanon president, I took a copy of the issue to his office at Marin Community Workshop in Mill Valley. Hurst was still furious about the attack on his friend in Berkeley. He had become increasingly fearful for his own safety and had told county supervisors Denis Rice and Barbara Boxer about the danger he felt he was in. Hurst previously had been unwilling to talk about Synanon violence, I had learned from Narda Zacchino of *The Los Angeles Times.* Now he was eager to talk.

Synanon attorney and vice-president Dan Garrett had outlined a policy of violence against foundation critics, Hurst said, adding that there were numerous witnesses. He told me of an incident in February, 1977, when Synanon members in Santa Monica caught a surfer urinating in the parking area of their beachside facility. The surfer was badly beaten, Hurst said, but not as badly as two teenage blacks from Watts who drove into the parking area with their girlfriends later that day. The males were held down and beaten; Synanon members kicked out the teeth of one of the boys, Hurst recounted. Hurst said he wasn't present for the attack but that another former Synanon official, Bill Crawford, was. He told me how to reach Crawford. In addition, Hurst had heard that two Synanon "goons" had "visited" an ex-member on the East Coast who knew about Synanon violence, to frighten him out of causing problems for Synanon. A commando unit/goon squad had been trained at Synanon's airstrip in Badger.

Hurst was interrupted by his secretary, who said there was a phone call for me from Gayanne, our receptionist at *The Light*. Morantz had called the paper to say he had just learned that Synanon members were being urged to attack him.

I managed to put my emotions on hold while I pumped whatever other information I could from Hurst. He soon had to leave for a meeting. Before he left, he agreed to let me come back to do a more complete interview for *The Light*.

Once I was outside in my car, I began to feel jolts of adrenaline. What Hurst had described was a terrorists' cabal. I needed to talk with someone in law enforcement. But who? Lieutenant Art Disterheft in Point Reyes Station would be concerned, but there seemed little he could do until Sheriff Mountanos left office in January. Art had told me in confidence that the only superior he still completely trusted was Captain Sid Stinson. But Art didn't know how Stinson felt about Synanon.

I had to pass the civic center en route back to Point Reyes Station. On impulse, I pulled off the freeway to drop in on Captain Stinson. I knew him only slightly, and he might not be interested in Synanon matters. However, I felt confident he would not pass along to Synanon anything I might tell him. Luckily, Stinson was in his office and had time to talk. Briefly, I sketched the escalating violence I was aware of without detailing what Hurst had told me. The captain, a stocky fiftyish man in a gray business suit, listened attentively. "I never did trust that organization," he grumbled. But instead of suggesting that his office might get involved, Stinson reminded me that "the old man," Sheriff Mountanos, was a friend of Synanon.

"I'm sure you're keeping all your notes on this hidden," the captain remarked. I said I was. "I don't want to alarm you," he went on, "but you ought to let somebody besides your wife know where they are. If any harm should come to you," he added with an unhappy smile, "those notes will at least give us an idea about where to start looking."

For the first time, I began to feel a trembling of fear that Synanon might actually attack *me*. "I'll tell Lieutenant Disterheft," I said shakily. Because Art was a friend as well as an officer, I knew I could trust him, that the notes would be secure unless something happened to me.

When I returned to *The Light*, I found Gayanne's scribbled note on Morantz's phone call. The attorney had learned the day before through ex-members that his name and address had been given out over Synanon's closed-circuit radio station, "the wire." Ex-members said calls had gone out over the wire for someone to find Morantz and "break his legs." Morantz had notified Los Angeles police and then bought a shotgun. He wanted *The Light* to know all this in case anything happened to him.

That evening, Cathy, Richard, and I held an urgent meeting. It seemed obvious to all of us that Synanon was preparing for more violence. "Dederich usually telegraphs his punches," Richard stressed. "He has to because he almost never gives a direct order if he can avoid it. He has to let members know what he wants and then sell them on doing it. It's a device to put distance between him and the act, so that afterward he can deny responsibility if he wants to."

Hurst had talked about Synanon training "goons" or "commandos," and Richard speculated the unit was probably being "sold" inside Synanon as something much more innocent than a "hit team." But, he added, "if they build something, they use it."

"That's all the more reason to take Morantz's danger seriously," Cathy responded.

"Hurst says we too are considered enemies," I noted, "although they don't talk about us personally—only *The Light*."

Cathy pointed out that even had we wanted to, there would be no safety in suddenly dropping the Synanon story; in fact, the more visible we were on Synanon matters, the safer we would be. An attack from Synanon would be immediately recognized as such as long as we were vociferous.

Richard and I argued for going directly to the cops. But, as Cathy pointed out, there were problems with that proposal. For one, we had already tried without success to interest the sheriff's office. For another, Cathy added, "a newspaper isn't supposed to be an arm of law enforcement. You compromise your reporter's role when you gather information for the cops instead of the paper. Ideally, you're supposed to publish an article and then send the cops a copy." The problem was, she added, "we don't have any of this stuff from Hurst nailed down enough to run it."

"You might also consider," Richard injected, "that being a reporter doesn't absolve you of your duty as a citizen to notify police if you know of criminal activity that is likely to occur."

I wanted to go to the FBI. The sheriff's office wouldn't do anything, I sneered.

"How much do you trust Art?" Richard wanted to know.

"Completely," I replied.

"Well, why don't you ask him whom we should talk to?"

Richard suggested. "He's a whole lot more likely to know than we are."

The next morning, Thursday, I called Art and told him I wanted to talk with him in person as soon as he could get free. Art came by *The Light*, and I filled him in on what Hurst had said. "We think Synanon has a goon squad to go around the country intimidating people," I noted.

Art knew someone in the Organized Crime Bureau of the attorney general's office: "I'll see if I can arrange a meeting with the guy." By bringing in an outside law enforcement agency behind the back of his boss, Sheriff Mountanos, Art was taking a chance, I realized. Art returned to his substation and called a little while later to say, "I got a hold of an agent. He's coming out to meet with us at noon tomorrow. He sounded interested; I was afraid he would say he couldn't get out here for a week."

At noon Friday, September 29, Cathy, Richard, Art, and I met at *The Light* with the special agent from the Organized Crime Bureau. The night before, I had typed up a list of violent incidents involving Synanon. We had already published stories on most of them; we needed more information on the others before we could cover them in *The Light*. Also included were lists of Synanon attempts at intimidation and of Synanon ties to other organizations, such as Cesar Chavez's United Farm Workers. We gave the agent a copy of the lists and asked him to destroy them once he was familiar with their contents. On one list was an account of the calls for an attack on attorney Paul Morantz, and I stressed the real danger Morantz might be in because of the probable existence of a goon squad.

The agent wanted to know why his office was being given the information instead of the Marin County sheriff's office. Art candidly told the agent about Sheriff Mountanos's friendship with Synanon. The agent nodded in understanding.

The meeting had been under way for about an hour when

Art got a call over his walkie-talkie. The burglar alarm at the Inverness Park home of rock star Jesse Colin Young had gone off. False alarms at the Young residence were almost a monthly occurrence, but Art had to check anyhow. "The one I don't check will be the one that's real," he explained as he rushed out.

The agent was the first official we had talked to in months who seemed personally concerned about our information on Synanon, and Richard and I began to tell him of our frustrations with government's failure to do its duty. Cathy soon began to worry that we were coming off as fanatics and kept trying to turn the discussion back to topics the attorney general might be able to deal with.

Art returned and stressed to the special agent that from his own knowledge of the Synanon situation, he believed our concerns were valid. The agent finally said that he would do a quick investigation regarding the information we had given him. If it checked out—"and I believe it will," he said—a report would be written recommending that his department begin a full investigation.

How likely was it that such a recommendation would be followed, Richard wanted to know. The agent shook his head gloomily. "Remember that group, People's Temple?" he asked. "We knew all about them before they went down to Guyana, but nobody cared enough to do anything."*

There would be a new attorney general in January, he noted, and the department might change directions. In the meantime, he was pessimistic about getting the department interested in violence by Synanon members "as long as they do it to each other and on their own property."

"You mean until somebody gets killed," Cathy interrupted.

"It could be," he responded unhappily. "I'm sure you know better than I," the agent added, giving us a meaningful look,

---

* Almost exactly seven weeks after the agent made the comment, nine hundred members of the People's Temple cult died in a mass murder/suicide in Jonestown, Guyana.

"that if elected officials start complaining, that can get things going. I'm just trying to be as honest with you as I can be."

When the agent left, Cathy, Richard, Art and I tried to evaluate how the meeting had gone. "He didn't hold out much hope," Cathy sighed.

"Yeah," commented Art, "but you also heard him tell us that the way to go about accomplishing something is to get the politicians interested."

"I can think of three who might help," I ventured, "our sheriff-elect, Al Howenstein; our district attorney-elect, Jerry Herman; and the foreman of the grand jury, Kirk Pessner."

The following week I called Howenstein, and he immediately agreed to contact the attorney general to second our concerns. A new grand jury had been impaneled since the one that wrote the Synanon report. Pessner was the new foreman. At my suggestion, the new grand jury had earlier called me in to summarize what I knew about Synanon. The jurors had little power beyond influence, and Pessner, when I called, said he would try to use his with the attorney general's office. My call to Herman went less well. Herman, the district attorney–elect, questioned whether it was "proper" for him to get involved, but since Art, who had worked in his campaign, would be along, he agreed to meet with me.

Synanon was a major story for *The Light* again that week. The foundation had filed a $55-million claim, a prerequisite to a lawsuit, against the County of Marin and thirty-seven county officials. The claim charged the county with abuses ranging from libeling Synanon to "discrimination" against the Synanon "religion." Nineteen of the officials named in the claim were grand jurors who had written the Synanon report. My story on the claim quoted County Counsel Doug Maloney as saying, "Synanon basically is involved in warfare with the county."

When I had finished the article, I phoned the special agent to find out how his investigation was going. To my amazement, he had already confirmed most of what we had told him. "The name of the Synanon goon squad," he revealed, "is the Imperial Marines." He named several people on it, including the former sheriff's reserves from Synanon, Art Warfield and Buddy Jones.

I was ecstatic. When the agent added that the Organized Crime Bureau was now working with Berkeley police in investigating the Ritter beating, I could barely restrain my excitement. "It's working!" I exclaimed to no one in particular after I hung up. I called Art to fill him in on the agent's revelations. "Wait until Herman hears about this Friday," I laughed. "We'll have him calling the AG's office for sure!"

"I don't know," said Art. "Apparently you guys didn't hit it off too well on the phone. He called me afterward and asked, 'What's with this guy Mitchell? Is he some kind of nut?' I told him, 'Mitchell's got some good information.' We'll just have to see what happens."

I couldn't understand why DA-elect Herman didn't want to talk about Synanon, but a worrisome possibility began to bother me. Herman had said one of the first people to encourage his campaign had been Synanon attorney Phil Bourdette. And Herman had received a couple of small campaign contributions from Synanon members. All that hadn't seemed important when I first found out during the spring campaign. Now it all seemed more significant.

On Friday, October 6, I drove over to Herman's office in the civic center. I got there ahead of Art, so Herman and I went into a conference room to talk while we waited for the lieutenant to arrive. Herman said he had an open mind about Synanon. I remarked that he was being very generous, since Synanon that week had filed a $55-million claim against the county and his office had just prosecuted four Synanon members.

But Herman said he had just talked with Jack Harrison, the newly elected Democratic Central Committeeman from Synanon; Harrison had explained to him that the four who beat Cardineau had just gotten carried away. I began to lead the conversation around to Herman's contacts with Synanon, and he bragged that he had earned the respect of Synanon's lawyers by his prosecution of the two ex-members who had stolen tape recordings from Synanon for *The Examiner*'s defense. Synanon would not have been able to get last month's $2-million settlement from *The Examiner* were it not for his prosecution of that "difficult case," the DA-elect proudly told me.

I was getting more and more uncomfortable, but held off challenging Herman until Art arrived. Art obviously had more rapport with the incoming district attorney than I, and I hoped Art would be able to set him straight. Art finally showed up, and the three of us went upstairs to get coffee before beginning our discussion. On the way, we passed Herman's boss, DA Bruce Bales, and Art's boss, Sheriff Louis Mountanos, walking engaged in conversation. We all offered greetings, but the two lame-duck officials only nodded curtly. As soon as we rounded a corner, Herman began to laugh merrily. "Bruce has been like that for weeks!"

When we returned to the conference room with our coffee, Art explained we had two reasons for wanting to talk to Herman. He related what the special agent had said about the need for elected officials to get the attorney general interested in Synanon. And, Art added, we felt Herman should know what was going on in Synanon. Herman's fellow deputy DA Michael Gridley had let his prosecution of the Cardineau case fall apart, I injected, because Gridley didn't realize that the attack might reflect Synanon corporate policy. It was a mistake, and Herman bristled into a defense of Gridley's abilities. What neither Art nor I knew at the time was that Herman was about to appoint Gridley his assistant district attorney.

There were witnesses, we said, who could testify that Synanon violence was directed from the top of the corporation. We gave him a revised version of the list we had shown the agent from the Organized Crime Bureau. Rather than accepting the information, Herman tried to debate each point. The mood quickly changed from a friendly conversation to a cross-examination. When we mentioned that Synanon members had harassed NBC producer Pat Lynch in New York, Herman said there was no evidence those were really Synanon members. Art replied with some irritation that "they had shaved heads and said they were from Synanon." I added, "And they were wearing Synanon buttons. Who else would go to the trouble?"

Herman also questioned whether Synanon's $60,000 gun buy had ever occurred, saying he thought reports of the purchase were just an ill-considered public relations ploy by Synanon to frighten off its enemies. Art countered that the attorney general's investigators were convinced the gun purchase was real and that they probably knew what they were talking about.

The more I tried to lay out a pattern of events for Herman, the more I found myself caught in games of legal semantics. "You can call it a conspiracy," Herman remarked condescendingly, "but under the law *conspiracy* has a precise meaning." Art, who was a lawyer as well as a sheriff's lieutenant, responded that we were talking about a "conspiracy *under* the law."

Finally, in a mistaken attempt to maneuver the tone of the meeting away from a legal debate, I stressed that unless the top of the attorney general's office was persuaded to take action, some people would be in danger. I added that Hurst had advised me that Synanon considered *The Light* its archenemy, and I was concerned for Cathy's and my safety. Rather than becoming sympathetic, Herman seized on the revelation to discount my information. "You're just frightened," he said as if trying to force a witness to confess. For the rest of the meeting, he systematically discounted each item on my list as "lacking objectivity."

By now, Herman and I were furious with each other. I angrily pointed out that his objectivity might be in question, considering the campaign support he had received from Synanon members. He shouted that he would not be "pressured" into investigating Synanon. If any investigating were to be done, he railed, it should be done by Art and his department. Art and I almost simultaneously corrected him—we were not asking him to do an investigation but rather to inform himself about what was going on.

Until now Art had tried to be a moderating force against mounting antagonism between Herman and me. Now he acknowledged the meeting was getting nowhere. Herman several times had tried to cut the meeting short so he could attend a coffee-and-cookie party for a retiring clerk in his department. I no longer saw any reason to hold him back, and gathered up all the documents I had offered him lest he pass them to Synanon.

Expressing all the contempt at his command, Herman said that if I insisted he would turn over to Mountanos my "little paper" listing Synanon violence. He started to add that he now expected a critical editorial about him in *The Light*, but cut himself short.

As we left, Art said he hoped Herman and I could talk about Synanon again in the future when our tempers had cooled. But once we had left the DA's section of the civic center, Art shared his frustration with me. "That ass is more in debt to Synanon than I realized," I remarked angrily. Art acknowledged, "The same thought crossed my mind."

"How'd it go?" asked Cathy cheerfully when I got back to *The Light*. Still in a rage, I filled her in on the meeting. "Before you do anything else," she said with sudden intuition, "write a memo to yourself on everything that was said." Hammering on my mechanical typewriter, I banged out the details of the meeting. As I did, I began to understand part of my frustration. Art and I had worked to get that ass elected because we thought he would improve the DA's office. We had been betrayed. In the conclusion of my memo, I typed, "Herman has all the charm of a terrified housecat; he claws even those on his side."

CHAPTER 13

A RATTLER IN THE MAILBOX

A few events in each lifetime crash into our consciousness with such impact that forever after we remember where we were and what we were doing when the news reached us. Almost forty years later, my father still remembered coming home from ushering at a Christian Science church in San Francisco on December 7, 1941, when a neighbor shouted out a window that Pearl Harbor had been bombed. About noon on November 22, 1963, my colleague roommate was trying to place a long-distance phone call when the operator told him President Kennedy had been shot. I remember my roommate shouting into the phone in disbelief and not completing the call.

On the morning of October 11, 1978, I drove to *The Sonoma Index-Tribune*, as I did every Wednesday, to have the following day's issue of *The Light* printed. A page 1 story in that issue, STATE PROBE OF SYNANON WIDENS, noted: "Among the allegations being investigated is a threat against attorney Paul Morantz, who has represented a number of Southern California clients in disputes with Synanon." By 8:15 A.M., I had dropped off the negatives for each page and was driving to a café for breakfast. I was half listening to San Francisco station KCBS on my car radio when a sudden excitement in the announcer's voice caught my attention. Los Angeles attorney Paul Morantz had been hospitalized after being bitten the previous evening by a four-and-a-half-foot rattlesnake hidden in his mailbox. Attorney Morantz, the announcer added, had won a $300,000 judgment against Synanon three weeks earlier. Morantz was expected to recover.

I wish I could say I was immediately overcome with grief for Morantz. But, like the Chinese, who were at war with Japan long before Pearl Harbor and were desperate for an ally, I greeted the news of the attack with unmixed joy. This was an act so vicious, I realized, that government could not fail to respond.

Immediately stopping the car, I ran to a pay phone and called Cathy at home. "They got Morantz!" were my first words when she answered the phone. I was excited. Cathy was terrified.

"I couldn't decide whether to stay here or go to school," she told me later. "If I drove to work, I would have to pass near Synanon. If I stayed home, I might get attacked at the house. My first reaction was complete paranoia. My second reaction was, 'How stupid! There's no way Synanon can get out of it this time.' Then, my third reaction was elation." Elated, but still shaken, Cathy drove to work.

My next call was to Richard. His response, as he later recalled, was "absolute confusion about what feelings to have. It didn't seem right to feel good about Morantz's misfortune, but the event was a vindication of our predictions." Richard tried to analyze Synanon's motivation in this bizarre crime and concluded, "It was a warning to Morantz that backfired."

If the attack was intended as a warning to leave Synanon alone, it came too late. Partially as a result of our meeting with the attorney general's Organized Crime Bureau, two state agents had visited Morantz in his law office the afternoon of October 10 to discuss what danger he might be in. The meeting ran late; Morantz had tickets for that day's World Series game in Dodger stadium, but the attorney realized he could not get through traffic in time to catch the game. Instead, he went home to watch it on television.

Morantz later described to us what happened next. "You have to realize this is a period of time when I was examining my car before I got in it, that when I came home I was looking around the bushes before I went into my house. I got into my house by opening the door, letting it swing back, and looking both ways. If my dogs didn't bark when I came home, I didn't go into the house. I had purchased a shotgun already at that time, so I was thinking. The Phil Ritter case brought it down to reality. I was very aware of it. With all that, not in my wildest imagination was I thinking of the possibility of a rattlesnake being in my mailbox."

The mailbox in Morantz's Pacific Palisades home was built into the front wall, with a grill-covered opening on the inside of the house. Morantz entered his house, let his two collies run out the front door to play, and carried some groceries into the kitchen.

"As I walked into the kitchen," he related, "I remember thinking something odd was stuffed in my mailbox. Because I first walked into the kitchen and put things down, I approached it from the side. I wasn't looking into it at all." Further limiting his vision, he added, was the fact that he was not wearing his contact lenses.

Morantz recalled vaguely thinking the object in his mailbox might be a scarf or a parcel post package. What he grabbed instead was an immense rattlesnake whose warning rattles had been cut off.

"I had a hold of it," he noted. As Morantz's hand pulled the rattler out of the mailbox, the attorney recalled, "I actually saw the head strike out and bite me. As it happened, my left hand swung into the air, and the snake went into the air and landed on my floor.

"The dogs were outside. After the thing bit me, I remember being aware they were coming back—maybe because I screamed. I had to lean over the snake to shut the front door [on the dogs], and the snake had recoiled. I remember I feigned once and then slammed the door. I went out the back door and out through the back gate of my backyard. As I went, I called out to my neighbors, 'Call an ambulance! I've been bitten by a rattlesnake. . . . It's Synanon!' "

A neighbor, Edie Ditmar, called paramedics while other neighbors made Morantz lie down in front of her house. All this had taken only seconds, but Morantz was already going into shock. "At that point, things begin to get blurry for me. . . . I remember thinking they [the paramedics] got there fast." Morantz was rushed to the County-USC Medical Center, where his condition was listed as "serious." The doctor attending him later said Morantz was "extraordinarily lucky" to be alive. He credited swift treatment with saving the attorney. As it was, Morantz's left arm and hand became badly swollen and blistered.

Back at Morantz's house, firemen who had accompanied the paramedics killed the rattlesnake, cutting off its head with a shovel. And neighbor Edie Ditmar told police she had seen two men place something in Morantz's mailbox earlier in the day.

Other information began to flood in to authorities. Police noted that prior to the attack someone had reported a suspicious car prowling alleys in Morantz's neighborhood. A highway patrolman reported he had stopped a vehicle with altered license plates in the area the day before.

The evening of October 11, Cathy and I stayed up to watch the 11 o'clock news on KGO, which had previously broken several Synanon stories. KGO staff were also feeling vindicated that night, and Synanon developments led off the broadcast. Los Angeles police had given out the license number of the getaway car, 427 HVG, and had issued an all-points bulletin for it to be stopped. The license, noted KGO's announcer, building to a climax, was registered to Synanon in Marshall.

"Wa-hoo!" shouted Cathy.

"They've done it!" I shouted back. "They've caught Synanon red-handed!"

Thursday morning at *The Light* was chaotic. A man who earlier had written a somewhat pro-Synanon letter to the editor came in to say, "I guess you were right. It was just like what people said about the CIA and nobody believed them. Then it turned out to be true." Several other readers came by to express concern about Cathy's and my safety. I jokingly pointed out we got our mail at the post office. As quickly as I could break away, I phoned Jack Hurst. He agreed I could come over immediately for an interview.

When I arrived at Hurst's office in Marin Community Workshop, the scene there was even more chaotic. Hurst was now clearly frightened. When I had been to his office before, the former Synanon president was being guarded by an attack-trained dog. A few days earlier, Hurst had left the dog in his Muir Beach home while running an errand. When he came home, the house's doors were open, the lights were on, and the dog was dead, hanged by its leash. He had beseeched the sheriff's office for protection and a permit to carry a gun. The sheriff's office had turned him down.

Hurst wanted to know if the district attorney–elect, Jerry Herman, could help him, and I briefly outlined my frustrating meeting with Herman. By the time I had finished, Hurst was in a rage. Grabbing a phone, he called the DA's office and demanded to speak to Herman. A secretary told him Herman was in a meeting. "He had better call me back immediately," Hurst roared, "or I'm going on NBC television in an hour, telling them Jerry Herman is refusing to act on Synanon."

I suspected Hurst was bluffing, but said nothing and waited to see what would happen. Ten minutes later, Herman called back. Hurst demanded Herman take some kind of action to make him and others safe from Synanon. Herman apparently began to object, for Hurst flew into a rage again. "I have reporters calling here from all over the country," he stormed. "I'm going on NBC nationwide! I have a reporter from *The Point Reyes Light* sitting in my office right now!" I gulped, fearing the district attorney–elect would suspect a setup, but Herman asked to speak to me. Hurst put me on the line.

"I feel bad about that meeting the other day," Herman offered apologetically.

I acknowledged, "We both got carried away."

Speaking very softly, Herman assured me, "I want you to know I am concerned. I'm not ignoring what's going on." However, he promised nothing specific.

As our conversation ended, a brain-damaged young man in his early twenties wandered into the workshop office and stuttered out a complaint about his anti-epilepsy pills. They were making him drowsy; his grandmother had advised changing the time he took them. Hurst showed immediate concern. "Your grandmother's right," he said, patting the young man's shoulder. "Take her advice." The young man smiled and wandered off.

Hurst had been a heroin addict and a burglar before becoming in 1959 one of Synanon's first "cures." He had risen within the Synanon corporation until he was on the board of directors and ultimately its president. But in the mid-seventies, Hurst, along with other "dope fiends" in Synanon management, had been slowly "squeezed" out. Dederich demoted him to "assistant motorcycle mechanic," and after a few months Hurst quit Synanon in 1976.

Now forty-six, handsome and graying, Hurst was again at the top of an organization, one that provided programs for handicapped youth. Until the Ritter beating, three weeks earlier, he had kept a public silence about Synanon. Now he was to become Synanon's most vocal critic.

My interview with him was difficult; the phones rang too often. The callers were indeed from NBC, from *The Los Angeles Herald Examiner*, from *The Berkeley Independent & Gazette*. There were calls from directors of the workshop, wanting to discuss a personnel problem. And there were calls from ex-members of Synanon. Some were passing information to him. Some had questions. Several had children still inside Synanon and were worried. Hurst was impressive, exuding what Ernest Hemingway admired most: grace under pressure.

Hurst was on the phone again talking to another reporter about Synanon: "They're heavily armed and very dangerous—and specifically trained in terrorist activities." Hurst hung up and looked sad. "I feel very bad about this," he sighed. "I'm doing something I swore I would never do—turn against Synanon. They saved my life. . . . If you discover your father is a flasher, you wouldn't denounce him in the papers. But this is more like the Mafia now."

The phone rang again; it was an ex-member calling from Los Angeles. Did Hurst know Lance Kenton and Joe Musico were the would-be-assassination suspects? Hurst said he did; he had just found out from a television reporter. "I think I'm next," he added.

Jack Hurst was one of the older "showcase" Synanon members who were, as Richard had once described it, "trotted out for the press whenever Synanon needed testimonials." He had been interviewed countless times and had once appeared on the old television show *What's My Line?* His public relations value had contributed greatly to his rapid rise within Synanon's hierarchy.

The story Hurst told me during telephone breaks was both impressive and revealing. An eleventh-grade dropout from Los Angeles's Franklin High, Hurst had first worked as a carpenter. He tried heroin a few times: "You start using it and you like it." Before long he was addicted. Addiction was expensive. Before long he was a burglar. "I was arrested for it in 1953," said Hurst. "I got sixty days' probation."

Hurst continued his heroin use until 1959. He went through one marriage and many jobs. "Then I went to Synanon. . . . I wanted to clean up. I had remarried by then, and I wanted to get the wife off my back." Secretly, he suspected that after a few months he would be back on the streets again, using heroin, but he never went back. "I got my problem cured, and I went to work for them as an executive." Soon he was managing Synanon's Santa Monica facility. "I did that for about six or seven years." In 1967, Chuck Dederich appointed Hurst to the corporation's board of directors. It was an unusual position. "It gave you power over other people," Hurst noted. Synanon's top officers "are an absolute monarchy." But within the leadership as everywhere else in Synanon, "Chuck Dederich has always had absolute power." To some extent, directors were so dominated by Dederich that they were little more than figureheads, he added. "You've got to have a board of directors; it's a nonprofit corporation." But the directors also had responsibility for carrying out Dederich's policies. "You need role models—people for the community to look up to," he explained.

And Hurst had more to offer Synanon than just leadership, administration, and public speaking. He was one of Synanon's best recruiters. Beginning in the late 1960s, the Synanon corporation needed middle-class executives and professionals, Richard had said, noting that a primary way of recruiting them had been through Synanon's game clubs. As Hurst talked, I realized that here was an opportunity to test some of Richard's theories. I asked Hurst about the recruiting.

"I was very good at it," Hurst replied. "We had eighteen hundred squares playing the game in Santa Monica. That's where most of the squares moved into Synanon." Did the new recruits really turn over all their possessions and money to Synanon when they moved in? "Most did," Hurst answered. "It could be anywhere from a few hundred to a million dollars. It was Synanon's biggest source of income for a while."

Synanon justified taking the wealth because members supposedly moved into Synanon for life. In fact, most eventually left. When that happened, did Synanon give members back their assets? "No way," responded Hurst, "although some have sued and gotten them back." Hurst, however, did not feel guilty about his recruiting: "Synanon was very attractive in those days. People lived better in Synanon, with less fear." Moreover, Dederich rewarded Hurst for his recruiting skill with lavish housing and promises of future wealth. "I was the number one citizen of Synanon in those days," recalled Hurst with a wisp of wistfulness. "I was the dope fiend turned fair-haired boy who lured the squares in."

Hurst's answer was exactly what it should have been, according to Richard's analysis of Synanon. So Richard was right about this too, I mused. Until that moment I had retained a touch of skepticism about Richard's theory of Synanon's motivations, although I had agreed with him on specific details of Synanon activities.

Richard had also claimed that while numerous members periodically disapproved of Synanon's policies, the members stayed in Synanon until the policies turned against them individually. Until that happened, Richard had explained, it was too difficult for most of them to leave; they would be broke, friendless, and unemployed. I asked Hurst how he came to quit.

The rapid influx of squares in the late 1960s did not sit entirely well with the longtime "dope fiends," noted Hurst. "They intuitively felt that when the squares came in, they would be squeezed out. And they were right. In 1968, he [Dederich] announced Synanon was going to go out of the dope fiend business. He was going to get every ex-addict out of management." Over the next eight years, Hurst continued, "he replaced every one of us with squares—a doctor or a lawyer, etc. I was running Santa Monica and [in 1975] Badger. Chuck just decided it was time I worked with my hands; I went to work as a truck driver and a mechanic. I lived like that for a few months and decided I didn't like it. I howled about the way Synanon was treating me and others, but that produced no change. It seemed like everything I had worked at for seventeen years had turned to shit." In 1976, with $82 and "a sack of clothes," Hurst left. "I went to live at my father-in-law's house and slept on the floor."

Four months later, Marin Community Workshop, which was foundering in squalid conditions, decided to hire Hurst because of his experience in running care facilities. Workshop directors called Ron Cook, who was then president of Synanon, and asked for a reference regarding Hurst. "Ron Cook said the only thing I did of any significance was as a motorcycle mechanic," Hurst laughed grimly, pointing out that he got the job anyhow.

Hurst was also bitter about what had happened to rattlesnake suspect Lance Kenton, the son of band leader Stan Kenton. Lance Kenton and his sister had entered Synanon a decade earlier. "I took them both in," muttered Hurst. "I even talked him [Stan Kenton] into Synanon for a while. He stayed there about six months. He left, but the kids wanted to stay." Referring to Lance Kenton, Hurst added, "Here is a kid who grew up in Synanon, one of the most bright and able." How can you take a young man like him, Hurst asked, and train him in violence? Now he's charged as a would-be "killer"! Hurst fumed.

Hurst was living with another veteran of Synanon, Mary Inskip. She had quit two months earlier after twelve years in Synanon. Hurst said Inskip was as angry as he over the recent violence and had notified Los Angeles police that Dederich had for months been urging members to attack attorney Morantz. He gave me the phone number of a law firm where she worked as a legal secretary. As soon as I got back to *The Light*, I called her.

Inskip confirmed that she had reported to Los Angeles police Dederich's repeated calls for an attack on Morantz. "What words did he use?" I asked. For months, she answered, Dederich had been on the wire growling, "When is one of you cowardly people going to go down there and break his legs?" Dederich had said it so often in various ways, she added, "it was like a drum beat."

Hurst had told me about Lance Kenton. I wanted to know anything she could tell me about Joe Musico, the second suspect in the rattlesnake attack. Inskip said Musico was a former veteran of the Vietnam War, where he had been "involved in excessive violence." She had been in a Synanon game with Musico in May when Musico had said "he would kill to protect Chuck . . . you don't pander to that urge! He's being used! He came to Synanon for some help, and [they] used him for cannon fodder!"

By now, Inskip had worked herself into a rage over the attack, and I used the opportunity to ask the question that would make or break an article: "Can I quote you by name on all this?" Her reply was adamant: "People should know! I have the right to tell the truth!"

"Then I can use your name?"

"Yes, you can. I'm that angry."

While all this was going on in Marin County, five hundred miles south in Los Angeles Morantz was being wheeled in his hospital bed into a conference with the press. His comments about being on Synanon's "enemies list" were reported in daily newspapers around the United States and made the evening news of all three television networks. CBS's Walter Cronkite called the crime "bizarre, even by cult standards." Flipping channels continuously, Cathy and I managed to catch the Morantz story on all the networks. By Friday, Kenton and Musico were under arrest and most Americans realized that Synanon could be a dangerous organization. A single rattlesnake bite had done more to arouse concern than *The Light* had been able to do with months of heavily documented reporting.

I spent most of that weekend at *The Light,* working on Synanon stories. There were five, including an editorial, for the October 19 issue. Besides the interview with Hurst, I wrote a brief history of Synanon. There was an update on Kenton and Musico's arraignment, which noted that band leader Stan Kenton had put up $25,000 to bail his son out of jail. But the big story was Mary Inskip's revelation that Dederich himself had solicited an attack on Morantz.

It would be almost a week from the time we got the information until we could publish it. Cathy was worried some other paper would scoop us: "Sometimes I wish we weren't a weekly." But, as with the Ritter and Cardineau beating stories, we would manage to break the news despite our schedule.

Monday evening we took the Inskip article over to our lawyer friend in Novato. Attorney Ladd Bedford suggested a few changes, which I argued about but eventually made. Bedford advised, for example, that we say Dederich called for "an" attack on Morantz—not "the" attack: "It's a small but important distinction." We all recognized that the article might result in a libel suit; Synanon had previously sued over far less critical reporting. But Cathy and I wanted to take the risk. "Well, then," Bedford said, "Damn the torpedoes! Full speed ahead." Since we couldn't pay Bedford for his advice, we bought a couple of pizzas and took them to his house for dinner.

When we got back to Point Reyes Station, we dropped a copy of the article off at *The Light* to be typeset and—for security—hid a photocopy.

We knew there would be considerable reader interest in the upcoming issue, and I began looking around for a dramatic page 1 picture to accompany the Inskip article. Someone had given us an old Synanon newsletter that included pictures of Synanon's "National Guard" receiving martial arts training. (The first twenty members to go through the training were the core of Synanon's goon squad, the Imperial Marines. Those who trained later were known as the National Guard.) We quoted the Synanon newsletter's ominous caption to the photo: "If trouble should occur, we're prepared to handle it. We don't need to call the police to handle our problems." Across the top of page 1, I stuck a banner in large boldface type: SPECIAL SYNANON ISSUE.

Knowing that there would be an unusually high demand for the paper, we printed four hundred extra copies. Even so, the issue sold out almost everywhere. Readers recognized we were taking a legal, if not physical, risk, and several stopped Cathy and me on the street during the following week to commend our "courage." Among those who stopped us were a few who had earlier dubbed us "fanatics," and it was a strain not to reply, "I told you so." That was certainly how we felt.

CHAPTER 14

TEAR GAS AND CHAMPAGNE

They were days of tear gas and champagne, those first weeks in October and November after the rattlesnack attack. Our special Synanon issue was barely on the streets when news media from all parts of the United States began deluging our newspaper office with requests for information on Synanon. When they learned how much information we had already published, many news organizations sent reporters to Point Reyes Station to read through our back issues and mine the mountain of public documents we had amassed on Synanon. Suddenly our revelations were getting the attention that we had hoped for during the past six months.

Our elation, however, was balanced with moments of anxiety about our own safety. In less than three weeks, two Synanon adversaries, Paul Morantz and Phil Ritter, had been nearly killed in surprise attacks. By now we had learned that prior to the attack on him, Ritter had not only been suing Synanon to regain the child stolen from him, he also had been helping lawyers for *Time* magazine fight Synanon's $76-million libel suit. Cathy, Richard, and I certainly had caused as much trouble for Synanon. Our efforts to get government to intervene had been scrupulously legal, but as far as we could tell, so had the activities of Morantz and Ritter.

The three of us reacted to the potential danger in markedly different ways. Richard was the least concerned. In the fall of 1978, Synanon still didn't realize that Richard was working with Cathy and me. He also believed that Synanon's violence was as carefully calculated as other activities of the Synanon corporation. Given the international publicity Synanon was then receiving, Richard doubted the corporation would attempt any new violence for the time being.

Cathy felt the danger the most strongly. Repeated urgings from well-meaning friends that we "be careful" unnerved her. "Why do people keep saying that?" she asked me more than once with irritation. "Don't they realize there really isn't very much we can do to protect ourselves?"

Cathy concluded that if any of us were to be attacked, the most likely victim would be me. Months later Cathy told me she had worked out a course of action for what she would have done had I been killed: "I was going to run a photograph of your bloody body on page one, and right next to it I was going to publish the complete list of Synanon violence we had given the Organized Crime Bureau. I had planned to get former students of mine to help put out that issue. Once it was out, I was going to go home and cry."

Consciously, I was not that worried. I agreed with Richard that this was not a time when Synanon would be likely to attack us. Yet, for all my outward calm, my body went on combat alert. At night when I was sleeping, if there was a noise outside or if the house creaked, I was awake in an instant. But with so much adrenaline coursing through my system, I also had tremendous energy; some of my most productive research on Synanon was ground out during this period.

And while there was no major violence following the rattlesnake attack, there were enough minor incidents to keep Cathy and me jittery. One of the grand jurors who had written the Synanon report began receiving anonymous threatening phone calls at night. Synanon cars tailed him as he drove through San Francisco. His locked mailbox was broken into, and a Synanon member accosted the juror's three-year-old daughter in a shopping center parking lot and asked why her father was doing "such mean things to Synanon." One of his fellow grand jurors came home one night to find a giant lizard nailed crucifixion-style to her driveway.

Synanon had for months consistently refused to return my phone calls, but my seventy-six-year-old father in Berkeley received a phone call from the Synanon legal department asking questions about me and *The Light*. It was an ominous indication that they knew who my father was and where he lived. When my father a few days later offhandedly informed me about the call, I wondered if Synanon was trying to intimidate us by making me concerned about his safety. Fortunately, my father was amused rather than concerned by the call, so I was not as upset as I might have been.

Upset and very worried, however, was Jack Hurst, the former Synanon president. He revealed to *The Light* and other news media that Synanon had threatened him through intermediaries. His girlfriend, Mary Inskip, began receiving ominous messages at work from anonymous callers.

By now county supervisors had asked the sheriff's office to protect Hurst, but Hurst had seen no evidence of any protection. He was still asking the sheriff's office for a permit to carry a handgun; he was still being turned down. Desperate, Hurst called me, hoping I could use my contacts in county government to help him, and I told him I would try. My first call was to Supervisor Barbara Boxer. She was surprised to learn that despite the board of supervisors' request, Hurst was not getting protection. She promised to look into the matter. My next call was to sheriff-elect Howenstein. Howenstein was in a difficult position, since he would not take office for two months; however, he said he would try to get Lieutenant Bob Gadini, whom he trusted, to intervene. As a result of that call, two officers visited Hurst and discussed his fears. But he still could find no evidence of protection on the part of the sheriff's office.

My frustration with the outgoing sheriff's failure to protect Hurst climaxed on the night of October 30. It was not twelve days since we had reported on Dederich's call for an attack on Morantz. To our surprise, no other newspaper had picked up the story. The problem, we eventually discovered, was that other papers were having problems confirming our information. The first paper able to do so was *The Los Angeles Times. Times* reporter Narda Zacchino had gotten the same information we had from Mary Inskip, Hurst's girlfriend. She had also found other ex-members who said the same thing. Publication of *The Times'* story was held up for several days while *Times* lawyers checked it over. On October 30, the story was finally cleared for the following morning's edition. Since Mary Inskip was the one ex-member identified by name as fingering Dederich, reporter Zacchino had promised to alert her just before the article came out. The impact of an accusation in *The Los Angeles Times* would be greater than one in *The Light*, and Inskip was worried about any possible retaliation.

About 9:00 P.M. Narda Zacchino called me at home. She had been unable to reach Mary Inskip. Did I know where she was?

Hurst and Inskip had moved out of their isolated home in Muir Beach to a "safe" place. I said I didn't know where they lived or how to reach them, but I pointed out to her that the sheriff's office had been directed to protect the couple; deputies must at least know how to reach them. I offered to have the sheriff's office contact the two. Relieved, Zacchino thanked me for taking care of the matter.

However, when I called the sheriff's office, the night sergeant revealed that no one on his shift knew anything about protecting either Hurst or Inskip, or how to reach them.

Following my call to Supervisor Boxer a week earlier, Undersheriff Larry Kelly had assured the supervisors that Hurst was receiving special protection. I had never trusted Kelly, who had been appointed by Sheriff Mountanos, Synanon's friend, and served at Mountanos's pleasure. However, Kelly seemed to be the only officer aware of protection plans for Hurst and Inskip, and I asked the night sergeant to call Kelly. A while later, I called back. The night sergeant said he had talked to the undersheriff, and "everything will be taken care of." The sergeant thanked me for my interest, and we said good night.

When I called Hurst at his office the next morning, he told me there had been no contact from the sheriff's office. He had learned about the *Times* story in that morning's *San Francisco Chronicle*. Angry, I called Sergeant Ray von Savoye at the West Marin sheriff's substation and asked him to find out what had happened. A few minutes later, Lieutenant Gadini called me from the main office. The main office still had not contacted Hurst or Inskip, he noted apologetically, and grumbled that the office was not doing its job.

I acknowledged the situation probably wouldn't improve until Sheriff Mountanos left office, that the lame-duck sheriff appeared unwilling to take any action that Synanon might view as unfriendly. Lieutenant Gadini interrupted me, again expressed his unhappiness with the situation, and added, "There are *some* things I probably don't want to know."

The incident left me burning with frustration. It appeared to me the sheriff and undersheriff were playing games when people's lives might be at stake. I considered Cathy and myself lucky to have deputies from the West Marin substation and not the main sheriff's office protecting our area. Deputies in West Marin were under instructions from Art to run extra patrols by our house. He offered to spend the night in our home if the danger seemed to get worse. And he advised me to keep tear gas in the house. In short, the local deputies were taking threats of danger from Synanon seriously.

I took the training required to get a permit to carry tear gas, and before long Cathy and I had a canister in readiness by our bed. For a few weeks we carried it with us when we went out at night—even if we just went outside to use our hot tub.

The hot tub on a deck outside our house was a large wooden vat similar to those used for fermenting wine. A friend and I had installed the tub and a small propane heater to warm the water. Such tubs for communal soaking have been popular in Japan for centuries and in the late 1970s enjoyed a sudden popularity on the West Coast.

Cathy and I, often along with Richard and one of his women friends, usually enjoyed a soak in the late afternoon or early evening to unwind from the pressures of the day—a sort of warm and cleansing cocktail hour. I remember several evenings sitting in the tub with Richard and Cathy, drinking white wine or celebrating developments with cheap champagne, and talking about Synanon. On a railing beside the tub lay our canister of tear gas. Happily, we never had to spray the tear gas—although Cathy nearly gassed us all one evening when she dropped the tub's hundred-pound lid on the canister.

Such relaxing was important, since our days at the newspaper had become incredibly busy. Reporters from the Associated Press, *The Los Angeles Times*, and *New Times* magazine were in our office for days on end. Others were there for shorter periods, all rummaging through our back issues and official documents, taking notes and asking questions. The flood of phone calls we received from various news media often had both our telephone lines tied up. When I returned to my desk after lunch one day, I found a jocular note from Gayanne, our receptionist: "You cannot leave again! We have heard from *The* [Santa Rosa] *Press Democrat, The New York Times*, and *The Washington Post*. They want YOU."

The Light's newsroom had only about 250 square feet of floor space, and most of that was covered by a large double-fronted desk for two, my desk, a large couch, a wood-burning stove, and a firewood barrel. With bookcases and filing cabinets thrown in, there wasn't a lot of extra space. And yet for almost a month we were constantly stepping over and around stray reporters from other news media as we tried to keep putting out *The Light*. A couple of times when particularly sensitive calls came in, I had to take them on the phone in *The Light*'s back-room shop.

Richard also found his life disrupted by the sudden demand for information on Synanon. He too got calls from various reporters, who heard about him from Cathy or me. Colleagues who knew about Richard's work with us were puzzled and sometimes skeptical. Several found Richard's collaborating on research with a couple of country editors too unorthodox. A couple of faculty members asked him whether such a project was wise in terms of his safety and his academic reputation.

About this time, all three of us began to notice a one- to two-month delay from the time a revelation about Synanon appeared in *The Light* until it appeared in other news media. The delay was first brought to our attention by a reader who commented, "Everytime I hear something about Synanon on television or read it in a magazine, I have this sense of déjà vu. And then I think, 'Oh, I know. That was in *The Light* weeks ago.' "

As one result of the delay, Richard found himself in a peculiar situation. Sometime after he had begun giving interviews, but before any of his comments appeared in print, he got a visit from Synanon, who still did not realize his involvement with Cathy and me.

He was walking down a long university hallway to his office one day when he saw two neatly dressed men standing in front of his door. One of them knocked, and Richard thought they might be book salesmen. As Richard approached, one of the men tried the door, found it unlocked, and looked inside. The man closed the door again, but Richard thought it strange that someone would open a door when no one inside had responded to a knock. He called out, asking the men if they were looking for him.

The men turned out to be Synanon members Leon Levy and Ted Dibble. They were on campus seeking speaking engagements for Synanon members. Earlier, they had been in the cafeteria, and a waitress, noticing the Synanon logos on their cases, mentioned that there was a professor in sociology interested in Synanon. Richard told Dibble and Levy that Synanon was a topic in a course he was teaching on utopian societies. Richard asked them to speak to his class, and added that he was working on a book about Synanon. Dibble noticed some clippings from *The Light* on Richard's desk and smiled. Nothing, however, was said about the paper.

The three agreed to schedule two class meetings; the topic for class discussion would be Synanon's development as a separate society—not current events. However, at the first meeting Levy and another Synanon member, Tom Quinn, gave a slide show on Synanon and a public relations–style description of the organization. Quinn, for example, told of his life with drugs before being saved by Synanon.

Richard tried to stay out of the discussion, but at the end of the class he told the Synanon members the presentation had not been quite what he had anticipated. He urged that they discuss Synanon as a society at the next meeting.

Levy came alone to the next seminar. This time the students questioned Levy repeatedly about the individual rights of Synanon members. What were the limits, they asked, of Synanon's power over its members? Levy had trouble describing any limits and finally suggested that in Synanon, "like everywhere else in the world," it was really a question of "how much the traffic will bear." Richard's students, in turn, had trouble understanding a society built in this fashion.

Levy made one more visit to the class, this time bringing along Mike Kaiser, Synanon's public relations director. By coincidence, Richard and Kaiser had grown up together. Kaiser noted this and called Richard "Richie," a name he had not used since childhood. Kaiser told the class Synanon was for him a religion, and in doing so illustrated something Richard wanted the class to see—how strongly Synanon members felt about living in the organization. The students began to realize the complexity of the Synanon issue.

After class, Richard said he wanted some objective information on Synanon for the book he was writing, and Levy invited him to dinner. A few days later Richard went to dinner at Synanon's San Francisco facility. His decision to go had not been easy. On the one hand, he believed Synanon was composed of rational people and that to generate violence by Synanon members required considerable effort by management. On the other hand, Richard worried that once he was on Synanon property, he might be subject to policies or rules of which he was unaware. A friend told him she would call the police if he didn't return by midnight. Laughingly he replied, "That's nonsense." He hoped he was right.

The evening turned out to be both pleasant and a waste of time. Richard concluded that his invitation to dinner was merely part of Synanon's public relations program designed to counter publicity over the rattlesnake attack. After dinner, Richard reminded Levy that he was interested in statistics for a book. Instead of information, however, Richard received an invitation to attend more meetings with Synanon members. Soon after this, articles began to appear in *The Light* and other newspapers quoting Richard's criticisms of Synanon, and I warned him it might be unsafe to continue visiting Synanon. I felt relieved when he heeded my advice.

Richard's visit to Synanon in the fall of 1978 was the only

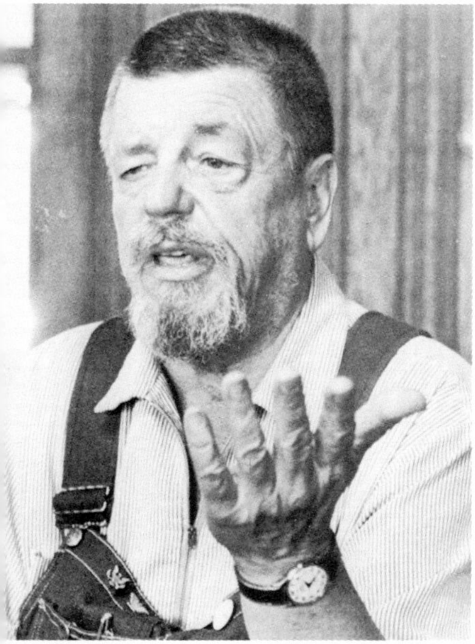

United Press International

Synanon founder Charles E. Dederich in 1977.

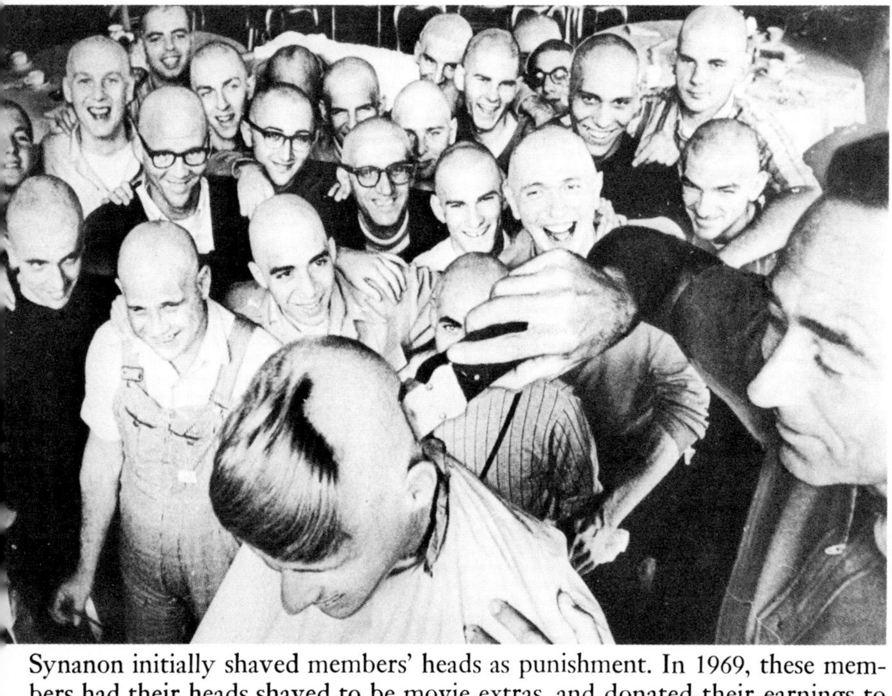

Wide World Photos

Synanon initially shaved members' heads as punishment. In 1969, these members had their heads shaved to be movie extras, and donated their earnings to the corporation. In 1975, shaved heads became regulation for male and female members.

Synanon corporate headquarters on Tomales Bay appeared tranquil, but buildings were beehives of business activity. Steel buildings in foreground housed offices of Synanon's main money-maker, its Advertising Gifts and Premium business (ADGAP).

Interior of ADGAP offices.

© Art Rogers

Newsroom/publishers' office of *The Point Reyes Light*, with publisher Cathy Mitchell (left) and office manager, Gayanne Lathrop.

San Francisco Chronicle, by Gary Fong

Sheriff's Lieutenant Art Disterheft, Dave Mitchell, and Richard Ofshe outside *The Point Reyes Light* offices.

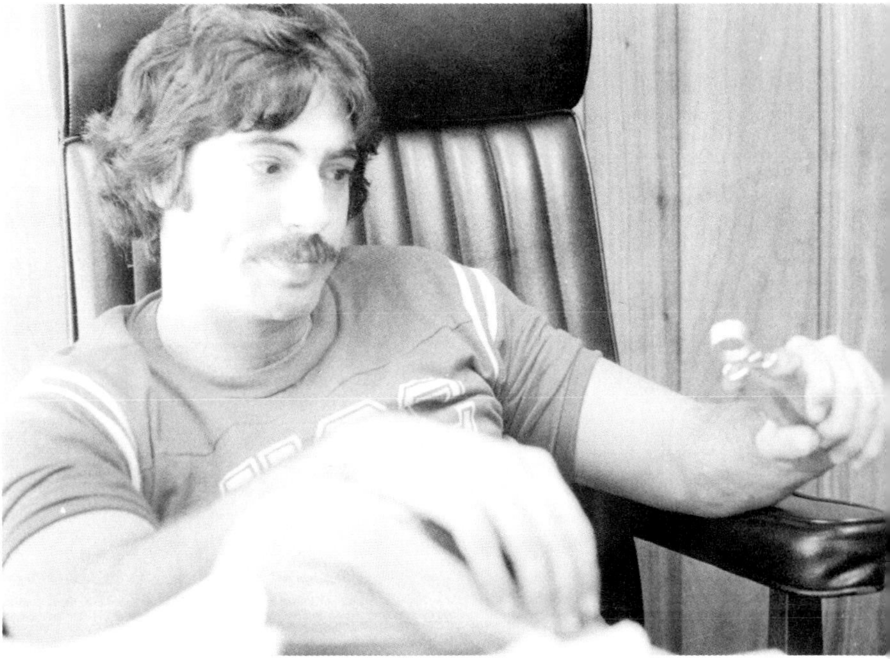

Attorney Paul Morantz exercises injured left hand.

United Press International

Los Angeles policeman Richard Grotsley shows 4½-foot rattlesnake which bit Morantz.

SPECIAL SYNANON ISSUE

October 19, 1978

TOMALES BAY PUBLISHING COMPANY

25¢

POINT REYES LIGHT

Vol.XXX, No. 27, Point Reyes Station, California

West Marin's Community Newspaper

SYNANON GUARD - These pictures from a Synanon newsletter distributed last December show the martial arts training and physical conditioning of Synanon's "National Guard." Noted the caption: "Synanon is developing its own form of a volunteer police department. We call it the Synanon National Guard. Like any other community, we're concerned about the rising crime rate in this country. So we're asking our most responsible adults to learn how to secure our property...If trouble should occur, we're prepared to handle it. We don't need to call the police to handle our problems."

Lawmen told of

Alleged call for attack on atty.

By Dave Mitchell

Los Angeles police and Justice Department investigators have received information from ex-members of Synanon alleging Synanon founder Chuck Dederich earlier this year repeatedly called for an attack on atty. Paul Morantz.

Morantz on Oct. 10 was bitten by a 4½-foot rattlesnake placed in the mailbox of his Pacific Palisades home by two men. Their car's registration was traced to Synanon's Marshall facility.

Morantz recently won a $300,000 judgment against Synanon for a woman who said last year she had been kidnapped by the organization and abused. He has also represented various clients in child-custody fights with Synanon.

Last Thursday, Synanon atty. Phil Bourdette in Badger, Tulare County, turned over to Los Angeles police two Synanon members suspected of the crime. Also turned over was the suspect vehicle owned by Synanon.

One of the suspects is Lance Kenton, 20, son of bandleader Stan Kenton. Kenton grew up in Synanon's West Marin facility and was in recent years living at Badger.

The second is Joe Musico, 28, a Vietnam veteran who entered Synanon over five years ago as a drug addict.

Atty. Bourdette told reporters Synanon will not provide lawyers for the pair and claimed Synanon does not condone unlawful acts.

But Synanon ex-members were quick to contradict Bourdette's claim. One of those who talked to lawmen is Mary Inskip.

Ms. Inskip left Synanon July 8 after 12 years in the organization. She now lives on the West Marin coast; her address is being withheld because she fears retaliation from Synanon.

The ex-member has told authorities she heard Dederich "several times" call for an attack on Morantz over the "Synanon wire."

She said, "This has been general conversation in Synanon for about a year - that he is bad and something should be done."

The call for an attack on Morantz was repeated so often "it was like a drum beat," said Ms. Inskip. Dederich would say, "When is one of you cowardly people going to go down there and break his legs?"

Continued on Page 9

Andrea Giacomini dies Sunday at 37

Andrea Giacomini, 37, president of Lagunitas School's board of trustees and wife of Supervisor Gary Giacomini, died Sunday in a local hospital.

The couple lived separately.

Mrs. Giacomini, a San Geronimo resident, had been admitted to the hospital a week earlier for an operation to remove a benign tumor of the brain.

Both the Lagunitas School trustees board and the board of supervisors meetings for this week were cancelled. Supervisor Giacomini, the Republican nominee in the 2nd Senatorial District, halted campaign appearances for now.

Mrs. Giacomini was a native of Eureka. She graduated from San Rafael's Dominican College and received a master's degree in psychology from Lone Mountain College in San Francisco. She served as a teacher and counselor in San Rafael schools, at Sir Francis Drake High School and at the San Geronimo Valley Nursery School.

In March, 1977, Mrs. Giacomini was elected to the Lagunitas school board where her husband had previously served.

She is survived by her husband; two sons, Andrew, 15, a sophomore at Sir Francis Drake, and Antony, 14, a freshman at Sir Francis Drake; her parents, Andrew and Neva Rosaia of Eureka; and a brother, Robert Rosaia of San Francisco.

A Mass of Christian Burial was held at 10 a.m. Wednesday in St. Raphael's Church, San Rafael. Entombment will be in Eureka.

Mrs. Giacomini's family has asked for memorial contributions to go to the Andrea Giacomini Memorial Scholarship Fund at the Lagunitas School District, P.O. Box 266, San Geronimo 94963.

Synanon update

Late Tuesday Joe Musico, one of the suspects in the snake-bite attack on atty. Paul Morantz, was arraigned in Los Angeles.

The district attorney's office there charged Musico with conspiracy to commit murder and conspiracy to commit an assault with a deadly weapon; added to both conspiracy charges was an allegation of "intent to do great bodily harm."

Musico was also charged with assault with a deadly weapon.

Lance Kenton, the second suspect in the case, is scheduled to be arraigned Friday. Last Friday he was released on $25,000 bail posted by his father, bandleader Stan Kenton.

Synanon has announced it will not provide defense for either suspect.

Park buy bill passes

An amended version of the omnibus parks bill passed U.S. Senators last Thursday and breezed through the House of Representatives on Friday.

Unless President Carter vetoes it, which is unlikely, it will ad 5,973 acres in West Marin to Golden Gate National Recreation Area and Point Reyes National Seashore.

In the only change affecting West Marin, 3.3 acres near Muir Beach were dropped from the original bill.

The excluded land is owned by Peter Lavalle, the Torres family, and Green Gulch Zen Center.

All other West Marin areas originally proposed by Congressman John Burton are included.

The bill includes conditions on use of the land drafted by Burton.

Among the bill's key features is a strong emphasis on the continuation of agriculture, including a program for lease-backs to present owners, present lessees or future lessees.

The main areas acquired are 1,625 acres on Bolinas Mesa at the Seashore's southern boundary and 3,724 acres between Olema and Samuel Taylor State Park at GGNRA's northern end.

GGNRA has also acquired new land for a southern entrance to the beach parking lot.

The Light devoted most of its October 19, 1978, issue to the rattlesnake attack and Synanon problems. The pictures showed training of Synanon's private police force. "If trouble should occur, we're prepared to handle it," noted a Synanon newsletter. "We don't need to call the police to handle our problems."

Meeting with California attorney general (left to right): Dave Mitchell, Attorney General George Deukmejian, Marin County Sheriff Al Howenstein, Grand Jury Foreman Kirk Pessner, Detective Sergeant Jim Riddell, Sheriff's Captain Sid Stinson, Lieutenant Art Disterheft, Richard Ofshe.

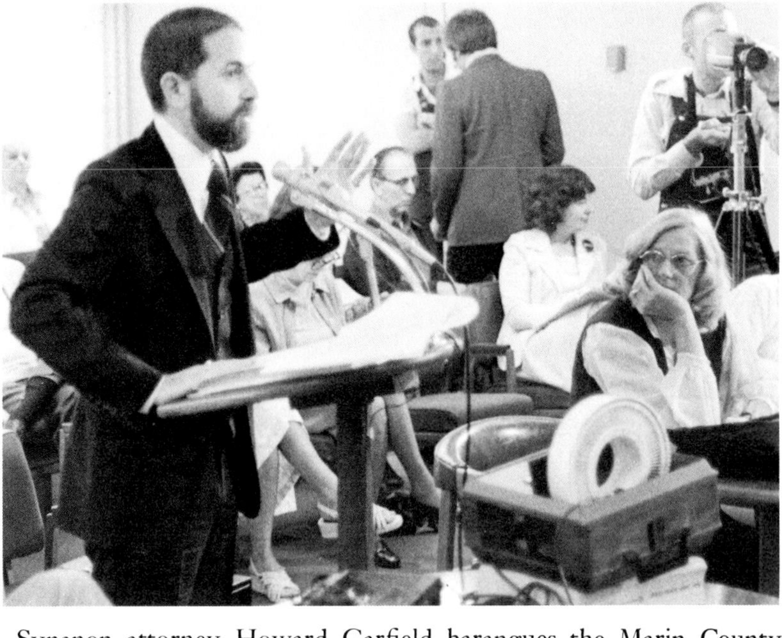

Point Reyes Light

Synanon attorney Howard Garfield harangues the Marin County board of supervisors. A Synanon member (at right) videotapes the supervisors' reactions.

April 19, 1979

25¢

POINT REYES LIGHT

TOMALES BAY PUBLISHING COMPANY

Vol. XXXI, No. 1, Point Reyes Station, California

West Marin's Pulitzer-Prize-Winning Community Newspaper

The Light wins Pulitzer Prize

PULITZER PRIZE WINNERS - David Mitchell (left), Cathy Mitchell and Richard Ofshe learned Monday that their efforts in producing editorials and articles on the Synanon Foundation had won a Pulitzer Prize for The Point Reyes Light. The Mitchells publish the newspaper. Ofshe is a professor of sociology at the University of California, Berkeley, and a Synanon expert. He served as an unpaid editorial consultant on Synanon coverage. (Neil Jacobs photo)

The Point Reyes Light Monday received American journalism's highest award, the Pulitzer Prize for public service.

The award was given for The Light's news coverage and editorials concerning Synanon Foundation Inc. The Pulitzer board called the Light's coverage "a pioneering expose."

Nominating The Light for the Pulitzer was San Francisco Chronicle reporter Ralph Craib, who has covered Synanon stories for his newspaper.

In a letter to Columbia University, sponsors of the Pulitzer competition, Craib wrote, "A $2.6 million settlement by the Hearst Corporation of libel and conspiracy suits brought by the Synanon Foundation effectively muzzled most of the American press in dealing with Synanon.

"Major news organizations were unwilling to risk the inevitable litigation certain to be pursued by an organization with a 48-member legal staff. Meanwhile David Mitchell and his co-publisher wife Cathy were printing week after week stories of beatings, of weapons, and of other strange practices in which this cult was involved.

"I have heard many, many of my colleagues speak with admiration of Mitchell's courage and dedication and, more particularly, of his vulnerability."

By coincidence, about the time Craib decided to nominate The Light, a reader in Inverness, John Rannells,

Continued on Page 5

DA won't prosecute old Synanon case

The Marin District Attorney's office this week announced it will not prosecute any members of Synanon involved in a December, 1977, incident with former member Lynn Worrell.

Miss Worrell told sheriff's deputies she was held against her will, threatened, and roughed up when she tried to leave Synanon. However, she did not report the incident until almost a year later, fearing retribution from Synanon, Miss Worrell said.

"It is the determination of this office that the evidence in this matter is insufficient to warrant the institution of criminal proceedings," the DA's office announced.

Sheriff Al Howenstein said a "major problem" with the case was Miss Worrell's delay in reporting the incident. When a year goes by before investigators can begin working on a case, he noted, the memories of witnesses "become vague," some witnesses move away, and "evidence of injuries is gone," the sheriff added.

Miss Worrell told authorities she finally reported the incident when other ex-members began reporting other vio-

Continued on Page 5

DRESS REHEARSAL - "Elizabethan Engishmen" and "Miwok Indians" braved fierce winds at Drake's Bay Saturday to run through a dress rehearsal of the pageant the Tamalpais Players will stage under the direction of Marion Hayes Caine June 16 as part of the celebrations of the 400th anniversary of the landing of Sir Francis Drake who stopped in Marin County on his circumnaviation of the globe. (Fred Graeser photo)

Landmark decision due on Bolinas home

The Bolinas Public Utility District is going to have to explain how it does what it does before Marin County Supervisors settle the fate of a woman living in a small shack on Alder Road without benefit of water, sewer service or electricity.

Supervisors last week heard the story of Phyllis Gould, who in 1975 first erected two small structures, without permits, on the small lot she owns at 179 Alder Road. Her case was before them as a nuisance abatement proceeding put together by the county's Building Inspection function. According to Chief Building Inspector Clay Gingerich, Mrs. Gould's living situation represents "the most flagrant violation" of building codes and health provisions of which he is aware.

Supervisor Gary Giacomini confirmed last week that this was about as flagrant a case of a 10' by 10' as could exist in Bolinas. He said the county's decision on this problem will be a landmark for en-

Continued on Page 5

Nude beach proposed

Nude sunbathing enthusiasts in West Marin soon may have a state-approved "clothing optional" beach on which to bask.

Department of Parks and Recreation Director Russell Cahill announced last week that the agency is considering designating eight state beaches as "clothing optional." The department will hold public meetings on the question in San Francisco, Los Angeles and Sacramento later this month and in May.

Red Rock Beach, approximately a mile south of Stinson Beach, is one of the areas under consideration. The beach is currently used partly by nude sunbathers.

Continued on Page 5

The April 19, 1979, issue of *The Light*.

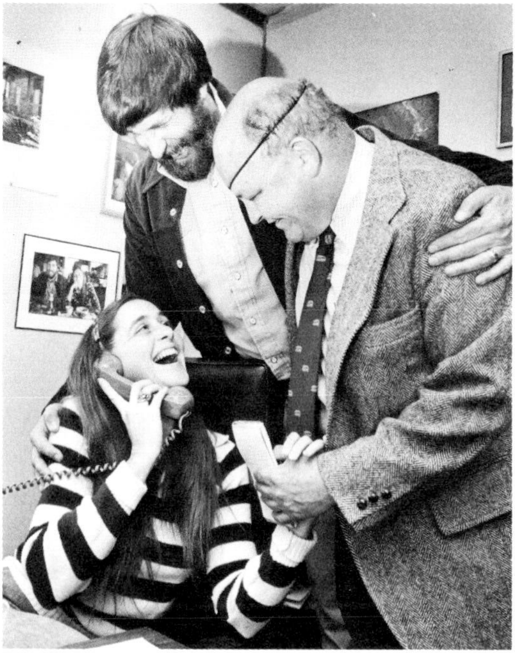

Wide World Photos, by Sal Veder

When the Pulitzer was announced, *San Francisco Chronicle* reporter Ralph Craib (right) showed up to cover the event and became part of the celebration. Craib nominated *The Light.*

Point Reyes Light, by Neil Jacobs

Synanon attorney Dan Garrett.

time any of us risked danger to gather information. There was an inherent risk in making our findings public, but we realized there was less danger of Synanon retaliating against us at home or at work than there was of Richard being roughed up inside a Synanon facility. We took seriously Dederich's growled warning during a television interview: "We never start anything. We never do, and never have. But *nobody* is going to mess with us! *Nobody!*"

Violence had put Synanon in the public eye, but violence was not our greatest concern with Synanon. We had come to realize how much the supposed charity was really being operated for the financial benefit of the Dederich family and a couple of other Synanon officers. Now that news media from across the country were paying attention to *The Light*, Cathy stressed this was the time to lay out whatever we could about financial irregularities and other problems on Synanon.

Ever since the Ritter beating, we had been in regular contact with numerous ex-members. Some of them had taken copies of Synanon documents with them when they quit. The most remarkable of these documents was a July 19, 1974, memo from Synanon attorney and vice-president Dan Garrett to founder Chuck Dederich.

In the memo, Garrett suggested that a case could be made for declaring "that Synanon is a religion." Synanon had been compared to a religion in a July, 1973, article in a magazine called *24*, Garrett noted. Since Synanon began with a defection from Alcoholics Anonymous and since AA's founders belonged to a fundamentalist group called the Oxford Movement, Synanon was "in the direct line of descent" from the Oxford movement, *24* magazine had suggested.

If Synanon were to officially become a religion, Garrett pointed out,

> we could very probably achieve a near immunity from recurring attempts to license Synanon. We have been

successful to date in securing exemptions from such licensing schemes in California and Michigan. However, the pressure toward licensing all agencies which do anything in the way of re-educating or rehabilitating dope fiends (or other unfortunates) is continuing. We can anticipate further attempts via the state legislatures in the near future. . . .

It also appears that there could be considerable advantages from a tax standpoint. Although the most recent legislation taxes unrelated businesses operated by religions on the same footing as those operated by tax-exempt charities generally, there is a 100 percent exemption included in that legislation for religions until the year 1976 for unrelated businesses in existence by 1969. *This means that even if the Internal Revenue Service is successful in sustaining its current argument that our Advertising Specialties Business is an unrelated business, we could nevertheless obtain a full exemption from income taxes for all income earned until 1976. That would amount to a very substantial sum of money. . . .* [Emphasis added.] In addition, no informational tax return is required for a religion, and this would eliminate the necessity which we now face for annual reporting to the Internal Revenue Service.

The last point which occurs to me is that we would eliminate a number of silly questions such as "When do they graduate?" and "Why do they have to obey?" Nobody "graduates" from a religion. . . . Insofar as obedience is concerned, it is always crucial to the practice of one's religion that one obeys the tenets of the faith.

The following year, 1975, Synanon's board of directors took Garrett's advice and declared that a major purpose of Synanon was to operate a church. Synanon was developing into a cult.

But Garrett's revealing memo was not the only bizarre bit of information ex-members had on Synanon's finances. Mary Inskip told me of Synanon management holding in-house lotteries for middle-level staff during 1976–77. Department heads, in her case attorney Howard Garfield, put names in a hat, Inskip explained, and those whose names were drawn received a total of over $100,000, she claimed. She herself had won $6,400 in cash and Bank of America stock. I was hesitant to publish this fact without verification, and called an investigator in the attorney general's office. The attorney general knew nothing about the lotteries and began looking into them, eventually confirming that at least $400,000 had been given away.

Inskip was defensive when I suggested there might be a legal problem with such lotteries. "*We never got much in salaries*," she remonstrated. A lottery winning "was considered salary" to compensate for "those little amounts of money" she had received as a Synanon employee. After twelve years in Synanon, her monthly pay beyond room and board was only $78, she pointed out.

Another financial peculiarity I learned about from ex-members was that Synanon had incorporated as Synanon Stiftung in the tiny European country of Liechtenstein. Liechtenstein was famous for its loose corporation and banking laws, which allow foreigners to create paper corporations there to dodge taxes overseas. The attorney general's investigators knew little about Synanon Stiftung except that *stiftung* was a German word for *charity*.

Still another revelation came from current Synanon members themselves, although indirectly. Members in the fall of 1978 were seen fairly commonly around West Marin: shopping, going out to meals, picking up the mail. From time to time they fell into conversation with outsiders. A number of *Light* readers were quick to pass back to us whatever gossip they picked up. Much of the gossip that fall concerned Synanon leaders buying real estate in Arizona and members traveling there for vacations.

We passed the rumors to the attorney general's office. Another reporter who found out about Arizona dealings was Bob Kroll at *The Berkeley Independent & Gazette.* Unlike *The Light, The Independent & Gazette* could afford to send someone to Arizona. Kroll went to Lake Havasu City, where he discovered that a newly formed Arizona corporation, Home Place, Inc., had bought a Best Western Motel, a warehouse, and residences. Signing the incorporation papers were Synanon vice-presidents Dan Garrett and Ron Cook. Dederich's name had also been listed but later crossed off. Kroll learned from the local paper in Lake Havasu City that Garrett had said the warehouse would be converted to a factory for manufacturing unspecified products—many of which would be sold to Synanon.

It was a nifty arrangement. Home Place, Inc., was a profit-making corporation run by officers of a nonprofit corporation. Synanon members could stay in the motel at Synanon expense, with Home Place, Inc., collecting the money. Once the manufacturing got under way, Synanon would have been able to buy the products from Home Place, Inc. The profits in both cases would go to Synanon officers. (Months later, the attorney general characterized the arrangement as "self-dealing" and moved to block it.)

The *Light* story outlining the financial puzzle created by Synanon came out in the October 26 issue, which went on sale at noon October 25, a Wednesday. It was the first issue after the special Synanon issue. *The Berkeley Independent & Gazette* that same afternoon published reporter Bob Kroll's extensive revelations about the Arizona business dealings to Synanon officers.

Two weeks later, Kroll followed up with a report that about sixty-five longtime Synanon members had received thousands of dollars in a distribution of the charity's money. The members had formed an investment group, the WMIR (We've Made It Rich) Club, and the club had invested $400,000 in blue chip stocks, options, and diamonds, Kroll reported. Altogether, Synanon members invested $130,000 in diamonds, $80,000 of that in Dederich's name.

The Kroll articles were followed by a series of articles in *The San Francisco Chronicle* written by Ralph Craib. The Craib articles methodically laid out how Synanon had built its financial empire, how contributions and sales were solicited, and how Synanon had managed to get over a million dollars' worth of goods and property from the U.S. government. On December 11, *The Wall Street Journal*, in a lengthy story stretching over three pages, named many of the corporations doing business with Synanon and making contributions.

There have been stories we have wished *The Light* could keep for its own. Not so the Synanon story. For one thing, there was much more to the jungle of Synanon's finances than we could ever explore on our own. For another, our main concern still was getting government to intervene. The more information that came out and the more public attention that Synanon received, the more likely it was the attorney general would have to start correcting abuses. As the deluge of articles continued, our spirits rose with the flood. Almost every day Cathy and I would call Richard, or he us, to happily read over the phone the latest Synanon story in some out-of-town paper.

There was one story, however, that I really regretted our not having done first. We had known since spring that sometime in 1977 Synanon had required vasectomies of many male members at all Synanon facilities. We had published the fact in a story on Synanon's fight with the California health department, but we had then let the story drop. One of the reporters who came to mine our back issues was Bob Anson of *New Times* magazine. When he found out about the vasectomies, he stayed with the story. His report in the magazine's November 27 issue, "The Synanon Horrors," included the grisly details:

> Like all of Dederich's notions, the childlessness was simply a suggestion at first—an idea casually planted at a game. At the next game, he articulated the idea more forcefully, and more forcefully still at the next. . . . Within weeks, what had begun as an apparently innocent intellectual proposition had, thanks to the devotion of Dederich's followers, swelled to a religious movement. From there, it was only a short step to the last order: Obey or get out.
>
> The rush to comply resembled a stampede. Within a week nearly 200 men had undergone vasectomies, performed in Synanon by Synanon's own cadre of doctors, working 10 hours a day, seven days a week. . . . A number of men entered the operating rooms supported by their friends, shaking and weeping. At one point in Tomales Bay, four doctors waited with scalpels at the ready while their patients were called out of a game, one by one. . . .
>
> For the women, the situation was far worse. Unlike the men, who merely had to give up the possibility of having children, the women were being asked to abort babies already in their wombs. When the childlessness policy came down, four women were pregnant, one of them more than four months. . . . Yet all of them wound up having abortions.

Since *New Times* had already sketched the scene, if we were to develop a new angle we had to make sense out of what happened. Throughout the next several months, as we got new information, we kept putting together more pieces of the puzzle.

Our first move was suggested by Richard. I called the California Board of Medical Examiners, which has power over physicians' licenses, and asked their reaction to the Anson article. Bob Rolland, executive director to the board, called "questionable" the ethics of performing vasectomies and abortions on patients who had agreed to the operations only under pressure. He asked me to send him the *New Times* article. I did, and the following week the board began an investigation.

Our first major breakthrough on the story occurred when we turned up a document filed in a custody case involving a Synanon child. The document was a transcript of a 1976 speech titled "Childbirth Unmasked," which Dederich had given to Synanon members to convince them of the need for childlessness. In the speech, Dederich repeatedly stressed that children are an economic liability to the Synanon corporation:

> . . . We haven't cashed in on any children. Really and truly. No children have made any contribution. There are just a few of them that have been here for quite a long time. They're still very, very young, and they're just barely getting to the point where they can earn a living. . . . They can't earn the kind of lifestyle that they have. We're not getting much for our money out of a Billy Beckham or like Carol Seigel's youngster. . . . So there's no profit to this community in raising our own children. If people want to have children, they probably shouldn't join Synanon. That's the way it will be 10 or 15 years from now. . . .
>
> This is a big issue in our community because every baby that *we indulge a Synanon female with* takes up a bed and somewhere between $100,000 and $200,000 worth of energy to be expended over a period of the next 18 years—which this religious community could expend on the child that is out there falling down on its face and growing up to be a criminal. . . . The problem is it's

too expensive. All the motorcycles in Synanon, all together, don't cost as much as to raise two children to the age of 16.*

In his speech, Dederich—despite having two children of his own—showed contempt for any maternal instincts female members might have. "The only reason to permit anyone to have children is to indulge the woman," he sneered, also commenting that having a baby is greatly overrated: "I understand it's more like crapping a football than anything else."

Another breakthrough in the story came still later when lawyers for *Time* magazine got copies of tape recordings made during what Synanon called the "Vasectomy Game and Meeting." (*Time* did not publish the information, but I got a copy when it was filed in an appeal.) The purpose of the game was to harangue recalcitrant men into accepting the surgery. On one of the tapes is part of a harangue against one unfortunate member:

"You seriously think that . . . it's going to be a rule in Synanon that everybody has their balls clipped *except you?* Right here and now you may as well make up your mind either to go about like [a Synanon man's name] did, getting yourself packed up and get out of here, or else to get your balls clipped!"

On another tape, a Synanon man can be heard trying to stammer out an objection to the surgery: "My gut keeps saying, you know, like this kind of Nazi feeling of, you know, mass sterilization."

But such objections were shouted down by other Synanon members: "If you want in Synanon a pluralistic representative form of government with everybody having the right to make a fool of themselves—the whole Bill of Rights and the Constitution—you're in the wrong place!" Explained another member: "You do live in a place where you've got to do what

* In 1978 Synanon had told Marin County it had 465 motorcycles.

you're told. I mean, we were not given a choice about sugar [prohibited by Synanon], we were not given a choice about aerobics [required exercises], you're not given a choice about your hair. There are a lot of things that you have to do because you're told that you have to do, and that's what you do in order to stay."

When it was all over, every man in Synanon who had been there at least five years had either quit or been sterilized. Except Charles Dederich.

CHAPTER 15

SYNANON'S "NEW RELIGIOUS POSTURE"

On Saturday evening, November 18, Cathy and I were driving home from Richard's Berkeley house when we heard on our car radio the first word of Congressman Leo Ryan's assassination in Guyana. By the next day, there were reports of mass suicides and murders at the People's Temple compound, Jonestown, in the Guyana jungle. Over the next few days the death count grew until the total was over nine hundred. Among the dead was cult leader Jim Jones.

Within a week, Americans realized there was something frightening about the control that cults can have over their members. Suddenly "the cult phenomenon" was more than ex-Beatle George Harrison happily greeting an audience with "Hare Krishna!" News report after news report documented the immense political power of cults, the wealth some cult leaders had amassed thanks to tax exemptions, and the amount of violence and other crime that could be traced to certain cult leaders.

The public concern was immediately recognized by Synanon officials in West Marin. Overnight, Synanon logos were removed from corporation vehicles.

On November 21, while the horror in Guyana was still unfolding, two dozen investigators from the Los Angeles police and district attorney's departments conducted a peaceful raid on Synanon's facility in Badger, Central California. Armed with search warrants, along with shotguns and flak jackets, the investigators seized numerous tape recordings. Deputy District Attorney Mike Carroll told reporters it was "merely a coincidence" that the raid came in the immediate aftermath of Jonestown. Others, including Synanon, were less certain.

Los Angeles authorities wanted the recordings for their investigation into the rattlesnake attack on Paul Morantz. If there was still any question about the atmosphere of violence within Synanon, the recordings answered it with horrifying directness. The key tape, which had been recorded on September 5, 1977, was labeled "The New Religious Posture," and on it Dederich outlined his vision of the Synanon "religion."

"We're not going to mess with the old-time, turn-the-other-cheek religious postures," Dederich on the tape told other Synanon members. "Our religious posture is: Don't mess with us—you can get killed dead, literally dead!" Particularly interesting to lawmen was Dederich's insistence that he would not let "greedy lawyers" destroy Synanon with lawsuits. "These are real threats," he snarled. "They are draining life's blood from us and expecting us to play by their silly rules. We will make the rules. I see nothing frightening about it. . . . A few people at Synanon are stimulated by the notion and somehow excited at the sound of cracking bones—as long as it isn't their own. . . .

"We're going to play by a different set of rules, our rules. . . . I am quite willing to break some lawyer's legs and next break his wife's legs and threaten to cut their child's arm off. That is the end of that lawyer. That is a very satisfactory, humane way of transmitting information. . . . There are people trying to destroy Synanon for profit. For money. . . . I want to get some son of a bitch in the basement. . . . I really do want an ear in a glass of alcohol on my desk. Yes indeed."

Dederich said he hoped that such terrorism would frighten not only current adversaries but also potential ones: "We could get response all over the United States in one year's time—Don't fuck with Synanon in any way. That's what I'm trying to do. That is the new religious posture. I think we will bring that about."

On December 2, less than two weeks after the raid that seized the tape recordings, Cathy, Richard, and I went out to dinner at the Inverness Coffee Shop. We were in good spirits, cracking jokes about Synanon and generally pleased that Los Angeles authorities were moving on the rattlesnake case. When it came time to order dessert, the woman who waited on us made some remark about "Dederich's arrest."

"What arrest?" all three of us wanted to know. The woman said she had heard on the radio that Dederich had been arrested in Arizona. "He was drunk!" she laughed.

We quickly finished dinner and drove to Art Disterheft's house. On the way, we heard on our car radio that Dederich had been arrested that evening in Lake Havasu City on charges of conspiracy to commit murder and solicitation of murder. Giggling with excitement, we stormed into Art's house, all of us competing to tell him the news. The arrest was certain to be on the 11 o'clock news, but Art didn't have a television. So he, his girlfriend, some visiting relatives, Cathy, Richard, and I caravaned across town to Realtor Cecil Asman's house.

Asman had not only a television but also good reception. Asman and his wife were in their robes, ready for bed, but with the news of Dederich's arrest, they too were ready to celebrate. Asman had loyally supported us as friends for months, and I suspect he too felt a measure of vindication.

In any case, he broke out a bottle of champagne; we had just toasted each other when the news came on. TV crews had been present for the arrest, and the film footage was extraordinary. There was Dederich—the reformed alcoholic who had supposedly developed a miracle cure for alcoholics and addicts—being carried out on a stretcher dead drunk.

Synanon attorneys, in fact, insisted Dederich was too drunk to understand the charges against him. The next day Dederich would be arraigned in a hospital room where he was being sobered up, the judge agreeing that the Synanon founder was in no shape to be hauled into court.

As we drove back to Art's house after the broadcast, Richard remarked that if there ever was a time we should take precautions for our own safety, this was the night. There was no way to predict, he warned, what the reaction would be inside Synanon to Dederich's arrest. Art repeated his earlier offer to spend the night with us whenever we needed protection. Richard and Cathy agreed they wanted Art in our house that night, and he came over, bringing a service revolver and walkie-talkie.

No one bothered us that night, but Monday we learned that similar precautions had been undertaken elsewhere by other Synanon critics, ex-members, and Synanon itself.

Synanon put its security forces on "red alert," and parked its fire trucks across the access roads to Synanon facilities in West Marin. Throughout the night, nine patrol cars from the highway patrol and sheriff's office cruised the roads around Synanon facilities in West Marin. In Los Angeles, lawmen beefed up security around Paul Morantz's home: "The entire operation is highly charged," Los Angeles Deputy DA Steve Trott told me over the phone. I also called ex-members Jack Hurst and Mary Inskip, who told me they were going into hiding. A woman still in Synanon had told them by phone oi talk among members, "Now Chuck's in jail thanks to Mary." They had called one of the local facility directors, who had stormed at them over the phone, "I hope you're satisfied!" Ironically, Mary Inskip was feeling sorry for Dederich. She and many other ex-members we talked to retained an affection or respect for Dederich long after they had begun condemning his calls for violence. "For every bad act Chuck Dederich has done," she had told me earlier, "he's done a hundred good ones."

Dederich's involvement in the rattlesnake attack was not the only allegation of Synanon violence then under investigation. We had learned from Captain Sid Stinson in the Marin County sheriff's department that lawmen were also looking into charges of assault and kidnapping lodged by an ex-member, Lynn Worrell. Worrell, twenty-four, had reported that a year earlier, when she tried to quit Synanon, she had been held against her will for four days, roughed up, and threatened. She had held off filing a complaint, she said, because she feared retaliation from Synanon. Now that other ex-members were coming forward with accounts of Synanon violence, Worrell had told the sheriff's office, she felt she could talk without having to stand alone.

For a month and a half, a deputy in the sheriff's office had been investigating her case but seemed to be getting nowhere. He had filed no report and seemed to be given little time to complete one. In fact, when it came to dealing with Synanon matters, the Marin County sheriff's office seemed in complete disarray. Sheriff Mountanos would be out of office in another month, but until he left, many officers were leery of being openly aggressive in dealing with wrongdoing at Synanon. Mountanos, in fact, had received a contribution from a Synanon officer after losing his reelection bid. The rattlesnake attack changed nothing. In the aftermath of the attack, the attorney general held a special meeting in Sacramento to organize a statewide investigation into Synanon. But when Mountanos and his appointee, Undersheriff Larry Kelly, returned from the meeting, Kelly announced it was uncertain whether the Marin County sheriff's department would participate in the probe.

The situation put immense pressure on officers such as Art, who believed the department had a duty to deal with Synanon problems. Art had been doing what he could on his own—protecting us, trying to get protection for Hurst and Inskip, and talking to the Organized Crime Bureau. But he was fearful of getting other deputies too involved. Art didn't know when some fellow officer would tell Mountanos what his lieutenant in West Marin was up to. One of the roles *The Light* played in the fall of 1978 was to break that impasse—although we did it quite by accident.

I had begun filling Art in on my conversations with his immediate superior, Captain Sid Stinson, and Art soon realized that there was someone in the main office who shared his concerns, someone he could talk to. When I told him that Sergeant Ray von Savoye, the officer immediately below him in the West Marin substation, also was critical of Mountanos's friendship with Synanon, Art was delighted. The three could be the core of a corps to keep tabs on Synanon.

When *The Light*'s story on Lynn Worrell's alleged kidnapping and assault was published in the December 14 issue, KGO-TV in San Francisco immediately broadcast the information. The next morning, Worrell called KGO reporter Joyce Shank, who had done the story, and asked her where she found out about the incident. Shank referred Worrell to me.

Worrell called, and I set up an interview for that evening to get whatever other information I could from her. Since Art was in the office when she called, I asked him if he wanted to come along. He did, and Worrell agreed that Richard could come too. She was anxious for her own safety, however, and set the meeting in her mother's apartment house, which was patrolled by security guards.

It was an unusual meeting. Shortly after dark we drove to

her mother's apartment on the east shore of San Francisco Bay. After lengthy questioning by security guards, we were escorted up to the apartment. Worrell and her mother had obviously prepared for our visit. Both were dressed up, and the apartment was immaculate. To our momentary chagrin, however, they told us Joyce Shank would also be arriving soon to film an interview. None of us had eaten, and we were in the process of ordering out for a pizza when Shank arrived with a cameraman.

Fortunately, the KGO interview was done quickly, since Shank wanted to get it on the 11 o'clock news. After she left, Art, Richard, and I began to question Worrell. Quickly we realized she had a lot to tell us. Miss Worrell had been in Synanon seven years, and in the months before she left, she had worked in "the Connect," Synanon's communications center. As such, she was in almost constant contact with Synanon's internal police force. She had done considerable work for Art Warfield, the former reserve deputy and member of the Synanon goon squad, the Imperial Marines.

Worrell told Art Disterheft where weapons were stored in Synanon's West Marin facilities. She knew the chain of command in each facility. And she had been a witness to Synanon violence. In detail, she laid out for us the beating a Synanon member, Cliff Zeppieri, had received as punishment during a Synanon "general meeting." Zeppieri's arm was apparently broken or dislocated and his nose was broken in front of 100 to 150 people, she told us. Zeppieri was held from behind in a "hammerlock," she explained, while five or six members punched him in the face and stomach. "At first he screamed," she recalled, "and then he just cried silently." Finally, he fell to the floor and was repeatedly kicked while he tried to shield himself.

Among those watching, noted Worrell, was a fifteen- or sixteen-year-old girl who had just entered Synanon. When the attack began, she started crying and asked what Zeppieri had done to deserve such a beating. (He was accused of planning to steal a motorcycle from Synanon.) Other Synanon members took the girl out of the room. Newcomers present watched the beating in stunned silence while old-timers standing behind them glared angrily at Zeppieri.

"Well, that was a hell of a story," I commented to Art and Richard as we drove back to Point Reyes Station after the interview. "But how the deuce can I verify it?"

Verification, however, proved to be amazingly easy. Unbelievably, Synanon had broadcast the beating over its internal radio station, "the wire." People at other Synanon facilities had been able to listen to it in their rooms. I called another ex-member, now living in Los Angeles. "Sure," he told me, "I heard it." His account was similar to Worrell's. I discussed the incident with Art, and we agreed *The Light*'s story on the beating would ask for anyone else with information on Zeppieri to contact Art at the local sheriff's office. Art was starting to make his activities public. By now Mountanos had less than two weeks to go in office. Art, Richard, and I had met with the incoming sheriff, Al Howenstein, and Howenstein had assured us that he realized the Synanon situation was dangerous.

The Zeppieri beating was covered in the December 21 issue of *The Light*. Normally, the next two weeks at *The Light* would be slow news weeks, since government activities are minimal during the holiday season. But our Christmas issue, which came out on a Tuesday, had just hit the streets when I got a call from Richard. Jack Hurst and Mary Inskip were leaving town, he told me. Richard had tried to arrange one last interview before we lost track of them, and Hurst turned him down. "It's time to call in whatever debts Hurst owes you," Richard insisted.

I called Hurst and explained our dilemma: there were things about Synanon management we could get only from him. "I've tried to help you get protection," I told Hurst. "Now I need help." Hurst reluctantly agreed we could have dinner with him and Inskip. I offered to pay, and Hurst named a sandwich shop in Sausalito where we could get "a quick bite." He and Inskip didn't have much time to spend with us, he explained, since they were in the midst of packing.

That evening, Richard and I met the couple outside the sandwich shop. To our relief, it was closed. One of the few restaurants that were open two evenings before Christmas in Sausalito was the lavish Valhalla Inn, owned by former brothel madam Sally Stanford, now a Sausalito city councilwoman. When Inskip and Hurst agreed to the Valhalla, Richard and I exchanged a knowing look: it was impossible to get a quick bite at the Valhalla Inn. As Richard and I drove to the restaurant, we hatched a plot. We would order every course the restaurant offered. This would be expensive but would drag the meal out for hours.

And what a meal it was! We had before-dinner drinks, stuffed-clam appetizers, aperitifs, several food courses, white wine, red wine, dessert, after-dinner drinks. Hurst drank a little wine but obviously still felt Synanon's onetime abhorrence of alcohol. Inskip was more relaxed about drinking, saying she wanted to celebrate. Nonetheless, Richard and I ended up drinking most of the wine.

With Richard tape-recording Hurst's comments and me taking down Inskip's remarks in a notebook, we talked and feasted for almost five hours and got much good information. The bill came to around $130; Cathy was not pleased.

Richard wanted to know why Hurst had stayed in Synanon seventeen years. Hurst spent his first couple of years in Synanon mostly recovering from addiction, but "then I took a look around. . . . I began to realize that I was in on what appeared to me to be a very fast-growing, exciting, unique, revolutionary corporation, and . . . I would have all the excitement of that. . . . I was investing my time in an organization that would carry me for the rest of my life, would allow me to live well, meet important people, and make a way for my wife, my children, and my brother."

Richard asked why Hurst had never gotten in writing something that would guarantee his expectations. "The whole organization was built on trust," Hurst replied. "Dope fiends have no trust." Whenever someone would ask for a written guarantee, Hurst explained, "it was merely ascribed to your disease. If you didn't trust Synanon, you were sick and crazy. . . . The ability to trust and have faith was the health you were striving for. From 1959 to 1975, I never doubted for a moment that I wouldn't be carried *grandly*." Hurst noted he had "assurances" from "Chuck himself. He said, 'You stick with me.' . . . I was thoroughly convinced I was making an investment. . . . I put time in this organization and that guaranteed me an annuity that I could cash in." Instead, Hurst was finally squeezed out of Synanon almost penniless, although he had thought he had $75,000 coming, and he laughed grimly at what a blow to his pride his fall from power had been.

While Richard and Hurst talked, I asked Mary Inskip about Synanon's relations with other cults. "For a while before I left," she answered, "there was talk of a coalition of Synanon, the Moonies, Scientology, and People's Temple—people who were doing a lot of good for the world and were misunderstood. The Sikhs, a militant Hindu group, were going to be part of the coalition too. Chuck talked it up enormously. He assigned that alliance-cultivating job to Sidney [Finkelstein, her former husband]." At one time, Inskip said, it looked like the coalition was assured. An official of the Moonies (Sun Myung Moon's Unification Church) was a periodic dinner guest of Synanon's legal department. The People's Temple became one of the larger groups receiving surplus goods through Synanon's "redistribution network." Inskip added, "We identified with them a lot because their media coverage was as unjustified as ours." But even before the mass murder/suicide of People's Temple members and Dederich's arrest, the coalition developed problems. "Synanon had a blowup with the Moonies," she recounted. "Chuck decided they were using Synanon for their benefit."

The following week, I used Inskip's account for a brief story in *The Light*, my confirmation of her story coming from an investigator in the attorney general's office. But the major story in that issue was on Synanon founder Dederich, whom we named West Marin's "Man of the Year" for 1978. The designation implied no honor but merely reflected Dederich's and Synanon's domination of local news that year. He was our gatefold.

CHAPTER 16

PUBLIC RELATIONS FOR A CULT

Near the end of 1978 and immediately after Charles Dederich's arrest, *The Light* received a letter to the editor from an Inverness woman. "I would like to suggest," she wrote, "that instead of high headlines fanning an already smoldering issue, the editor invite our close neighbors at Synanon to meet with local folks in dialogue."

The letter seemed to me to reflect a major misunderstanding about Synanon. However, I too was not eager to see conflicts erupt between townspeople and Synanon members. As Cathy, Richard, and I saw it, Synanon's general membership was as much a victim of Synanon leaders as were outsiders whom Synanon management wanted attacked.

"Synanon members," we wrote in our December 7 editorial, "are confused and upset by the arrest of Dederich—in part because of their isolation except under carefully managed situations. We urge West Marin residents to show understanding and restraint in dealing with Synanon members. This is a time for sympathy—not recrimination."

But the letter put us in a dilemma. We were being challenged to arrange a meeting, and I doubted such a meeting would resolve anything; Synanon spokesmen could not be trusted. We had caught Synanon attorney Howard Garfield lying about the existence of an airstrip and medical clinic. We were familiar with Synanon's use of half-truths to deceive government. And we took seriously Dederich's oft-repeated comment, "It's all done with words."

By now we shared along with state authorities the opinion that Synanon was in the control of criminal leadership. Synanon members/employees were not robots, we felt, but they obeyed corporate policy. Unfortunately, we were faced with a number of West Marin residents who were products of a 1960s attitude: no problem's so bad that it can't be fixed through improved communication. And they wanted to communicate with Synanon. In an editor's note, which followed the letter to the editor, we suggested the meeting be set up without our help: "We could do it ourselves but fear Synanon's resentment to *The Light* might doom the effort in advance."

Synanon, of course, read the exchange and contacted the letter writer to set up a meeting. It was held on January 6 in one of Point Reyes Station's meeting halls, the Dance Palace. At the insistence of Synanon, the organizers agreed that no pictures could be taken or tape recordings made during the meeting. A possible reason for the conditions soon became clear.

Synanon sent to the meeting a handful of members headed by Synanon director Dan Sorkin, a former San Francisco radio "personality." After organizers announced the meeting's ground rules, Sorkin gave a twenty-minute talk on Synanon. Sorkin began by saying there had been a lot of "spoof" about Synanon in the news media. Synanon members had not placed a rattlesnake in attorney Paul Morantz's mailbox, Sorkin insisted. Morantz had done it himself and had now admitted it, he said. Sorkin read a newspaper clipping that seemed to confirm the claim. It was a bizarre assertion, but it would be several days before the means of his deception were uncovered.

Sorkin did not deny that Dederich had called for someone's "ear in a glass of alcohol" but insisted Dederich had said it during a "Socratic" dialogue called a "think table," in which participants "take any position." As a result of so much false information being circulated about Synanon, said Sorkin, the corporation's ability to find new members had been damaged. "We used to have an intake of one thousand a year," he said. "We're down to less than sixteen per month."

Bad publicity had also hurt the corporation's ability to make money, Sorkin reported. "We've lost a lot of our original business. We work for our money, and it's getting harder and harder to work for our money." Synanon's Imperial Marines, which the attorney general's office described as a goon squad, was just a "security group," Sorkin claimed. "We decided to put together a security group—just like any other corporation."

People reacted to the Sorkin presentation immediately and bluntly. "It's such blatant crap," remarked an Inverness resident, Lance Brown, from the floor, following Sorkin's presentation. "It was a well-put-together public relations statement." One townsperson told of doing carpentry work on Synanon projects that had no building permits. Rancher Gambonini recited his story of being attacked by Synanon members in 1975.

Of the two hundred townspeople who crowded into the meeting, only a couple defended Synanon, but one of those who did drew heavy applause. Christopher Thorsen of Inverness spoke emotionally of Synanon members and townspeople both "fighting for survival. We are both part of a country where the government is killing people. We're awfully good Germans." The news media, Thorsen continued, were manipulating members of the public into hostility against each other. West Marin, he raged, was "a sanctuary" from a "government that wipes out whole countries of people." The Vietnam War had been over for six years, but antiwar rhetoric still held its force, and the audience cheered.

However, it was one thing for a townsperson to attack the news media and quite another for Synanon. When Sorkin tried blaming "media manipulation" for changing Synanon, Michael Jayson of Point Reyes Station responded, "Nixon said that all of his problems were caused by the press." And Inverness resident John West grumbled that Sorkin's blaming Synanon troubles on the press was a "weak" excuse.

By now the meeting had evolved into a heated debate, which wasn't what the organizers had wanted. Moderator Kevin McVeigh had hoped for something more along the lines of sensitivity groups, what someone in the crowd dubbed the "touchy-feelie" approach. McVeigh briefly stopped the meeting and suggested everyone "hug" the person sitting next to them; but no one did, and the meeting reverted to acrimony.

While Cathy and I felt obliged to keep silent, Richard was under no such constraint. Was it true, he asked Sorkin, that Synanon members were not offended by the attack on Gambonini? Richard had watched the discussion begin to wander and brought it back to serious topics with jarring directness. "I want to know why Tom Cardineau was beaten!" he demanded. Then, referring to two youthful outsiders briefly taken prisoner by Synanon members, he asked Sorkin to tell "why the kids had their heads shaved."

The bluntness of Richard's questions, I later realized, followed the form of "indictments" in a Synanon game. And Sorkin responded as he would in a game. "We obey the law!" the Synanon director countered with a show of anger. More angrily he added, "We get a lot of violent people in here! Anyone who breaks the law goes to jail!" Then, referring to the rattlesnake suspects Kenton and Musico, Sorkin shouted, "So far there hasn't been a shred of evidence against these guys!"

Lowering his voice, he added that if the case against Kenton and Musico were proven, "they should go to jail."

Sorkin was again asked to explain the attack on Gambonini. Gambonini was well liked in the ranching community but had a shy, halting manner of speaking. Sorkin tried to duck the question by mocking Gambonini. "Everyone knows what Alvin Gambonini is like," the Synanon director sneered. His condescension drew an outburst of angry muttering from the audience, and Sorkin dropped the topic.

I was beginning to feel quite pleased about the matter. Confronted with questions about Synanon violence, Sorkin could react only with a show of emotion and contempt; for a moment the ugly side of Synanon was on the stage for all the town to watch.

The meeting, which ended with coffee and cookies supplied by Synanon, resolved nothing in the community, but it did stir up quite a flap in San Francisco Bay area news media. Ralph Craib, who covered the get-together for *The San Francisco Chronicle*, predictably quoted Sorkin's assertion that Morantz had planted the rattlesnake in his own mailbox. Synanon immediately complained that Sorkin had said no such thing, that he had merely read a clipping from *The Van Nuys* (Los Angeles County) *Valley News.*

Craib got hold of the *Valley News* article and discovered what Sorkin had done: he had read part of the article, omitting some key phrases. The article covered Morantz's October 13 hospital press conference. As the lawyer had been wheeled into the conference, he remarked that for a decade he had tried to warn people about groups like Synanon. Here is what the article said, with the phrases Sorkin omitted in italics: " 'I was going to call a news conference, but a reporter told me no one would come. I needed a bigger event. *The problem has been getting authorities to listen.*' Morantz then said, *in a manner dismissing the idea as ridiculous*, 'So I put the snake in the mailbox and let it bite me.' "

Since no one had been allowed to tape-record the meeting with Synanon, *Chronicle* reporter Craib was in a dilemma. His solution was to poll several other journalists and two professors who had been at the meeting, among them Richard and me. The unanimous answer was that Sorkin had left out the qualifying passages, and the *The Chronicle* published the fact in responding to Synanon's complaint.

Following the meeting, Cathy, Richard, Art, and I had driven across the county to San Rafael, where Al Howenstein had just been sworn in as sheriff and was throwing a dance. We wanted to join the celebration, but I also wanted to confirm with Howenstein some plans for a trip to Southern California.

For over a month, I had been trying to arrange a meeting with the incoming state attorney general, George Deukmejian, to lay out before him the problems with Synanon. As I quickly discovered, getting the attorney general of the most populous state to meet with us was about as easy as getting an audience with the president. My first approach was made through a mutual friend, the just-retired state senator from our area, Peter Behr. The problem, as I explained it to Behr, was this: local deputies and the incoming sheriff realized that Synanon was a statewide law enforcement problem; investigators in the attorney general's office had also determined that Synanon leaders were breaking the law; but their recommendations to superiors were being ignored. It was the same problem we had observed in several other state and county agencies. The only way to break the impasse in the attorney general's office, we now believed, was for law enforcement officials from Marin County, along with Richard and me, to convince Deukmejian to himself take an interest in Synanon.

Behr called an aide to the incoming attorney general, who said Deukmejian would contact me. When Deukmejian never did, Behr called again. He was assured that Deukmejian would meet with us and would call me to schedule a time. I had filled

Howenstein in on the plans at each step, and he seemed enthusiastic. But as time went by and Deukmejian still had not called, the incoming sheriff asked me what was going on. Recalling my earlier frustration in trying to set up a meeting between Richard and the board of supervisors, I was determined not to suffer another fiasco. I began calling Deukmejian's office two and three times a day, even though the calls were long-distance and expensive. "The sheriff of Marin County is waiting for an answer!" I repeatedly stressed to Deukmejian's staff. They kept promising call-backs that never occurred.

"You are embarrassing State Senator Behr," I finally told a Deukmejian aide. "He has been told by your office that the Duke will meet with Sheriff Howenstein. Howenstein needs to arrange travel plans. These brushoffs just can't go on."

Deukmejian finally called. He felt it was too soon after he took office to meet with us, he told me, but if I insisted, he would. I insisted, and the meeting was scheduled for January 11, 1979, in Los Angeles.

On the morning of January 11, Art and I met at *The Light* before dawn and drove together to the civic center. There waiting for us were Sheriff Howenstein, Captain Sid Stinson, and Detective Sergeant Jim Riddell. Also showing up for the trip was Kirk Pessner, foreman of the grand jury. At the Oakland airport, we were joined by Richard.

There were so many of us that some problems were inevitable. Captain Stinson sent airport security into hijacker alert when he forgot that he had a service revolver in his attaché case and it showed up on the x-ray machine for carry-on luggage. Since none of the officers was in uniform, Captain Stinson had to show his police identification and received a "polite request" that in the future he tell the airport when he planned to travel with a gun.

The seven of us arrived in Los Angeles expecting a couple of cars and drivers from the attorney general's office to pick us up, but the office had underestimated the size of our group, and had sent only one car and driver. The car could have carried six of us comfortably, but with the driver there were eight. Moreover, Richard and Sergeant Riddell were planning to stay on in Los Angeles and had brought luggage.

I suspected one reason Sheriff Howenstein had brought so many of us was to impress upon the attorney general the seriousness of our mission. Instead, we arrived at his office looking like a phone booth full of college students. Sheriff Howenstein rode from the airport on my lap. My feet were so tangled with the grand jury foreman's that I fell backward out of the car and onto the curb when the door was opened at our destination.

We were all in good spirits. Attorney General Deukmejian was not. His office was in a tall steel-and-glass building in downtown Los Angeles. (He also had an office in Sacramento.) After being cleared by two sets of guards, we were ushered into a waiting room, and Howenstein was summoned to a premeeting meeting with Deukmejian. The attorney general was impatient. He wasn't sure why he had been pressured to meet with us. He didn't understand why Richard and I had come along. The meeting would begin at 10:30 A.M. "Call me out of the meeting at eleven fifteen," Deukmejian told a secretary. To Howenstein he commented, "Let's get this damned thing over with!"

Howenstein then led the group of us into a large conference room. One wall was almost solid windows. The other three were covered with historic photos of Los Angeles. The ubiquitous conference coffeepot was in the corner. Moments later, in walked Deukmejian, a short, slender man, flanked by an even shorter press aide and the assistant attorney general, Michael Franchetti.

As we sat down at an immense table consisting of several smaller tables placed together, Franchetti gave me a hard look: "Everything said at this meeting is off the record." His clothes were so crisply starched and pressed, his every hair so perfectly in place, that I found myself thinking of a men's-shirt ad. "Is that understood?" Franchetti broke sharply into my thoughts. I said it was, since, as the sole media member in the room, I was clearly his chief concern.

As it turned out, I heard nothing new anyhow. The seven of us took turns filling Deukmejian in on the Synanon problem. Richard's presentation particularly seemed to impress the attorney general. When the secretary came in to pull Deukmejian out of the meeting, the attorney general waved her away, and the meeting continued for another half hour.

When it ended, Franchetti asked Sheriff Howenstein if "that guy," meaning Richard, "is getting protection." The sheriff said Richard was. I, meanwhile, had taken out my camera and was busy lining up everyone, including Deukmejian, for a picture. Art was amazed at my audacity and whispered to Captain Stinson, "That guy's got brass balls." Stinson laughed: "He's had to, just to get this far." At the last minute, I handed the camera to Deukmejian's press aide and had him snap the picture; I couldn't stand not being in this historic photo.

On the way home, I pulled an in-flight magazine out of the seat pocket and found that the issue included a recap of the news for 1978. There, as one of the major news events of the past year, was a photo of a Los Angeles lawman holding the rattler that had bitten Paul Morantz. Pacific Southwest Airlines later got one of Synanon's routine demands for a retraction for running the photo. It may have been one of the few times an in-flight magazine was threatened with a libel suit. PSA ran the demand as a letter to the editor in a later magazine but made no retraction.

Richard stayed in Los Angeles with Detective Sergeant Jim Riddell in order to gather information for the Lynn Worrell case; she was the young woman who had complained of being held against her will and roughed up when she tried to leave Synanon.

One of Howenstein's first acts as sheriff had been to make Richard a consultant to the sheriff's office. The position was unpaid but gave Richard access to considerable information for his research. Howenstein had several reasons for wanting Richard to be involved in the Synanon case. Not only was he an expert on Synanon matters, but he could interview ex-member witnesses in their own terminology; he knew the "Synanon lingo," as it was called. Art had commented to the sheriff on this after the three of us interviewed Worrell. By referring to events in Synanon in terms Synanon members used, Richard had been able to jog her memory much more successfully than had Art, who didn't know the lingo.

And there was a third reason why Sheriff Howenstein wanted Richard as a consultant: he gave credibility to the sheriff's concern about Synanon. Because of former Sheriff Mountanos's known friendship with Synanon management, other law enforcement agencies around California had been quietly refusing to share information on Synanon with the Marin County sheriff's office. Howenstein realized this; so did we, thanks to tips from the attorney general's investigators and Los Angeles police. Several lawmen had told us they feared the recently departed Mountanos had allowed friendships to overcome his better judgment.

Richard and Sergeant Riddell's first stop after leaving the attorney general's office was at the Major Crimes unit of the Los Angeles police department. The unit is an elite squad within one of the best police forces in the United States; it gets the *big* cases. And in January, 1979, the Major Crimes unit was working on a couple of very big crimes—the "hillside strangler," who had murdered a series of young women, and "the rattlesnake in the mailbox," the alleged Synanon members' conspiracy. The unit had its own office, its walls covered with pictures of the strangler's victims and its desks littered with Synanon files and pictures of rattlesnakes. For a couple of hours, Richard and Sergeant Riddell traded information and hunches with the Major Crimes officers. As the discussion went on, Richard noticed an investigator from the attorney general's office sitting apart from the group, listening but saying nothing. Richard gave his analysis of how Synanon controlled its members and was pleased to observe the state investigator nodding in agreement at several points. "Synanon members are not a bunch of crazies," Richard emphasized, and for once he had an audience sophisticated enough about cults to realize he was telling the truth.

For two days Richard and Sergeant Riddell tried unsuccessfully to get together with a key witness in the Worrell case, and Richard visited rattlesnake victim Morantz. Overnight Richard had become part of law enforcement, and he was thoroughly enjoying himself. "I feel like Philip Marlowe," he told me laughingly over the phone.

On Richard's third day in Los Angeles, Synanon called a press conference in the Pacifica Hotel; the purpose of the conference was to build opposition to efforts then under way to extradite Dederich from Arizona to California for trial. Cesar Chavez, the Reverend Ralph Abernathy, militant black lawyer Flo Kennedy, and other celebrities friendly to Synanon had been assembled to denounce extradition, claiming it would probably kill Dederich in his weakened condition.

Kennedy said Dederich was being prosecuted because he had allied himself with the poor and oppressed. Dederich had been "niggerized" by government and the news media, she insisted. She was skeptical of the charges against the Synanon founder. "You have rattlesnakes out here," she remarked, adding that it could be "assumed" the snake crawled into Morantz's mailbox on its own. Chavez, while disagreeing with Synanon's gun purchases, commented, "That doesn't mean we disagree with Chuck's right to health."

Synanon doctors by now were claiming Dederich was suffering not only from alcoholism but also from a heart condition and a mild stroke. The week following the press conference, however, Synanon attorneys dropped their opposition to extradition when Los Angeles prosecutors agreed Dederich could be freed on $100,000 bail once in California. No bail had been allowed in Arizona. Dederich was flown to California in an air ambulance, and once he was in the state, his health seemed to improve remarkably.

After the press conference, Richard and *San Francisco Chronicle* reporter Ralph Craib, who had covered the get-together for his paper, drove to Paul Morantz's office. Soon after they arrived, an ex-member of Synanon, Ben Parks, joined them. He was carrying a pistol. Having supplied information on Synanon to law enforcement, Parks was clearly concerned for his own safety. Morantz too was feeling the pressure of being in danger. Police were constantly at his house for security. "My personal life is destroyed," he told Richard. Even the officers in the Major Crimes unit admitted to Richard that they were concerned for their own and their families' safety. Particularly upsetting, said one officer, were indications that Synanon might have tried to locate officers' homes by running checks on their cars' license plates.

In Los Angeles more than in Marin County, Synanon had created a climate of fear. The anxiety was contagious, and by the time Richard returned to Northern California the next day, he was worried about his and our safety.

For the moment, Synanon had also ended Richard's private life. The Monday after his return from Los Angeles, Richard spent five hours interviewing a former Synanon doctor. Tuesday, at Sheriff Howenstein's request, Richard briefed the Marin County Board of Supervisors on Synanon. Wednesday he spent the morning going over the Synanon situation with a reporter from KPIX-TV in San Francisco. That afternoon he talked with relatives of a Synanon woman; they hoped they could get her to leave. In the evening he interviewed a former longtime member of Synanon.

Friday Sheriff Howenstein issued a pistol to Richard and had

Sergeant Riddell train him how to use it. Richard had never fired a gun before in his life and ran through many rounds of ammunition at a pistol range before he learned to shoot accurately. That evening, he and Sergeant Riddell went to San Francisco's black ghetto, Hunters Point, to interview a teenager who had left Synanon.

Saturday, Richard met with Art to discuss the Worrell case, the meeting taking place in the hot tub at Richard's home in Marshall. Sunday, Cathy and I sat down with Richard to review the week's developments. Richard was to be called as an expert witness in a Synanon child-custody case. His following week would be spent with the lawyer for an ex-member who wanted to get a child out of Synanon. And in between all these meetings, his trips between Marin County and Berkeley, and his work with the sheriff's office, Richard had to teach classes at the University of California. He found himself swinging between exhilaration and exhaustion.

CHAPTER 17

WHO GETS THE BOY?

Despite coming out only once a week, *The Light* published over one hundred articles and editorials on Synanon in 1978, and as 1979 began, we were starting on our second hundred. From the start, a majority of those readers who commented on our coverage had encouraged us to stay with the story. Of course, we had our critics, but their numbers steadily fell as events confirmed our concern about Synanon. A handful of critics remained, however, and in January, 1979, one of them complained in a letter to the editor: "*The Point Reyes Light*'s Synanon coverage continues ad nauseam, dominating the local news. In reality, the events at Synanon affect few people outside its boundaries. Why should it loom so large in the local press. . . . Harassment of an experimental community such as Synanon either in the press or through the various arms of officialdom is a threat to everyone who makes the choice to live unconventionally. I think it is time for *The Point Reyes Light* to lighten up and leave this story."

The letter drew a flurry of rebuttals from other readers. One man commented in a letter to the editor: "*The Light* has kept on the Synanon story in a very professional way, unwrapping it week after week as one would peel off the layers of an onion. . . . They deserve a Pulitzer prize for their achievement, not irrelevant criticism."

Without our knowing it at the time, other readers had also concluded we deserved a Pulitzer. But no one was really certain how a paper got one. One reader in nearby Nicasio, we found out later, wrote a letter recommending us for a prize; not knowing where to send it, he mailed his recommendation to *The Wall Street Journal* and asked that paper to forward it to whoever awards Pulitzers. A couple in Inverness wrote their son-in-law Anthony Lewis, a Pulitzer winning columnist on *The New York Times*, asking how the prizes were awarded. Lewis picked up an entry form from Columbia University, the Pulitzer sponsor, and sent it to them. His mother-in-law, Mrs. Sooch Rannels, brought it by *The Light* in mid-January. Also feeling we should get a prize was Ralph Craib, who covered Synanon for *The San Francisco Chronicle*. In mid-January, Craib told me he was preparing a letter of nomination. The deadline for submitting an entry was February 1, and on the last weekend in January, Craib with his wife and two daughters drove out to the Point Reyes National Seashore for a picnic and dropped off his letter.

Cathy, Richard, and I were extremely flattered that several people believed our investigation worthy of a Pulitzer, but only Richard thought there was much chance we might win one. Since Richard wasn't a journalist, Cathy and I felt he was naive about the reporting competition *The Light* would be up against. But it was such an honor to even be considered for a prize that we filled out the entry form and compiled the required twenty clippings for a scrapbook. Since we wanted to include editorials along with news stories, we could not enter the investigative reporting division. Instead we entered the Meritorious Public Service category.

Our part-time ad designer, Teresa Marks, assembled the scrapbook, finishing late in the afternoon of January 31. By then we had missed the outgoing mail in Point Reyes Station, but I assumed I could drive across the coast range to San Rafael and still get the scrapbook in the express mail to New York. We called the main San Rafael post office to find out its deadline and discovered we had only forty-five minutes. The trip would take that long in good weather, and this day rain was falling. By the time I got the scrapbook wrapped and was out the door, I had only forty minutes. Wheels spinning on the slick pavement, I roared out of Point Reyes Station.

On the winding road below Nicasio Reservoir, I accelerated to sixty miles per hour, and once on the reservoir's causeway, my little Ford Fiesta was splashing along at over ninety. Getting scared, I slowed to eighty. Lucas Valley Road was the fastest route over the coast range, but it was narrow and winding, forcing me to slow down. I was still driving far above the speed limit, however, when I caught up with some guy in a station wagon. There were few places to pass, and every time we came to one, the station wagon would speed up. I flashed my lights; it refused to pull over. I honked, it would not let me by. My watch told me that unless I could pick up time, I was going to miss the express mail—and likely my one shot at a Pulitzer, however unlikely.

Finally I saw a chance to pass and took it, narrowly getting past the station wagon before sliding into a curve. Accelerating hard, I kept the car on the road, and once out of the curve, I checked my watch again—still a chance!

But now the driver of the station wagon was angry and, despite my speed and the rain, began tailgating. As soon as I reached flat land in East Marin, I accelerated to over eighty, but the station wagon stayed with me. "You idiot," I shouted silently. "I'm not in a contest with you." I squeezed my own anger into a grip on the steering wheel. The way I was driving, any distraction would probably prove fatal.

Just before the freeway, I had to slow for a red light, which changed just as I reached it. The station wagon swerved past me in a turn lane and, once in front of me, slammed on its brakes. I avoided a crash by veering off the road and into a dirt lot. Barely slowing down, I cut across the lot and onto the on-ramp to the freeway. The station wagon was gone, but now I was in rush-hour traffic; luckily, the heavier flow was in the other direction. Cutting back and forth through traffic, I raced into San Rafael. The post office was next to an off-ramp, and I pulled up with a minute and a half to spare. Leaving my car in the middle of the parking lot, I ran inside. "Will this package get to New York by tomorrow?" I anxiously asked the postal clerk.

He looked at the clock on the wall, then at the address, and then back at the clock. "I suppose it will," he drawled, "but you cut it pretty close."

"I'll allow more time in the future," I sighed in relief, and drove back to Point Reyes Station—very carefully. By the time I reached *The Light*, weariness had set in. I dropped into the chair at my desk and grunted to Cathy, "You wouldn't believe what that trip was like."

She smiled. "I can imagine."

"No you can't," I assured her.

Despite the excitement of getting our entry in the mail, within a week we had pretty much forgotten about the Pulitzer awards. Dominating our attention was a child-custody case being tried in San Rafael, the Marin County seat. The father in the case was a former Synanon member, Dave Fagel, who was trying to get custody of his four-year-old son, Dmitri. Fagel's former wife, Valerie Law, still lived in Synanon with their son. Fagel's attorney, Sam Jackson, hoped to get the child away from her by showing that Synanon was not a fit place to raise a child.

The hearing ran for almost two weeks in late January and early February and at the request of Mrs. Law, it was closed to the public when she complained that too much publicity could create a "circus" atmosphere. Judge Henry Broderick, who presided over the case, at first refused to close the hearing, relenting after she then argued an audience would intimidate her from adequately representing herself, as she planned to do.

Both Richard and Art had been summoned as witnesses for the father, as had a number of former Synanon members. Cathy covered the first day of the hearing for *The Light* and found herself in the company of reporters from *The San Francisco Chronicle*, *The New York Times*, *The Pacific Sun*, and KGO-TV. Conspicuously absent was the reporter from *The San Rafael Independent-Journal*, which was still publishing articles supportive of Synanon.

When Judge Broderick ordered the press and public out of the courtroom, this crowd of reporters and witnesses formed a small-scale Synanon convention in the hallway. There were also a handful of current Synanon members, who had been called as witnesses for Mrs. Law, and they kept to themselves. A few would talk with ex-members, but none would talk with reporters. It was the first time Cathy had talked with any ex-members other than Jack Hurst. (By coincidence, Hurst had come out of hiding long enough to divorce his wife and, while all this was going on, was sitting in an adjacent courtroom.) Cathy was surprised to discover that all the ex-members, most of whom had flown in from Southern California, knew who she was. Several remarked on *The Light*'s "Is Anyone Listening?" editorial, and in general the ex-members were friendlier to her than to other reporters.

Most of the ex-member witnesses had held important positions within Synanon, and as Cathy and Richard eavesdropped on their conversations, sometimes joining in, the two picked up some remarkable bits of information. Ed Arkin, a former Synanon accountant, revealed that the corporation had placed a lien on corporate property to guarantee payments to Dederich in his retirement. Ex-member Marjorie Cohen confirmed for Cathy something Richard had already suggested: that Synanon violence could be traced to a seemingly minor incident in 1973. In a game Dederich had gotten angry with a woman and had poured a can of root beer on her head. Since even minor physical aggression was absolutely forbidden within Synanon, Dederich had then felt under pressure to explain his action. When he rationalized it was done "to teach her a lesson," he began a major break from Synanon's policy of nonviolence. Within two years, Synanon members were physically attacking people to teach them a lesson.

Until now, Cathy had thought of Synanon in terms of incidents, not personalities. Curious, she watched the ex-members. What kind of people, she asked herself, could get caught up in something like Synanon? Her first discovery was how articulate and forthcoming the ex-members were. Several had no hesitation in talking about Synanon violence and financial chicanery. All felt they had moved into Synanon because of idealism or other sound motivations and that Synanon had betrayed them.

Marjorie Cohen's husband, Iz, had been a baker before the couple moved in. When they entered in 1971, they sold their bakery and gave Synanon virtually all their assets—about $50,000. They left with some Synanon furniture and their own motorcycle. Art Disterheft, besides being a sheriff's lieutenant and an attorney, was also a better than amateur cook and had won prizes for his bread and pies at the county fair. He and Iz Cohen for a while killed time in the courthouse corridors discussing how to bake a perfect loaf of French bread. Richard, more interested in research than recipes, asked Cohen about some act of violence, but Cohen insisted he wasn't in Synanon when the incident occurred. "Yes you were, Iz," interjected Arkin, the former accountant. But Cohen had been sincere, and Richard again realized how ignorant many Synanon members were of what was going on elsewhere in the corporation.

Cathy was particularly taken by Bill Crawford, a former member of Synanon's Board of Regents, an advisory body made up of members with high status. Crawford, a soft-spoken man wearing wire-rim glasses and a tweed suit, graciously told

Cathy how much he admired the "Is Anyone Listening?" editorial. Crawford, forty-nine, had been in Synanon most of his adult life and still wore a Synanon ring on his finger. He reminded Cathy of a high school history teacher, and she later was horrified when Crawford testified to having taken pictures for Synanon's legal department of victims before and after they were beaten. He had done this several times, and the next day I brought up one of the beatings and asked how he had reacted at the time. "I was sick to my stomach," Crawford told me. "Most of us who were there were too ashamed and upset to talk right after it happened."

One ex-member witness who would not talk to Cathy was Jim O'Donnell, the former director of Synanon's Santa Monica facility. Throughout the day, there were continual murmurings among the former members that O'Donnell would give some powerful testimony. What he was going to testify to neither he nor the ex-members would say. But Cathy was told over and over, "He's going to do something very brave."

Finally, O'Donnell was called in. Cathy and others in the hall took turns peeking through a small window in the courtroom door, but there was no way of telling what was being said inside. After about an hour, O'Donnell came out again. He looked shaken, and immediately a series of ex-members solemnly lined up to hug him silently.

Although the press was barred from the hearing, the judge had put no prohibition on reporting testimony—if reporters could learn of it from lawyers or the witnesses themselves. O'Donnell would not reveal what he had said, but both Fagel, the father, and his lawyer, Jackson, were cooperative and they confirmed that O'Donnell's testimony had indeed been powerful.

O'Donnell had described for the court an incident in Santa Monica when some people driving past the Synanon facility had shouted an insult aimed at Dederich. The Synanon founder immediately ordered a group of Synanon men to kidnap the people, bring them back to Synanon, and "break their legs," O'Donnell testified. He added that Synanon vice-president Dan Garrett had then modified the order: there should be no kidnapping, and the assault should take place outside Synanon.

O'Donnell also described an attack on two black teenage couples who had driven into an underground Synanon parking area. One of the youths had attended a program at Synanon for disadvantaged teenagers the previous summer and apparently wanted to show his friends the place. On this occasion, the founder's son, Chuck Dederich, Jr., had conferred with Synanon's legal department and then ordered the young men to be beaten, O'Donnell testified, to teach the youths "to not mess with Synanon."

Other ex-members described incidents of child abuse. Art told of violent incidents involving Synanon members in West Marin, and Richard explained how Synanon management controlled the lives of members. But for those following the case, the testimony of Crawford and O'Donnell remained the most dramatic.

When it was all over, Judge Broderick awarded Fagel increased—but not total—custody of his son. The judge seemed aware that he was being asked to rule on more than a child's upbringing—in fact, on Synanon as a whole. To avoid doing this, the judge stressed that Mrs. Law, the mother, was untypical of other parents in Synanon. Because she worked in the Synanon school she was in daily contact with her child. Most Synanon parents saw their children only occasionally. And the judge also noted that, were Dederich still in charge of Synanon, the father would have received total custody.

Richard and I suspected Dederich continued to dominate Synanon more than Judge Broderick realized, and were disappointed for the father. But we were overjoyed at what the hearing had brought to light. At last Synanon management's campaign of violence was on the public record. It looked as if a noose was dropping over the necks of the Synanon corporation. When we learned that the attorney general's office had ordered a transcript of the hearing, we began to hear an accompanying drumroll.

CHAPTER 18

HOW LEGAL A LEGAL DEPARTMENT?

As far as Cathy, Richard, and I were concerned, the essential problem with Synanon was its financial exploitation of members and the public. Many members turned over their wealth to the corporation and worked for extremely low pay, believing they were building a utopia where they would live for the rest of their lives. In time, however, most members found some demands on them intolerable and left—with little or nothing to show for their contributions.

The public was being exploited in several ways. The corporation was making wealthy people out of a handful of corporate leaders, but as a supposed charity was paying no income taxes. Businesses and individuals who contributed to Synanon did so believing their donations were all going to rehabilitate addicts, alcoholics, and juvenile delinquents. In fact, after 1968 few of Synanon's activities involved rehabilitation, and the contributions were used mainly to help a wealthy corporation become even wealthier. Synanon invested in the stock market, bought real estate, and even dabbled in foreign currency exchange.

Because of its low-paid work force and its aura of charity,

Synanon's pen, pencil, and knickknack distributorship had an unfair advantage over competitors, we believed. And because the corporation routinely ignored zoning and building codes, Synanon was able to do things on its property that more law-abiding neighbors could not.

If there had never been a rattlesnake attack or a beating of Phil Ritter, these abuses likely would have continued unchecked, the three of us felt. But Synanon's violence and attacks on the news media finally brought about the public scrutiny that should have been there all along.

Cathy and I tended to see the violence as a symptom of Dederich's overconfidence. The Synanon founder had gotten away with so much for so long that eventually he overplayed his hand. Richard, while not disputing this interpretation, added another factor. It was Richard's contention that the Synanon leaders found themselves trapped by California's charitable trust laws. Dederich and his fellow leaders could live extremely well off the charitable corporation's money—but only as long as they were running the show. Ultimately, the public owned Synanon through its status as a nonprofit corporation. The leaders were only highly paid managers. They could not sell their interest and retire. Technically, they had no interest to sell, although they talked as if they did. "Synanon is a little company we put together to pay the bills," Dederich remarked in the mid-1970s.

But as long as the Dederich family and friends ran Synanon, there would always be the danger that a dissident faction within Synanon or an outside agency would challenge the way Synanon was being run, Richard theorized. To try to block outside interference, Synanon had declared itself a religion, he noted, adding that to eliminate potential dissidents within the organization, Dederich had carried out a series of conformity tests. It was this combination of strategies that gave Synanon its cult quality, for the strategies drove out all but the most dedicated members.

As Richard saw it, the three major conformity tests were the mass vasectomies and abortions, the requirement that all couples be broken up and paired off with new people, and the introduction of violence. Internally, these strategies appeared to be successful. Externally, they were a disaster, turning Dederich from a folk hero into a criminal defendant.

The "new religious posture" tape recording seized by Los Angeles lawmen in their raid on Synanon's Badger facility revealed Dederich inside Synanon propagandizing for violence, Richard noted. The tape was recorded on September 5, 1977, and in the recording Dederich acknowledged that his policy of violence would drive out some members:

> I keep thinking of the militant posture, militant defenses, don't tread on me—or something like that. . . . And I think . . . taking this kind of posture will decimate our population once again because it means doing something which is, you know, doing something different, which is the most frightening thing in an other-directed society. . . . And I think we'll decimate our population, which is good. And we'll take very definite stands. We will accelerate a very offensive defense against the ungodly. . . . We've already tested it out in various small, tiny, minuscule ways—by beating up the Dinuba punks, by beating up the San Francisco punks, by chasing the dingbats around with our "Hey Rubes" and so on. We're beginning now—most ineptly—to throw people down stairs in Santa Monica. We won't be as inept as this in another six months. We will not be inept at all. . . . We started quite a while ago with the Imperial Marine deal and so on. We're doing that, taking our best people and putting them into this kind of situation, and it is our intention to do just exactly that. We're not going to mess with the old-time, turn-the-other-cheek religious posture. . . . We're going to crack some bones.

After this recording was seized by Los Angeles police, Synanon's lawyers claimed that Dederich did not necessarily mean everything that he had said, even though events seemed to bear out the policy. But Richard pointed out to Cathy and me that Dederich and Synanon attorney Dan Garrett had said almost the same thing publicly in a press conference a month after the tape was recorded.

The press conference was held in Badger during October, 1977. And although the Synanon leaders outlined the same policy of violence, very little of it was quoted by reporters, who apparently believed it was all hyperbole. Later the press and public would realize that Garrett and Dederich had meant what they said.

"Don't tread on me," Dederich had remarked to reporters. "That's why we're all sitting in this country—because some guy said that. The word's getting around. Watch! I understand. I'm getting feedback [from] people away from Synanon, you know. That's what they said [is] the word: don't attack, don't fuck with Synanon. It's getting around, what! That's the way I want it." Garret chimed in: "And it's around Marin County. . . . You know, where we caught a couple of guys who were loaded in a pickup truck trying to run three of our young ladies, who were kids, you know, children on bicycles, trying to run 'em down. Ran them in the ditch two or three times. And we caught the cocksuckers. And we hauled them in and shaved their heads and turned them loose. Now, you know, that was so shocking to everybody that nobody bothers us up there anymore."*

Events such as the Badger press conference that occurred outside Marin County were known to Cathy and me at the time only insofar as they were covered in the news media.

* This incident, as described in Chapter 7, indicates that the sheriff's report had two, not three, bicyclists involved. Sheriff's deputies disputed whether the two men in the pickup truck tried to run anyone off the road, but agreed with Garrett on what Synanon members did to the pair.

In mid-March of 1979, the two of us realized that so much of the Synanon story was in Southern California that we would have to take a trip south. Los Angeles courts were full of Synanon litigation, and *The Light* needed to know what had been filed in those cases. So in late March, Cathy and I flew to Southern California for three days of research. It would be the most expensive news-gathering expedition in the paper's history.

Our trip took us to courthouses in Santa Monica and Los Angeles, where for hours Cathy and I skimmed through hundreds of pages of court filings in various civil cases looking for material we didn't already have. Much of what we read were tedious disputes over the interpretation of state laws. But here and there in the mountains of court records we found declarations suggesting that not only Dederich but also Synanon's legal staff was at the core of an immense criminal conspiracy.

In a declaration made under penalty of perjury, a former member of Synanon, Mike Flynn, revealed:

> I have listened to Synanon lawyers advise the community that, as to people who harass us, we should try to get them on the property so that we can beat them up. Such discussions were given by Dan Garrett, Phil Bourdette and Adrian Williams [Synanon's main lawyers]. Mr. Williams once told me in person that if there are no witnesses, you can beat the person up and then later say that the person was trying to hurt you so you had to hurt them. I have heard lawyers say that we should pick our shots and hurt a few people so that the word would get out not to mess with Synanon. Mr. Williams has told me that guilt and innocence do not matter but only what evidence can be produced in court.
>
> The lawyers have also discussed the art of telling partial truths in a way that will benefit Synanon. They

> have said that you can say something in such a way as to make an innocent act look terrible.
>
> Synanon lawyers have also discussed filing suits against any lawyer who sues Synanon. They have said that big corporations do that. It has been suggested that if you slap a bunch of lawsuits on a guy, he will not be able to overcome it.

Another former Synanon member, Ben Parks, had similar comments. He described "general discussions by Synanon attorneys—that they would harass anyone who tries to sue Synanon and that they would file countersuits against anyone who did so. It has been stated that they would gang up on any attorney who filed a lawsuit against Synanon so that he would not be able to do anything. Dan Garrett, a Synanon attorney, and Dan Sorkin [a corporate director] have referred to these strategies as 'legal terror tactics.' "

Still another ex-member, Dan Ross, described the plans of Synanon lawyers to harass Jack Toulchin. Toulchin was a former member who, with his wife, had entered Synanon with the expectation of having a child and living out his life there. When Synanon adopted the policy of childlessness, Toulchin and his wife still wanted a child; as a result, they had to leave. "The Synanon attorneys," said Ross in his declaration, "stated that they would teach Jack Toulchin a lesson for filing a lawsuit against Synanon. . . . They would see to it that he was fired from his job. They indicated that they would make it so unbearable for his attorney that his attorney would be sorry that he fooled around with Synanon. The Synanon attorneys indicated that they would find dirt about Mr. Toulchin's attorney."

But perhaps the most damning allegation we found was in a second declaration by ex-member Mike Flynn. Flynn was in Synanon when the Imperial Marines, Synanon's goon squad, was created and trained. "People who went through this training," he declared, "told me that they were being told that they might have to do things that might cause them to go to jail. This fit in with the general talk in Synanon, which was to the effect, 'How much are you willing to do for Synanon? Are you willing to go to jail?' I was also informed that Synanon lawyers would counsel these people on what to do if they were caught. And after a particular beating, lawyers would go over the incident to discuss mistakes so they could have a better legal position on the next occasion."

The more Cathy and I discovered in the court filings, the more indignant we became. "They're not just shady lawyers," I hissed to Cathy across a table in the Los Angeles county courthouse. "There's stuff here that says they're out and out mobsters! Why haven't they been disbarred? Where the hell is the state bar association?" I became so nettled that when we returned to Point Reyes Station, I photocopied my copies of the declarations and sent a bundle to the state bar. When I later discovered the bar was already secretly inquiring into the conduct of the Synanon lawyers, I was somewhat mollified.

But before Cathy and I left Los Angeles, we dropped in on rattlesnake victim Paul Morantz in his law office on Wilshire Boulevard, over a Wells Fargo bank. It was a small law firm with unpretentious offices. Morantz was even less pretentious. It was a Saturday, and he had driven to the office in a football jersey inscribed "USC," where he had attended law school.

Morantz, thirty-three, was tanned and athletic-looking. He was a sports fan, he acknowledged, and a dedicated volleyball player. The snakebite to his left hand had ruined his set, he complained, and throughout our conversation he kept squeezing a gadget to strengthen his grip.

The attorney was depressed. Young and handsome, with a successful law practice, Morantz should have been enjoying the good life—if that is possible in Los Angeles. Used to towns where we could make a U-turn whenever we chose and where winds off the ocean kept the air clear, Cathy and I were uncomfortable, even claustrophobic, in the traffic congestion and smog of Los Angeles. At times we were caught in traffic jams that stretched for miles along the freeway. "There are just too many people here," sighed Cathy at one point, rolling up the car window and turning on the radio.

But Morantz seemed to love Los Angeles and resented the threat of Synanon violence, which was preventing him from enjoying it more. It was difficult to take a woman friend out, he complained, when he was still under part-time police protection and watching out for Synanon. It was even more difficult to work on other legal cases; he was too preoccupied with his legal fights against Synanon. Besides working with police as the victim in the rattlesnake case, Morantz was suing Synanon for $32 million over the incident and was involved in three other civil suits and countersuits with Synanon. Gloomily Morantz told us he expected to be tied down by Synanon cases for at least two or three more years. The more he talked about all this, the unhappier he got. I remembered Morantz, before the rattlesnake attack, excitedly telling me about the Frances Winn kidnapping case. Now he sounded weary, and his voice was so low that Cathy and I sometimes had difficulty understanding him. The only time he became at all animated was when the conversation drifted into sports.

We would stay in contact with Morantz over the next year, and as time passed his warrior spirit began to revive. But the only evidence we saw of it that Saturday in Los Angeles was a newspaper picture he had stuck on the wall behind his desk. The picture was of a snake-killing mongoose.

After we left Morantz's office, Cathy and I spent the night with two friends in Laguna Beach before returning home. Morantz's depression had infected both of us. And the fact that the attorney general had not acted against Synanon despite what we now knew was outlined in court records discouraged us even more. Adding to our woes were mounting financial problems. Cathy had taken a semester's leave from her teaching job to work more on our Synanon research. The junior college had cooperated when she explained her need for a leave, but the academic dean had worried aloud about her safety. "Do you have a gun?" he asked. "We have a big dog," Cathy laughingly assured him. She didn't tell the dean our big dog was ten years old and crippled with arthritis. In fact, though, the loss of Cathy's income was more of a problem for us than was the potential threat from Synanon.

Sitting in our friends' living room overlooking Laguna Beach and the ocean, Cathy and I tried not to be gloomy guests. The effort became much easier when a call came in from Richard. The Hewlett Foundation in Palo Alto had just awarded us a $15,000 grant to conduct our Synanon research, Richard reported with excitement. It was an unusual grant for the foundation to make, he explained, since Hewlett normally funded big civic and cultural projects. Hewlett helps to build symphony halls.

Cathy and I chortled with relief; we wouldn't have to borrow money. Cathy took the news as a sign that "things may yet work out for the good guys." Moments before, our spirits had been dragging along in the dust; now they were soaring. We had now been on the Synanon story for over a year, and for almost the entire period our emotions had been swinging wildly between jubilation and despair. Synanon had committed so many outrages, and yet no government agency seemed able to come to grips with the corporation. But every time we would uncover some new damaging piece of evidence against Synanon, our hopes would zoom. Surely now, we would tell ourselves, the impasse would be broken. But weeks would pass with no agency acting, and our depression would return. Richard, Cathy and I, Morantz, a host of state investigators—we were all developing manic-depressive tendencies, it seemed. Our frustration was almost intolerable, but we knew too much to drop Synanon for more rewarding projects.

Ultimately, we realized, Synanon would not be straightened out until the California attorney general acted. Stories in *The Light* alone could not force the attorney general's hand, but there was something else that might: the myriad of lawsuits Synanon had brought against the news media. "The attorney general has only public safety to worry about and so can take his time," I commented bitterly to Richard after the trip to Southern California. "But *Time* and ABC have money at stake. That's why they're so much more aggressive in going after Synanon."

The lawsuits, as the three of us saw them, were the result of one more Synanon strategy that worked inside the organization but backfired on the outside.

When *Time* magazine on December 26, 1977, described Synanon as a "kooky cult," the management of Synanon was spoiling for a fight. The Hearst corporation had just settled the Synanon libel suit for a world-record $600,000 and was on the verge of settling the Synanon conspiracy suit for $2 million. The news media seemed no match for Synanon's aggressive legal staff, and Synanon management declared a "Holy War" against Time, Inc.

An internal Synanon memo later acquired by *Time*'s lawyers denounced the *Time* article but also revealed that Synanon management expected the Holy War to be good for Synanon's internal morale. "Synanon thrives on adversity," the memo quoted Dederich's daughter Jady as saying. The memo went on to note: "The Holy War against *Time* unites people in Synanon as other battles did in the days that built Synanon."

The memo was written on Febuary 23, 1978, just after Synanon filed its $76-million lawsuit against *Time*. Written by Synanon public relations officer Skip Ferderber, the memo was addressed to corporation director Dan Sorkin. The "first major step" in the Holy War, Ferderber announced, would be a "letter-writing campaign to Hedley Donovan, *Time* editor-in-chief, by all Synanon residents expressing outrage at the treatment of Synanon at *Time*'s hands."

Some nine hundred letters to Donovan followed. One letter writer vowed "to dedicate my life to harassing you and your family." Warned another, "I will do everything in my power to help Synanon rid the earth of vermin such as yourself and Time, Inc." Dederich himself went on Los Angeles television to describe the Holy War: "I want to make them [*Time* executives] as nervous about the safety of their children and their grandchildren as I am about mine."

As the Holy War grew, *Time* attorneys complained in an Oakland superior court about "a continuing series of threats, insults, and other acts of harassment directed by [Dederich] and his followers at top executives and other personnel of Time, Inc." The attorneys cited a phone call from a man who said he was from Synanon, warning that there was a bomb in the Time-Life building. The forty-eight-story building was evacuated, but the bomb threat proved to be a fake. After U.S. Customs agents received calls that Hedley Donovan would be smuggling drugs into the United States on an October 19, 1978, flight from Europe, customs agents held the *Time* editor at a New York airport, searched him, and interrogated him at length. Donovan finally convinced agents he was a target of Synanon harassment and that Synanon members were constantly following him around to cause him trouble. Accompanied by customs agents, Donovan left the airport building and found the ubiquitous Synanon members waiting for him. The agents apologized.

Similar tactics were used against the news staff of KGO-TV, the ABC station in San Francisco, after it broke the story of Synanon's gun purchases. Synanon filed a $42-million suit against KGO-ABC, and KGO staff suddenly found themselves victims of a campaign of harassment. Posters falsely claiming that KGO anchorman Van Amburg "pays for sex" appeared on utility poles around the homes of KGO staff living in

Marin County. Van Amburg was falsely quoted on other signs as referring to "niggers and faggots." News director Pete Jacobus found himself being characterized on signs as a Nazi who wanted more "blood and guts" on the air.

The television station began receiving unordered shipments of food—six cases of Coke on one occasion, a dozen pizzas on another. A contractor showed up at Van Amburg's house, saying he had been instructed to put on a new roof; Van Amburg had to explain the hoax.

Also receiving harassment was NBC producer Pat Lynch after the network aired her four-part series on Synanon. Members threatened her on the street and hung around her apartment building, harassing her when she entered and left. For a while I got almost daily long-distance calls from Pat Lynch, who filled me in on the latest annoyance.

Synanon members also interrupted stockholders' meetings of Time-Life and ABC, and the members hinted that both corporations' executives and their families were in danger and had best take precautions. Cathy, Richard, and I were familiar with Synanon's harassment of Marin County grand jurors and wondered if we too would become targets. It was a disturbing possibility, but we knew no way of blocking it.

We had learned from testimony in the Fagel child-custody case that Synanon had mounted an extensive internal-propaganda campaign to rally members against the common enemy—*Time*. And during the town meeting with Synanon, a fireman who had been invited to breakfast at Synanon remarked about posters he had seen in Synanon warning: KNOW YOUR ENEMIES. Four *Time* executives were listed below. A Synanon member who responded claimed the fireman "lacked a sense of humor."

But Synanon clearly took harassment of the news media seriously. Synanon management had created "Synanon Committee for a Responsible American Media" (SCRAM) to coordinate the Holy War. It was the outgrowth of an earlier group, "Synanon Committee for a Responsible American Press" (SCRAP), which had been formed for the fight with the Hearst corporation. Besides harassing journalists, SCRAM conducted demonstrations and picketing. Synanon also contacted other cults for help in the effort. Soon some Synanon protesters—like their counterparts in Scientology—were showing up at demonstrations in gorilla suits to mock their adversaries.

The Hearst corporation had been worn down by such harassment, but *Time* was not about to make the same mistake. A successful lawsuit against the magazine would only encourage more. By the end of 1979, *Time* would have spent over $2 million on pretrial legal costs. One pretrial hearing that went on for several days in the fall of 1979 was probably the most intensely fought motion for summary judgment in American legal history, a *Time* lawyer was to whisper to us during the hearing. At the start of each day's courtroom battle, both sides would bring in cartloads of legal ammunition. Synanon would wheel in cases of documents on large plywood dollies, *Time* would bring their boxes of documents in on hand trucks, and the crates of papers would fill the front row of the courtroom's spectator section.

Much as Cathy, Richard, and I knew about Synanon in the spring of 1979, we would still be startled in the fall when *Time* revealed how much of the Synanon horrors had been tape-recorded and in other ways documented by Synanon itself. I suspect my own shock came through in a story I would later write for the November 8, 1979, issue of *The Light*:

> "In Synanon . . . you can go into a room . . . with 75 other people and sit there and you say, I am going to be fucking one of these people, and I don't know whom, and I am not going to have anything to say about it."
>
> The speaker is a Synanon member, whose comments were tape-recorded two years ago. In late 1977, Synanon

founder Charles Dederich launched a game of musical beds in which almost all couples in Synanon—married or unmarried—were directed to take new sexual partners.

Synanon called the game "changing partners," and Dederich at the time told *The Independent-Journal*, "I thought, 'Wouldn't it be fun to perform some kind of emotional surgery on people who were getting along pretty well?' "

The Independent-Journal reported 460 members had taken part and quoted Dederich as saying, "What happened is what I thought would happen. People fell madly in love with their new partners . . . I'll bet you that most of these are going to stay together a lot longer than the average American couple."

Through court cases now underway a different picture of what really happened is coming to light. What was "fun" for Dederich was agony for many Synanon members. One member, whose comments were tape-recorded, worried, "Maybe it's that, that I'm afraid of most, that we're going to become two pieces of meat in the open market of Synanon."

Another member described how the new partner she received tried to make her submit to him: "He pursued me and tried to physically beat it into me that I had to be with him. That convinced me that I shouldn't be with him, but only after the second time that he beat me."

Dederich in talking about "changing partners" commented, "I'm a statistician," and perhaps in reflection of this Synanon kept extensive statistics on members' sexual affairs.

Not only were some members' comments tape-recorded, all members were directed to fill out a questionnaire on their trading of partners.

Time magazine in defending itself against a $76-million Synanon libel suit got copies of the recordings and questionnaires, and Synanon struggled in court for months to keep *Time* from making the materials public.

When *Time* got the materials from Synanon, they were sealed by a court order. In October of 1979, the California attorney general's office asked the court for copies, and the court agreed the attorney general could get many of the materials.

But before the attorney general received them, Synanon lawyers appealed to the First District Appeals Court in San Francisco to keep the materials sealed.

At this point, an incredible goof occurred. Lawyers for Synanon accidentally filed as public documents in the appeal the very materials they were trying to keep secret.

In mid-October, two newspapers—*The Light* and *The San Francisco Chronicle*—one day apart found the documents, *The Chronicle* published some excerpts, and Synanon lawyers learned in horror what had happened.

Within hours after reading *The Chronicle* story, Synanon lawyers filed an "emergency application for sealing of records." The attorney general's office objected, explaining to *The Light*, "It's like shutting the barn door after the horse is out."

On November 5, 1979, Appeals Court Judge Wakefield Taylor agreed and denied the Synanon request.

The documents revealed that many more Synanon members swapped lovers than the 460 reported by *The Independent-Journal.* Analysis of the Synanon questionnaires by *Time* lawyers found at least 729 members swapped—some several times.

Noted *Time* lawyers: "Of the 729 persons who completed the forms after switching mates, 311 confined themselves to one new sexual partner, 237 had two, 57 had three, 13 had four, and three had five (and) 108 did not respond to the question."

Time lawyers described how new sexual partners were

paired up "in a large room" at one Synanon facility: "The participants yelled out the names of those with whom they wanted to spend the night. When two people wanted the same person, the situation was resolved either by the community or by the flip of a coin."

In a now-public tape recording, one Synanon member gave this description of the scene: "It was a crazy night, and everybody was going bananas, making phone calls, answering the telephone, running off to bed with a bowl of fruit in hand and a new wife and two sticks of incense in the other. . . ."

Said another member: "A lot of people in Santa Monica were grabbing someone and saying, 'Let's go fuck so we can get this thing on.' "

Still another commented: "Like Chuck [Dederich] says, 'Yeah, just grab anybody. It works with anybody.' "

For some Synanon members, the experience was a chance to escape the outside world's taboo on promiscuity. Reported one member: "There is a gimmick to this whole changing partners deal. We've got a real little loophole, and that is that you can make it with anybody that is in Synanon."

"I feel sexually, totally liberated," said another Synanonite. "I thought I would never want to screw or even could screw another man, and now there are at least three of them that I would like to screw, and I know that I will screw every one of them."

An older woman paired off with a 20-year-old-man remarked, "If I do this to [him, name withheld] and bring him through his initiation, in about 12 years when he's 32, then he can initiate [her daughter, name withheld]. He can say, 'And your mother taught me this.' "

But what was exciting and liberating to some Synanon members upset many others. "I was confused," wrote one member on the questionnaire. "[I] also felt I was doing something strange, against what I was brought up to believe."

Another member "felt pressured to choose a new partner . . . complete resistance, sadness, and sense of loss . . . Not many immediate rewards other than going through the process with everybody."

"Mine was not . . . an experience of euphoria at first," a Synanon member wrote, "I felt betrayed, adulterous, and very unhappy at first."

But as Dederich's sister-in-law, Delores, explained in a recording, members accepted that their choice was either to go along with the swapping or leave Synanon (which a number of members did).

"I was listening to the wire [Synanon's internal radio station] that afternoon," said Delores Dederich. "This person being ordered to live with that person and this person being ordered to give up that person . . . There is no way to stay and not do this thing."

Many of those who accepted what was happening to them did so believing they were serving the Synanon movement or Synanon "religion." Here is how some explained their experience:

- "I am a tool for Synanon. Synanon does have a right to tell me anything to do."
- "Others know better than I what kind of marital partner I should have."
- "Synanon will take care of me if I follow the directions."
- "I do not have a choice about giving 100 percent to the relationship. It is my contract with Synanon to do so . . . My relationship with Synanon is steel."
- "One's mate is secondary when there is a higher principle involved [Synanon.] Religious purpose heightens individual love."

• "I can make it work with anyone as long as it seems to be a good match for Synanon."

• "The only thing that's important to me is Synanon . . . even more important to me than this person that I love."

Delores Dederich and her husband Bill left Synanon following "changing partners." She realized the effect on her emotions of Synanon's pressure on her to give up her husband.

In a tape recording made before she left, the Synanon founder's sister-in-law said, "Sometimes I think, my God, I think I've lost every bit of feeling that I have, that I'm a zombie."

What disturbed us about what these documents revealed was not the sex itself; it was Synanon management's willingness to cause so much suffering among the members. And equally disturbing was how many members unthinkingly acquiesced to management's taking control over one more part of their personal lives.

The article was one of the few instances where *The Light* discussed sex in Synanon, although we could have written volumes. Because Synanon members all the way up to Dederich and his late wife, Betty, discussed their sexual activities and problems in Synanon games, the general membership knew quite a lot about each other's sex lives. Adding to members' lack of privacy about sex was an institution tried in Synanon during the first half of 1977, "star charts." The charts were graphs drawn on poster board and displayed in public rooms of different facilities. Down the left side of the graph were the names of couples listed alphabetically. Married couples were in one group, unmarried couples were listed below. The rows of boxes to the right of the names were days of the month. Couples were expected to stick stars in the boxes to indicate the quality of their sexual activity each day—gold stars, blue stars, and red stars indicated varying degrees of fulfillment. Black stars were disasters. No star meant no sex that day.

Several former members noted that the charts were introduced to encourage members to spend more time on sex. Synanon management at the time was complaining that couples spent too much time watching television and not enough time being attentive to each other. Couples who had too many black boxes after their name were "gamed" about their sex problems. One older couple adamantly refused to participate in the star charts, but most went along—although not always honestly, ex-members told us.

Further depriving members of privacy in sexual matters was the pressure on younger members to get permission from older leaders before engaging in sex. Couples who were not living together were expected to sign up to use bedrooms designated for sexual activity. Such things as status and good behavior affected how long members had use of the bedrooms.

As a result of all this, the ex-members we talked to could quickly tell us which Synanon members had previously had homosexual experiences and who suffered from impotency. Not only had such information come out in games, but many of the games were also broadcast over the Synanon wire for all members to hear.

Twice I was tempted to publish some of this information. Synanon, after all, had tried to distress various local journalists by spreading false information about their sexual activities. Our information could be confirmed, but we never used it. I didn't want to be guilty of the same cruelty and crudeness that I resented in Synanon management.

CHAPTER 19

MANAGING *THE LIGHT*

Once in joking with Cathy, I suggested that the story of our Synanon investigation should be called *Startled Innocence* v. *Complacent Corruption.* Synanon leaders for years apparently believed they could get away with repeated lawbreaking; in that respect, they could be considered complacent. But mainly I was referring to what innocents we were to the politics of criminal justice. When we started our investigation, it never occurred to us that getting California's criminal justice system to act against wrongdoers would require the same sort of lobbying and news media attention that is needed to get a tax bill passed or a new highway built.

Before the state finally acknowledged late in 1979 that Synanon had been acting "unlawfully," Cathy, Richard, and I met with five state assemblymen or their aides, the state superintendent of education, the state director of health services, two state senators, an official of the state Department of Industrial Relations, the attorney general of California, and Governor Jerry Brown. We had also had innumerable discussions with Marin County officials and middle-level state staff.

After one long meeting with aides to Assembly Speaker Leo McCarthy, I wearily remarked to Cathy, "The Constitution guarantees our right to petition the government for redress of grievances, but it fails to warn us what a chore that can be."

Since most of the officials were not readers of *The Light*, our discussions usually amounted to filling them in on what had already been revealed in the paper. Several were bemused that a tiny weekly had undertaken what seemed the near-impossible task of bringing Synanon and its leaders to justice. And one of the results was that we were repeatedly asked to explain the workings of *The Light* and our own roles in the investigation.

It was easy to explain Richard's and my roles. He was the theoretician; I was the investigative reporter. But what was Cathy? My eventual answer was a metaphor drawn from World War II: "Think of me as General Patton fired up and running around in the field. Richard has been General Eisenhower, assimilating information and devising a strategy. And Cathy has been President Roosevelt, in charge of the home front—meaning *The Light*—and having ultimate authority over our coverage and editorial campaign."

Cathy used that authority sparingly, but on two occasions she refused to let articles I had written run in the paper. On both occasions, she felt, probably accurately, that I had allowed a measure of self-righteousness to flavor the articles. One of the articles she rewrote. The other was abandoned.

To understand Cathy's role, it is necessary to understand what a juggling act it is to operate a small weekly newspaper. There are so many bits of information, so many ads, so many people with specialized talents that have to be assembled to produce each issue, that Cathy and I often referred to the paper as "the weekly miracle."

The Light at this time had four part-time employees and one full-time reporter, besides Cathy and me. With so much of the staff part-time, we suffered through continual turnovers. Cathy did most of the interviewing and hiring. Cathy could operate every piece of equipment at the newspaper, and when an employee called in sick, it was often Cathy who had to pinch-hit. Despite her seven years in reporting, Cathy did not touch-type, but after a typesetter quit in June, 1978, Cathy typeset an entire issue with her hunt-and-peck typing. It was an exhausting effort, but the paper came out on schedule.

Cathy liked to think of herself as the practical member of our team, who kept Richard and me from becoming carried away in our eagerness to expose Synanon. But at other times, she would admit, "I'm a gambler," and once told me, "When I was a kid in Tennessee, whenever we had family reunions we all ended up playing poker together." Cathy's willingness to take risks made her almost unique among the newspaper business managers we knew. She realized when we published the Cardineau beating story in March, 1978, that Synanon might sue us out of business over it, and yet she refused to be frightened off. Later, she took the same stand when we were about to publish the story about Dederich calling for an attack on attorney Morantz. But perhaps the biggest gamble either of us took was the decision to buy *The Light*, when it was on the verge of bankruptcy.

As might have been anticipated, our living together and working together was sometimes difficult. We could not always separate our business relationship from our personal one, and disagreements in one setting would carry over into the other. Our brief separation in 1977 resulted in large part from too much togetherness.

Cathy was both more blunt and more shy than I. More than once I heard her tell readers who had called to complain about some article that she would hang up on them unless they were more polite. But she was often uncomfortable in large gatherings and protected her privacy ferociously. After our Synanon investigation had become somewhat well known, *The New York Times* called her for information on us. It was a typical interview until the reporter asked Cathy her favorite recipe. Cathy firmly refused to say, insisting it was none of the public's business. By the end of 1978, I had finally come to acknowledge this side of Cathy, and we were trying to make room for each other's differing temperaments. As a result, we were getting along better than we had in years.

Cathy's business responsibilities at *The Light* kept her in the office when Richard and I in 1978 were off tracking down information on Synanon, and there were times she resented not being able to join in more on the adventure. So when her leave from teaching began in early 1979, Cathy started going out more often on Synanon stories.

One of the news-gathering trips Cathy took in the spring of 1979 was to Sacramento. She and Richard met with state Department of Education officials to find out how the department came to be giving so much federal surplus property to Synanon. The corporation had picked up surplus ranging from furniture to airplanes. Education officials by then had become suspicious of Synanon but claimed Synanon conformed to the law. Synanon was calling itself an educational institution, to be eligible for the federal surplus. This was done by defining normal activities of the corporation as classes; kitchen workers, for example, were said to be enrolled in a cooking class.

About noon, Cathy and Richard ran into a staffer from the attorney general's office. The agency had been conducting an investigation of Synanon for months. Investigators had compiled reams of information, but the officials over them seemed uninterested. The attorney general's office, like most bureaucracies, had had more problems demanding attention than time to deal with them. Under those circumstances, bureaucracies tend to take the easy shots, and Synanon was anything but an easy shot.

The staffer apparently felt he was among friends, because he candidly revealed to Cathy and Richard that he was unhappy with his agency's inaction. "It's beginning to look like the whole thing's going to be shelved," he remarked with a gesture of hopelessness.

Cathy offered sympathy, but it dawned on her that without directly saying so, the staffer hoped *The Light* could somehow put pressure on his department. He predicted that Marin County District Attorney Jerry Herman would soon drop the Lynn Worrell kidnapping case without filing charges, and that would leave the rattlesnake case in Los Angeles—which was limited to one incident—as the only case in California remaining against Synanon.

Cathy and Richard returned from Sacramento depressed. Something had to happen, but they didn't know what.

CHAPTER

20

THE PULITZERS ANNOUNCED

It was Easter Sunday, 1979, and Richard had come over to our house for Easter dinner. Although we had met Richard only because of our common interest in Synanon, he was now a friend as well as collaborator. All of us were worried about the disintegration of state efforts to bring Synanon under control, but this evening we refused to let Synanon intrude upon our conviviality. Cathy and I had cooked a big dinner. Richard, who had brought a bottle of wine, told stories of growing up in New York City. We took turns recalling the various routes that had brought us all to do graduate work at Stanford University. Although the three of us had been at Stanford at the same time, neither Cathy nor I had met Richard until a year before. It was a pleasant friendship to have formed.

"We sometimes have our differences, but I do like Richard," I remarked to Cathy the next morning as we dressed for work.

"Both of you pontificate so," she laughed.

As I pulled on a turtleneck shirt, a thought darted into my Monday-morning mind: this is the middle of April. Cathy said the Pulitzer Prizes were awarded in mid-April. What day in April? I didn't know. God, I thought, wouldn't it be amazing to win? If the miracle should happen, I don't want to be photographed looking like I just came off a ski slope. You're a country editor—dress like one, I thought, and took off the turtleneck and tucked a favorite red-plaid shirt into my blue jeans. I commented to Cathy, "I think it'll be too warm for a turtleneck today." I was secretly embarrassed at being presumptuous enough to think we had a chance. It had been several weeks since I had thought much about the Pulitzers. There had been too many frustrations with Synanon. I didn't want to get my hopes up about something else only to be disappointed there too.

As was usual in our division of labor, I cooked breakfast. The window by our breakfast table looked out over green hills of pasture rolling to Tomales Bay. The morning air was brilliantly clear, making the white hulls of sailboats moored offshore stand out against the water. Cathy smiled. "Springtime at last."

Down at the office, however, it was a typical Monday morning. I took a couple of classified ads over the phone since Gayanne, our classified ad manager/receptionist, did not come to work until nine o'clock. After going over the front-page-story list with reporter John Madden, I sat back with a cup of coffee to read the morning *San Francisco Chronicle.*

Around nine o'clock the phone rang and Cathy answered. It was a reporter for *The Washington Post.* He had heard a rumor that a San Francisco Bay area weekly might win a Pulitzer Prize. He had checked with two prominent local weeklies, *The Bay Guardian* and *The Pacific Sun*, and neither had entered. The *Post* reporter said he had called *The San Francisco Examiner* and asked what Bay area weekly was "doing something out there." *The Examiner* had suggested he call *The Light.* Had we entered? the reporter asked. "Yes," Cathy screamed. "We entered our Synanon coverage."

"Well, you may have won," said the reporter. "But you won't know for sure until noon your time." Cathy wanted to know how the reporter got the rumor. He had picked it up, the reporter said, while trying to learn if *The Post* had won anything.

It was heady news, and I told the staff and called my father. The next call we got, however, was disappointing. Sheriff Al Howenstein reported that the district attorney's office had decided against prosecuting the case involving former Synanon member Lynn Worrell. Worrell was genuinely nice and sincerely felt she had been mistreated when she tried to quit Synanon fourteen months earlier. We had been tipped the case might be dropped, but I was still disappointed. I wrote the story and tried to get some editing done.

Cathy meanwhile realized better than I what could happen if we won the prize: the chaos would destroy our production schedule. As a result, she set aside all other work and began pounding out rewrites and editing copy at a furious pace.

From about 11:45 A.M. on, I checked my watch every few minutes. Noon came and went. About five after, I decided that the rumor had been just that and wandered across the street to Cheda's Market for a chocolate ice cream cone. Back in the newsroom, I edited a feature story on medical self-help while slurping on the cone.

The phone rang. It was the Associated Press calling: Congratulations! *The Light* had just won the Pulitzer for Meritorious Public Service. I set the cone down and shouted to Cathy, "We've won! We've won the Pulitzer! All over *The Light*, staffers broke into laughs and yells and exchanged hugs.

As the ice cream cone melted onto my desk, I gave AP a brief interview. When I hung up, Cathy was on another line answering questions from UPI. I also talked to them for a few minutes, but the commotion in the office was making it hard to hear the wire service reporter. Reporter Madden dashed to the market across the street for a bottle of champagne, popped a cork, and passed out glasses. By now, *The San Francisco Examiner* was on another line, and Cathy was giving someone else an interview on the third line.

"Call Richard," Cathy interrupted her call to shout to Gayanne. As soon as there was a free line, Gayanne did.

I came on the line: "We've won the Pulitzer!"

Richard whooped elatedly. "I have to see a student first, but then I'll be right over."

Richard had an appointment to see a woman who would take the oral exam for her doctorate the next day. She was nervous and seven months pregnant. As quickly as he could, Richard reassured her she was well prepared, then canceled classes for the day and hurried out to his Porsche. With a tape deck blasting the final concert of Bob Dylan and the Band, Richard roared over the Richmond–San Rafael Bridge and out to Point Reyes Station, laughing and shouting, with only himself to hear.

Within an hour of the Pulitzer announcement, *The San Francisco Examiner* had a reporter at *The Light*. So did *The Los Angeles Times*. KGO-TV reporter Joyce Shank flew in by helicopter. NBC and CBS arrived with camera crews. Two literary agents called to sign us up. Relatives tried to phone and, when they couldn't get through, sent telegrams. Cathy called her father in Tennessee and started crying with joy as she told him the news. Cathy also called her mother in Florida, who called back at 3:30 P.M. to say we were on Walter Cronkite's evening news on the East Coast.

Cathy and I were interviewed by so many radio stations we lost track of whom we were talking to. The radio broadcasts inspired more calls from friends. Fifty or so readers had already showed up at *The Light* with dark beer and champagne when Richard arrived. The delay with his student kept him from being photographed by any of the national news media, which were under the earliest deadline. As a result, Richard never received the same news media attention that Cathy and I did, although *The Independent-Journal* and *The Light* carried pictures of the three of us together.

Lieutenant Art Disterheft, learning of the news, dropped by his house to tell his companion, Susie Sasso. "He was in uniform and on the verge of crying," she later told us.

Sheriff Howenstein called back. His second call of the day, this one full of congratulations, was much happier. *Chronicle* reporter Ralph Craib, who had nominated *The Light* for the prize, arrived to a hero's welcome. He had a story to write, but most in the crowd were pushing champagne on him and trying to get him in photos.

Mrs. Sooch Rannels, who had brought us the Pulitzer entry forms, hurried in breathless. It was a heroine's welcome for her.

Synanon's former president, Jack Hurst—then in hiding—called with his and Mary Inskip's congratulations. Other calls came from ex-members Lynn Worrell and Jerry Newmark.

I was interviewed by the BBC calling from London and by an Australian radio station calling from Melbourne. A French magazine wanted to translate stories from *The Light.*

The party went on for six hours; then Richard, Cathy, and I went over to Cecil Asman's house to have dinner and watch ourselves on television. In a daze, Cathy and I finally slipped into bed around midnight, only to have *The Des Moines Tribune* wake us up with a 6:00 A.M. phone call. Over breakfast, we watched ourselves on *The Today Show* and *CBS Morning News.*

Tuesday morning at *The Light* was more of the same. James Reston of *The New York Times* called me with some questions. ABC arrived with a camera crew. So did Channel 10 from Sacramento. *Time* and *Newsweek* lined up interviews for Wednesday.

But we still had to get out that week's paper. Fortunately, two readers who were retired newspaper editors volunteered to help write and edit the final stories. Five of Cathy's junior college students drove down to help with paste-up. On page 1, we stuck a banner headline in 96-point type—a size too large for normal use and referred to in newspapering as "going-to-war" headline type. It read: THE LIGHT WINS PULITZER PRIZE.

It was only the fourth time since the Pulitzer Prizes began in 1917 that a prize in any division (public service, reporting, editorials, etc.) had gone to a weekly newspaper and not a daily, and that added greatly to the news media attention we received. In recent years the Meritorious Public Service award had gone to *The New York Times* (1972), *The Washington Post* (1973), *Newsday* (1974), *The Boston Globe* (1975), *The Anchorage Daily News* (1976), *The Lufkin* (Texas) *News* (1977), and *The Philadelphia Inquirer* (1978).

Since the Pulitzer Prize for Meritorious Public Service is the highest honor in American journalism, it was not surprising that the national news media were interested in our award. But it was other weekly newspapers that seemed to take the most delight in it. Reporters on weeklies are used to a certain amount of condescension from their brethren on big-city dailies, and many weeklies took our prize as a confirmation of the importance of weekly newspapering. An editor in Canada wrote us: "As editor of a twice-weekly paper here in the heartland of Southern Ontario, I am surrounded by chain dailies which see us as a collection of social notes and birth announcements. . . . My staff and I are deeply indebted to you both for indicating to all readers that weeklies and community newspapers do in fact carry news." An editor in New York wrote: "We, too, are a small weekly [about 2,300 circulation] with a staff of four. The issues here are usually quite local, but suddenly—because of our proximity to Indian Point [nuclear installation]—we have found ourselves right in the middle of the Three Mile Island nuclear accident aftermath. After reading of your award I got to fantasizing—Well now maybe this nuclear thing. . . ."

In nominating us for the prize, *Chronicle* reporter Craib had written Columbia University, sponsors of the Pulitzer awards: "A $2.6-million settlement by the Hearst Corporation of libel and conspiracy suits brought by the Synanon Foundation effectively muzzled most of the American press in dealing with Synanon.

"Major news organizations were unwilling to risk the inevitable litigation certain to be pursued by an organization with a 48-member legal staff. Meanwhile David Mitchell and his co-publisher wife Cathy were printing week after week stories of beatings, of weapons, and of other strange practices in which this cult was involved. I have heard many, many of my colleagues speak with admiration of Mitchell's courage and dedication and, more particularly, of his vulnerability."

The awarding of any prizes—Olympic medals, Academy Awards, or Pulitzers—inevitably sparks a round of speculation as to what the judges based their decision on. Published reports about awarding of the 1979 Pulitzers generally emphasized the dangers *The Light* faced, rather than our writing.

I was asked by so many reporters what I thought were the reasons for our winning that I was finally forced to come up with my own guess. It seemed to me that *The Light* won its Pulitzer not so much for investigative reporting as for its editorial campaign demanding that the government correct abuses at Synanon. The paper was required to submit twenty clippings to the Pulitzer jury, and of the twenty, thirteen were editorials. That is, almost twice as many editorials as news stories made up *The Light*'s entry.

The editorials constituted the main difference between *The Light*'s coverage of Synanon and that of other newspapers. Our editorials continually made a moral issue of the Synanon situation, while other papers covered it as a somewhat bizarre news story. The result was that readers of other papers, such as *The San Rafael Independent-Journal*, saw developments at Synanon as one more bit of tomfoolery in a county, Marin, already known for outlandish lifestyles.

That there was something fundamentally different between the rigors of Rolfing and institutionalized cruelty at Synanon generally escaped *I-J* management—often to the frustration of several *I-J* reporters. In an attempt to be tolerant of unconventional behavior, *The Independent-Journal* initially ignored the fact that many Synanon members were being exploited, that some behavior of Synanon's leadership was vicious, and that certain corporate acts appeared to be essentially criminal.

To be sure, *The Light* broke a number of Synanon stories, but the newspaper's real role was to arouse the moral outrage of its readers. In an interview with *The New York Times* on our winning the Pulitzer, Art, the sheriff's lieutenant, recalled my slamming a fist on a table and exclaiming, "It ain't right, Art. It ain't right." Ultimately, I theorized, Cathy, Richard, and I won the prize because we saw our responsibility as an obligation to keep reminding the public "It ain't right."

CHAPTER 21

WHAT IT ALL MEANT

I remember the months that followed the Pulitzer announcement as auraed in a haze of euphoria. We were "heroes," or so said *Quest* and *Penthouse* magazines. Governor Jerry Brown held a reception for us in his office. Thousands of feet of television footage were shot of us. The three of us appeared on *The Tomorrow Show* after giggling—as probably many other program guests do—while we were chauffeured to the studio in a limousine complete with bar and TV.

Our readers took up a collection to send Cathy and me to the Pulitzer luncheon at the National Press Club in Washington, D.C. The University of California paid Richard's way. ITT put us up in its suite at the Sheraton-Carlton in Washington, a suite worthy of a visiting head of state. Richard and I were invited, while in New York, to watch the *NBC Nightly News* live from the control booth, and discussed journalism with John Chancellor afterward. We were three kids in the Disneyland of national attention, and we loved it.

I gave the commencement address at the College of Marin. Cathy addressed graduating sixth-graders at the two-room Nicasio School. She and I spoke to groups as far-flung as the Mississippi Press Association and the World Press Institute in St. Paul, Minnesota.

Richard gave lectures at Yale, Columbia, the University of Massachusetts, and the American Sociological Association. He was the toast of the sociology profession, and scholarly magazines invited him to write articles.

We met hundreds and hundreds of people. I delighted in it; Cathy sometimes was overwhelmed. Richard on four occasions considered falling in love.

Too long a diet of such attention would not be good for anybody. I suspect the years of adulation from his followers figured mightily in shaping Charles Dederich's personality. But for the three of us it was a wonderful moment of exhilaration. Our faults were excused, our efforts respected. It was for me the end of youth. The ancient Romans considered men *adulescens* until they were thirty-five, and perhaps we are. In the wake of the Pulitzer, I discovered the pressure to prove myself in the adult world was finally over.

Also experiencing a life change in the aftermath of the Pulitzer was *San Francisco Chronicle* reporter Ralph Craib. When I had first met him, I was reminded of those reporters who pounded the police beat in movies of the 1930s. He was stocky of build, with a black patch over one eye. He had fought in Europe during World War II and seemed tough enough to get an interview from Al Capone. But I had also seen Craib in tender moments with his adolescent daughters and appreciated his total lack of condescension toward me despite his much greater experience in newspapering.

Craib also had felt the pressure of covering a potentially dangerous organization. There were no threats made against him, but Synanon, as *Time* magazine attorneys pointed out, had created "an atmosphere of terror." When *The Chronicle* in January, 1979, sent Craib to Los Angeles to cover a Synanon press conference, his family was anxious. As Craib left, his eleven-year-old daughter, Betsy, gave him a note and asked him to hold on to it "so you will know I will always love you, no matter what happens."

Craib had been in newspapering thirty-seven years, starting as a copy boy on *The Oakland Tribune*. He had eventually worked his way up to editorial writer on *The Chronicle*. It was the "country club job" on the paper, he once told me with a laugh, relaxed work at good pay. But eight years earlier, Craib had a disagreement over an editorial with publisher Charles Thieriot. Had he not been a Guild member, Craib would probably have lost his job. As it was he was demoted to reporter. "It was quite a blow to brother Craib," he had once admitted to me.

The day the Pulitzers were announced, Craib made such a noisy commotion in the city room, I later learned from a *Chronicle* editor, that much of the newsroom thought he had won. When it came out that he had nominated us, he was treated like a hero by the San Francisco press corps.

Reporters on the rival *San Francisco Examiner* were as enthusiastic as those on *The Chronicle*, since several *Examiner* reporters felt management had sold them out when it settled Synanon's libel suit. One *Examiner* reporter offered to pay for all Craib's future drinks at the M&M, a press bar he frequented. Craib was flattered but after three drinks killed the tab.

As an Associated Press picture of Craib celebrating with Cathy and me was wired across the United States, *Chronicle* management asked him to write an editorial congratulating *The Light*. Then he was given a couple more editorials to write. Finally, he was asked if he would like to resume writing editorials on a steady basis. Charles Thieriot was now dead and the disagreement long forgotten. "I don't have to start for a month," he told me exuberantly one afternoon in the M&M.

"Have to?" I asked in bemusement.

"I'm working on a couple of Synanon stories," Craib answered, "and I want to finish them first."

Cathy, Richard, and I also had unfinished business with Synanon. "While we're in the public eye," Richard had suggested, "we ought to keep reminding people that despite all the brouhaha, the state has yet to take action." It seemed good advice, and our public appearances inevitably included a call for state action. One of my comments was reprinted in newspapers from *The Miami Herald* to *The Hongkong Standard:* "If there is one arch-villain in this story, an unindicted co-conspirator, it's the Charitable Trust Division of the attorney general's office." I told an Investigative Reporters & Editors conference, "The only thing we can do is keep laying out in front of people: Look, you've got an attorney general who's sworn to protect the citizenry. And he ain't doing it, and we all know he ain't doing it. And we're going to keep rubbing his nose in the fact until he does something."

With other state agencies we took the same approach. When Governor Jerry Brown held a reception for the three of us and *The Light*'s staff, we used the opportunity to remind Brown how ineffective the administrative branch of California government had been in dealing with Synanon. The capital press corps had been invited to the reception, and several television reporters showed up with camera crews. The cameras were rolling as I asked Brown to look into the Synanon matter, and after some discussion, he promised he would. A month later he made good on the promise: his office organized a task force of state agencies to coordinate efforts to bring Synanon under normal regulation.

The meeting with Brown was revealing in a couple of ways. The NBC affiliate in San Francisco broadcast our Synanon discussion with Brown, but lawyers for at least one other station refused to let its footage be aired, fearing that a candid discussion of Synanon—even between three Pulitzer winners and the governor—might attract a Synanon lawsuit. But the meeting also revealed how effective the combined attention of several news media can be in forcing government to pay attention to a problem.

The renewed news media attention on Synanon in the wake

of our Pulitzer was also recognized in the attorney general's office. Investigators' reports that had been languishing in file cabinets were suddenly on the table. A state prosecutor, Deputy Attorney General Charles Just, was assigned to Synanon matters and began putting together a case covering Synanon members' violence. Even the attorney general's Charitable Trust Division became a little more aggressive. By the end of 1979, the division had filed a complaint in Marin County demanding that Synanon leaders return to the organization's general fund over $1.5 million. The complaint charged leaders with "unlawfully" spending Synanon's money—mostly on themselves.

Synanon, however, had a different interpretation of the state action. "Vile" press coverage was damaging Synanon's good reputation, claimed a Synanon spokesman. Synanon attorneys charged that Attorney General George Deukmejian was carrying out a "vendetta" against the Synanon "church." Synanon's repeated complaint was that the press focused only on Synanon's and Charles Dederich's problems while ignoring the good both had done.

But our own and other news media's findings had already shown how serious those problems had become. And they revealed how vulnerable to abuse are the laws dealing with tax-exempt corporations and churches. America's loose system of tax exemptions encourages the growth of authoritarian economic groups such as Synanon, we concluded; and Synanon is not the only group whose leaders have been able to live unduly well off the work of their followers/members/patients.

Such groups are often in conflict with the laws and regulations of government because their leaders, in effect, claim a separate sovereignty. The leaders would like de facto sovereignty because American laws prohibit many of the activities used by the leaders to control and exploit their work force.

Because political feudalism is virtually dead, the surviving institution most resembling these groups' authoritarian and hierarchical structure is organized religon. But the resemblance is in organizational structure, not in content. Taxing agencies, we discovered, have had trouble finding a difference between a church starting a business and a business starting a church. Our message to legislators who write the tax-exemption laws was that they must learn to make the distinction and then enforce it.

We also came to feel that if you examined the development of Synanon from a rehabilitation program into a cult, you could see how easy it was to shed any pretext of leaders working for the group and replace it with a structure whereby the group worked for Synanon leaders.

In summary, Synanon began in Santa Monica in 1958 as a drug and alcohol rehabilitation program, and over the next few years gained national prominence. Sociologist Lewis Yablonsky in the 1960s called Synanon "a breakthrough in the treatment of drug addiction." U.S. Senator Thomas Dodd lauded Synanon as "a man-made miracle on the beach in Santa Monica." Synanon founder Dederich was widely credited with doing what no one else could do: cure narcotics addiction. Less widely known was how few addicts took the Synanon cure and then were graduated to productive lives in the outside world. Many of those who were cured were quietly absorbed into the Synanon corporation as employees.

Dederich himself later came to deny that Synanon's cure would have a lasting effect on many former addicts once they left Synanon. In 1971 he admitted, "We once had the idea of 'graduate.' This was a sop to social workers and professionals who wanted me to say that we were producing 'graduates.' I have always wanted to say to them, 'A person with this fatal disease will have to live here all of his life.' I know damn well if they go out of Synanon, they are dead."

In 1968, Synanon deemphasized its rehabilitation program for addicts and began touting itself as an "alternative lifestyle community." It began recruiting professional and other middle-class people looking for an escape from the chaos of the 1960s.

At the same time, Synanon's various business ventures were booming, and Synanon used the fact to help recruit middle-class members. "Here's your chance to get in on the ground floor of something that's going to be big" was the oft-repeated recruiting slogan. The business growth Synanon predicted did occur. Synanon's major money-maker, its Advertising Gifts and Premiums distributorship, grew from a gross income of $1.2 million in 1968 to $9.58 million in 1978.

In 1974, Synanon went through another change. Synanon as an alternate-lifestyle community was deemphasized, and Synanon the "cult" emerged. In 1975, directors of the Synanon corporation amended Synanon's articles of incorporation to declare that "one of the primary purposes of the corporation is to operate a church." A major reason for the change, Synanon internal documents later revealed, was to protect the corporation's tax-exempt status and to block state efforts at imposing licensing on Synanon. But by 1977, Synanon lawyers were referring to the "cult" at Synanon.

Accompanying these name changes was a steady broadening of Dederich's power over the membership. On tape recordings made in 1975–76, Dederich described his new role in the new Synanon. The remarks were edited by Synanon into a pamphlet called "Chuck Dederich Talks About Synanon Home Place."

Home Place was the resortlike retreat in Badger, a remote site in the foothills of Central California, where much of the Synanon leadership lived in the late 1970s. Dederich decided to move there after a tour of the site in 1975. The new facility would "provide a grand lifestyle for everyone," Dederich proclaimed—providing one was part of Synanon's elite. "Everyone in Synanon does not have to enjoy what we've got . . . ," Dederich said. "We're the highest paid people in Synanon. We live off the fat of the land up here at the Home

Place. We all live better. We eat better. We have shorter working hours. Very shortly, we'll have on the average the best living quarters. We're supposed to do this, to be kind of like a royal family."

Commenting on another occasion about the Badger retreat, Dederich observed: "Everybody keeps thinking this is part of Synanon. There is no connection with Synanon. Synanon's a little company we put together to pay the bills, really and truly. We literally have some millions of dollars to put into this experiment." The "experiment," he explained, was "to squeeze more sensation out of life."

Dederich gave his "experiment" a high-sounding title, "Research into the Business of Living," and declared, "We are exploring how to increase and enhance the happiness quotient of people." What the experiment really sought to discover, Dederich revealed, was how well he and others of Synanon's elite could live off the corporation's tax exemption. "Synanon exists on government money," he noted. "Everything we use here in Synanon, with the exception of our little Mickey Mouse personal effects . . . is the property of the people of the United States. We are subsidized by this government to carry on our experiments."

That comment was made in September, 1975, and a month later Dederich returned to the topic on another tape recording: "When a community of people . . . begins to get what it worked for, then it goes into a new phase of its life. It begins to move out of development and over into decadence. It begins to decay. Now there's nothing wrong with that. In other words, I can't tell whether it's more fun to live in a developing society or a decaying society. One of the research projects that we want to carry on down here—see if we can do this simultaneously—is we want to develop and decay at the same time."

Unbelievable as it seemed to those of us who came upon the "Dederich Talks" pamphlet, the state and federal governments in the late 1970s were unknowingly subsidizing an "experiment" by Synanon leaders in how much pleasure they could get out of decadence.

"Our evening dinners, night after night and week after week, are quite possibly the most gracious dining in the entire state of California," Dederich rhapsodized in October, 1975. "The way we dine, the time we take doing it, the sound of it—people are having a good time. . . . There's a wonderful leisure about it which would not be rivaled anywhere in California. This had come out of our attention to that intangible thing that we're building down here: this research into living. This research into living."

The Synanon founder suggested that newcomers could be easily used to do the "dirty work" for the tax-exempt corporation's elite—"scrubbing the floors, schlepping the pots. . . . The good ones [newcomers] we keep, the rest we throw back. That may be a permanent part of Synanon. It may be that a resident of the Home Place will never wrestle another pot. Why do that when we got slews of dingleberries coming in here every day looking for what they can steal? Let's work their ass off. Now the good ones we'll keep. Maybe."

As Synanon evolved from an alternate-lifestyle community to a cult, not only did the leadership live better, the demands on the general members became heavier. One Synanon member described the process on a tape recording subpoenaed by *Time*'s lawyers: "You do live in a place where you've got to do what you're told. I mean, we were not given a choice about sugar [prohibited], we were not given a choice about aerobics [required exercises], you're not given a choice about your hair. There are a lot of things that you have to do because you're told that you have to do, and that's what you do in order to stay."

The demands on members escalated through the late 1970s, ranging from orders that both sexes shave off their hair, to requiring all men who had been in Synanon longer than five years (except Dederich) to have vasectomies, to making almost all members swap spouses and lovers. A Synanon member commented on the escalation in a tape recorded in 1977: "All Chuck has to say is, 'To stay in Synanon everybody has to go out and kill a gook or something. That'll be the next thing.' "

One effect of the increasing demands was to drive out all but those most committed to Synanon in its new cult form. From a high of about 1,700 members in 1972, Synanon by 1980 was down to less than half that number. The tax-exempt corporation, however, continued to grow in wealth, in part by selling off some of its vast real estate holdings at a profit.

A year after we won the Pulitzer, *The Light* was still chronicling developments at Synanon. Synanon was besieged by civil lawsuits, criminal cases, and investigations, but was fighting back. Our own research had revealed how many times before Synanon had faced crackdowns by government, only to have its lawyers uncover an escape route, and there was no certainty that even now Synanon leaders would be brought to justice. Here are some of the highlights of the months that followed our prize:

MAY, 1979—A Synanon financial statement revealed that Dederich was continuing to receive a $100,000-a-year-for-life consulting fee from Synanon.

JUNE, 1979—California's Board of Equalization for the second consecutive year denied Synanon's application for an exemption from property taxes. The state and federal governments, however, continued to allow Synanon income-tax exemption.

JUNE, 1979—Synanon subpoenaed me for deposition, along with *The Light*'s notes and sources, including those that were confidential, on Synanon. With *pro bono* legal representation from the San Francisco law firm of Heller, Ehrman, White and McAuliffe, I invoked a reporter's shield law and refused to turn over confidential information.

JUNE, 1979—California Governor Jerry Brown announced the creation of a state task force to investigate Synanon.

AUGUST, 1979—*The Light* learned that Dederich aide Walter Lewbel had taken the Fifth Amendment when asked in a secret pretrial hearing about events allegedly leading up to the rattlesnake attack.

AUGUST, 1979—Synanon put up for sale its 64-acre Tomales Bay facility. Asking price: $6.75 million.

OCTOBER, 1979—Synanon reactivated its $45-million libel and conspiracy suit against the Marin County government. The amount sought was over $200 for every man, woman, and child in the county.

NOVEMBER, 1979—*The Light* revealed that Synanon leaders had made provision for leaving the United States should that sometime become necessary.

DECEMBER, 1979—Synanon sold off well over $100,000 worth of vehicles equipment, and furnishings during a two-day auction in San Francisco.

DECEMBER, 1979—The California attorney general's Charitable Trust Division drafted a complaint against Synanon. The complaint asked a court to oversee future spending by Synanon and demanded that money wrongfully spent by Synanon leaders be returned to the organization's general fund.

Synanon went to court in an attempt to block the attorney general from filing the suit but was ultimately unsuccessful despite repeated appeals. Finally, U.S. Supreme Court Justice William Rehnquist ruled that the attorney general was acting properly, and the complaint was filed.

DECEMBER, 1979—Synanon filed a $1.25-million slander suit against Cathy, Richard, and me. Heller, Ehrman again came to Cathy's and my defense, the University of California to Richard's.

DECEMBER, 1979—The California Press Association named Cathy and me California's "Publishers of the Year."

JANUARY, 1980—*The Light* revealed that at least a dozen Synanon members, including Dederich and other leaders, had taken the Fifth Amendment in pretrial depositions and interrogatories when asked about Synanon violence.

FEBRUARY, 1980—Synanon dropped its $76-million libel suit against *Time*, claiming it could not afford to match *Time*'s legal expenditures, which by then were approximately $2 million.

MARCH, 1980—Acting on a complaint from United Press International, the National News Council investigated Synanon's efforts to silence news media coverage of problems at Synanon. The council found that Synanon lawyers in 1978–79 alone had on 960 occasions threatened libel suits against the media.

Michael Dorais, attorney for California Newspaper Publishers' Association, was quoted in the report describing the three of us as being "on a kamikaze mission" in crusading against Synanon abuses.

Dorais also noted some people think Synanon is dying. "I'm not sure that's true," he said. "I think they may be a very viable organization still."

APRIL, 1980—After moving out of Synanon, attorney Dan Garrett was interviewed in *The Pacific Sun* and noted: "This is probably surprising to you, but [Synanon's ADGAP] the advertising specialty business did a little bit less last year than it did the year before: $9.5 million or $10 million compared to $11 million. But

Synanon actually netted more last year than the year before; it was more profitable."

MAY, 1980—Synanon settled out of court for an undisclosed sum a $1-million damage suit brought by rancher Alvin Gambonini over his 1975 beating by Synanon members. Synanon also agreed to drop two lawsuits it had filed against Gambonini.

MAY, 1980—During a deposition with lawyers for ABC, Synanon founder Charles Dederich remarked, "*The Point Reyes Light* has about as much circulation [then 3,050] as a small high school paper, and nobody takes it very seriously."

JULY, 1980—Charles Dederich, Lance Kenton, and Joe Musico pled no contest to conspiracy to commit murder in connection with the rattlesnake case.

Much on our minds was the comment to us by an attorney general's investigator in September, 1978. Referring to the People's Temple cult, he had said: "We knew all about them before they went down to Guyana, but nobody cared enough to do anything."

INDEX